S0-BBY-794

JOURNAL FOR THE STUDY OF THE OLD TESTAMENT SUPPLEMENT SERIES
218

Editors
David J.A. Clines
Philip R. Davies

Executive Editor
John Jarick

Editorial Board
Robert P. Carroll, Richard J. Coggins, Alan Cooper, J. Cheryl Exum,
John Goldingay, Robert P. Gordon, Norman K. Gottwald,
Andrew D.H. Mayes, Carol Meyers, Patrick D. Miller

Sheffield Academic Press

Defining the Sacred Songs

Genre, Tradition and the Post-Critical Interpretation of the Psalms

Harry P. Nasuti

Journal for the Study of the Old Testament
Supplement Series 218

BS
1430.2
.N378
1999

Copyright © 1999 Sheffield Academic Press

Published by
Sheffield Academic Press Ltd
Mansion House
19 Kingfield Road
Sheffield S11 9AS
England

Typeset by Sheffield Academic Press
and
Printed on acid-free paper in Great Britain
by Bookcraft Ltd
Midsomer Norton, Bath

British Library Cataloguing in Publication Data

A catalogue record for this book is available
from the British Library

ISBN 1-84127-028-8

CONTENTS

Contents

PREFACE

The Psalms have been at the center of my scholarly interests ever since I first studied them with Samuel Terrien at Union Theological Seminary (New York) more than two decades ago. They were the subject of the doctoral dissertation I wrote under the direction of Robert R. Wilson at Yale, subsequently published in the Society of Biblical Literature Dissertation Series as *Tradition History and the Psalms of Asaph*. A number of the undergraduate and graduate courses that I have taught at LeMoyne College and Fordham University have focused on the Psalms, and these texts will undoubtedly continue to both challenge and inspire me for many years to come.

The present work represents over 10 years of wrestling with the question of the role that genre should play in the current post-Gunkel era of Psalms scholarship. While the long period of this book's development is to some degree due to a series of time-consuming administrative appointments, it is also a tribute to the vibrant nature of Psalms research at the present time. The continued stimulus of contemporary Psalms scholars often required me to rethink and extend my own work. What follows is obviously heavily indebted to the work of such scholars, as well as to the work of those who preceded them in the Psalms' long interpretive history.

This book also owes a great deal to a number of institutions and individuals who have provided me with many different kinds of support. For financial support, I am grateful first of all to the Catholic Biblical Association of America. A Young Scholars' Fellowship from the Association in 1988 made possible the first research on this book. I am also grateful to Fordham University for two faculty fellowships, during which time much of the present work took shape. During one of these fellowships, I had the privilege of residing at the Ratisbonne Christian Center of Jewish Studies in Jerusalem and working at the libraries of the Ecole Biblique and Hebrew University. To all of these institutions, I extend my sincere thanks.

Parts of this work were read at various scholarly conferences over the past 11 years, at which occasions they profited from the feedback of a number of my colleagues. An earlier version of chapter two was presented at the 1988 national meeting of the Society of Biblical Literature, while part of chapter six was presented at the 1993 national meeting of the Catholic Biblical Association. A draft of chapter three was discussed by the Continuing Seminar on Literary Theory and Hermeneutics at the 1989 meeting of the latter Association. I am indeed grateful to all those scholars who gave me the benefit of their insights at these times.

In a similar way, I would like to express my appreciation to all the students who have taken my Psalms courses over the years. Their questions and comments have often caused me to clarify and revise what has resulted in this work. To one of these students, Kenneth Share, I owe a special debt of gratitude for his extremely careful and insightful proofreading of the present work. I look forward to the stimulus of future students for further insights on these and other biblical texts.

Among my many supportive colleagues at Fordham, I am especially grateful to Mary C. Callaway, my Old Testament colleague and current chair, both for her unfailing personal and official support and for the continuing inspiration of her passionate engagement with the biblical text. Sincere thanks are also due to Robert B. Robinson, Professor of Old Testament at the Lutheran Theological Seminary at Philadelphia, for his specific comments on various parts of this work and for the many heated discussions about hermeneutics we have shared since we met in graduate school. For helpful advice on certain aspects of chapter two, I am indebted to Professor Nicholas Constas of Harvard University. I am also most grateful to my editor, Miss Rebecca Cullen, for her careful work with this manuscript and her patience with its author.

In a more general way, I am grateful to Professors Brevard S. Childs, James L. Kugel, and Roland E. Murphy, O. Carm. of Yale, Harvard, and Duke Universities for their example and their encouragement throughout the years. Special thanks are also due to Joseph Browne, S.J., whose wise guidance has seen me through many rough spots in the writing of this book and beyond.

My deepest thanks, of course, must go to those who have suffered through the writing of this book in the most intimate way—namely, my family. My son, Peter, grew up hearing about this work, and I am truly indebted to him for being a continual reminder of what really matters in life. In my wife, Jane, I have been shown God's grace beyond any deserving and all measure. To both of these most important persons in my life, I dedicate this book with sincere gratitude and with love.

ABBREVIATIONS

BZAW	Beihefte zur *ZAW*
CBQ	*Catholic Biblical Quarterly*
ConBOT	Coniectanea biblica, Old Testament
HSS	Harvard Semitic Studies
HTR	*Harvard Theological Review*
Int	*Interpretation*
JAAR	*Journal of the American Academy of Religion*
JBL	*Journal of Biblical Literature*
JSOT	*Journal for the Study of the Old Testament*
JSOTSup	*Journal for the Study of the Old Testament*, Supplement Series
JSS	*Journal of Semitic Studies*
NIB	*New Interpreter's Bible* (Nashville: Abingdon Press, 1996).
SBLDS	SBL Dissertation Series
TDNT	Gerhard Kittel and Gerhard Friedrich (eds.), *Theological Dictionary of the New Testament* (trans. Geoffrey W. Bromiley; 10 vols.; Grand Rapids: Eerdmans, 1964–)
TU	Texte und Untersuchungen
VT	*Vetus Testamentum*
ZAW	*Zeitschrift für die alttestamentliche Wissenschaft*

Chapter 1

INTRODUCTION

Perhaps no book of the Bible has been able to sound both so broadly and so deeply as the book of Psalms. While some biblical books have waxed and waned in popularity throughout history, the psalms seem to have remained broadly accessible to every age of believers. There has never been an age in the history of Judaism and Christianity which has not found itself attracted to the book of Psalms.

This attraction has been as deep within each age as it has been broad throughout the ages. Even though other times may not have been as likely to hear laborers singing the psalms in the fields as that of St Jerome, these texts have always figured large in the personal piety of individual believers. Certainly, they have played a consistently important role in these believers' communal liturgical practice. In addition, the psalms have been a major concern for every generation of scholars and commentators. Indeed, they have often called forth such scholars' most creative and perceptive efforts.

When one prays or studies the psalms, one finds oneself in a wide and glorious company. It is a company that ranges from the desert fathers for whom the psalms formed an essential part of their being, to young children for whom Psalm 23 is one of their earliest introductions to Scripture. It is a company that encompasses an exceptionally large number of theological giants, men like Augustine, Jerome, Luther, Calvin and Bellarmine, as well as Saadiah Gaon, Rashi, ibn Ezra and David Qimḥi. And it is a company that even in our ever more specialized age includes both theologians such as Barth, Bonhoeffer, and Buber and biblical scholars such as Gunkel, Mowinckel, Westermann and Brueggemann.

It is, however, not enough to celebrate the breadth and depth of the psalms' reception throughout their history. It is also necessary to reckon with the rich diversity of this reception. For while all ages unite in extolling the virtues and central importance of the psalms, these same ages display no such accord as to how these texts are to be understood. One should, of course, not expect a consensus over such a wide range of centuries. Nevertheless, the many interpretive voices surrounding the psalms pose a dilemma for the modern interpreter that should not be underestimated.

What, after all, is one to do with the theological giant of another age who insists that the bone-chilling approval of infanticide found at the end of Psalm 137 is really an exhortation to eliminate one's small sins by dashing them against the rock of Christ? How is one to deal with that other theological giant who sees the psalms not as prayer but as an alternate exposition of the law? What does one do with the widely accepted traditional view that David was the author of all the psalms, even those which reflect events many years later than David's own time? And what is one to make out of those expositors from Augustine to Bonhoeffer who see Jesus as the true speaker of the psalms?

The Changing World of Modern Psalms Scholarship: The Central Question of Genre

Until recently, the answer of mainline scholarship to such questions has been clear. While agreeing with previous interpreters' exaltation of the psalms and even respecting their endeavors as appropriate and fruitful for their own times, modern scholars have tended to say that their efforts were basically misguided and of little consequence for the present.

As a result, the study of such interpreters has been felt to have only historical interest, a way of understanding previous ages but not of understanding the psalms themselves. For the latter task, only the dominant historical-critical approach (particularly in its form-critical manifestation) has been accepted as an appropriate method. Though modern scholars have often been aware of (and even influenced by) the work of their more traditional predecessors, their first allegiance has clearly been to more contemporary critical methods.

Indeed, the book of Psalms may well be seen as one of the great success stories of modern biblical criticism. It is almost impossible to conceive of any twentieth-century psalms commentary that does not reflect the form-critical advances of Hermann Gunkel, as least in its more definitional aspects.[1] Both liberal and conservative works routinely use such categories as lament, hymn and thanksgiving to describe the various psalms, often with wide levels of agreement across the standard ideological spectrum. Most annotated Bibles reflect these genre categorizations as well, thus bringing form-critical definitions of the psalms into the consciousness of even the most casual of Bible readers.

This is, of course, not to say that twentieth-century psalms scholarship has been merely a slavish repetition of Gunkel's work. Certainly, scholars such as Sigmund Mowinckel and Claus Westermann have proposed significant modifications to fundamental aspects of Gunkel's system. Moreover, not every commentator has stressed the full nature of all that Gunkel envisioned by form criticism. In particular, Gunkel's crucial concept of life setting has often received a somewhat perfunctory treatment.

Nevertheless, even if one were to limit the modern appropriation of Gunkel's system to its most formal taxonomic aspects, one should not underestimate how useful that system has been for modern interpreters. By defining individual psalms according to the larger category of genre, the modern interpreter has been able to see each psalm in the context of a group of similar psalms. The awareness of this group's common elements has in turn allowed for a sharper recognition of the unique aspects of individual psalms. Form criticism has, at the very least, provided a literary context out of which one can interpret each individual psalm.

In view of this strong consensus as to the utility of Gunkel's system, certain recent movements in psalms scholarship are worthy of note. Particularly interesting are attempts by authors such as Westermann and, especially, Walter Brueggemann to propose different groupings for the psalms. To be sure, neither scholar has any desire to challenge the overall thrust of Gunkel's system. Instead, both view themselves as moving beyond Gunkel to a more inclusive theological level.

Westermann and Brueggemann differ as to how they envision this theological move beyond Gunkel. What is, however, common to both scholars is that this theological move has resulted in a change as to the grouping of the psalms in terms of genre. While these authors will be

---

1. Gunkel's two major form-critical masterpieces on the psalms are: *Die Psalmen* (Göttingen: Vandenhoek & Ruprecht, 1929) and *Einleitung in die Psalmen: Die Gattungen der religiösen Lyrik Israels, zu Ende geführt von Joachim Begrich* (Göttingen: Vandenhoek & Ruprecht, 1933).

discussed in detail throughout this book, a brief overview at this point might help to illustrate the significance of their departures from the standard form-critical consensus.

Along these lines, Westermann has tended to de-emphasize the connection of form to life setting and to focus instead on the relationship between the larger theological categories of praise and lament.[2] It is these larger categories which he sees as basic to the confessional life of ancient Israel and those who follow in its footsteps. For Westermann, Israel is especially characterized by praise for God's specific actions on its behalf, a praise that Westermann calls 'declarative' in contrast to the praise that is 'descriptive' of God's more general characteristics.

Important here is the way these new categories cut across Gunkel's genres. Thus, for example, Westermann's declarative praise may be seen to undergird even the psalms of lament, since the latter genre both calls for the type of specific divine intervention celebrated in that type of praise and even anticipates such praise in its own structure.

Brueggemann uses Westermann's interplay of praise and lament to construct a threefold system of orientation, disorientation and new orientation.[3] Psalms of orientation may be seen to use descriptive praise to celebrate an ordered world and a trustworthy God, while psalms of disorientation (especially the lament) describe the loss of that ordered world and call for God to act. Psalms of new orientation, on the other hand, use declarative praise to recount how God acted to overcome the distress of the person praying.

As in the case of Westermann, Gunkel's genres are not entirely forsaken by Brueggemann, though they are revised in accord with the latter's larger theological interests. Brueggemann also is similar to Westermann in that these theological interests affect the way that he sees Gunkel's key category of life setting.

Again, it is clear that neither Westermann or Brueggemann sees his work as overthrowing Gunkel's basic system and the form-critical consensus. Nevertheless, both have proposed major modifications as to

2.   See his analysis in *Praise and Lament in the Psalms* (Atlanta, VA: John Knox Press, 1981), as well as the detailed discussion later in this work.

3.   For an outline of this system, see especially Brueggemann's article, 'Psalms and the Life of Faith: A Suggested Typology of Function', *JSOT* 20 (1980), pp. 3-32, and his book, *The Message of the Psalms: A Theological Commentary* (Minneapolis: Augsburg, 1984). These works undergird much of what Brueggemann has written on the psalms elsewhere.

how one groups the psalms into categories and how one defines these categories. What has prompted these developments?

On the one hand, these changes may be traced to a normal refinement and furthering of the form-critical agenda. Westermann's work, in particular, may be seen as an attempt to realize Gunkel's call for a literary history of forms in ancient Israel. Much of his work on the psalms is devoted to a description of the changes that the genres of praise and lament undergo throughout Israelite history. Surely, Gunkel would have approved of the general thrust of Westermann's work, even if he might have argued for different genre categories and more sustained attention to life setting.

There is, however, another side to these recent developments, one which is particularly evident in the work of Brueggemann, though it is to be found in Westermann's writings as well. This other factor is the manifestly theological concern of both authors. For both Westermann and Brueggemann, the way one groups the psalms has theological, as well as *religionsgeschichtliche* significance. Such theological interests were not absent in Gunkel, but they were clearly not his dominant concern.[4]

It will become clear over the course of this book that this combination of sharpened theological interests and different genre groupings of the psalms is neither unusual nor accidental. Indeed, when one looks back through the history of the psalms' interpretation, one is struck by the way changes in the theological understanding of the psalms have often been accompanied by changes in the way the psalms have been grouped. In such a way, one can point to a history of interpretation in which theological interests go hand in hand with literary concerns.

Such a correlation of theological and literary concerns is especially intriguing in light of the present climate of biblical studies. The past few years have witnessed a revival of interest in the literary interpretation of the Bible. This literary revival is, of course, a wide ranging movement with many different manifestations. One important question, however, is the ultimate purpose of reading the Bible in a 'literary' way. Is the goal of such a reading 'aesthetic' in the sense of a general

---

4. The subtitle of Brueggemann's *The Message of the Psalms (A Theological Commentary)* is indicative of this change in emphasis. It is significant that both Westermann and Brueggemann have contributed Old Testament theologies to the field, something which was not a major concern for Gunkel. Gunkel instead appears to have considered himself much more of a historian of ancient Israelite religion.

enjoyment of poetic forms and literary artistry? Or is the greater appreciation of the literary aspects of the Bible only a step towards a larger goal? If so, to what extent does this goal have a theological component?

What the history of psalms interpretation helps us realize is that even though these are clearly major theoretical questions for modern interpreters, they are by no means new questions. Rather, such questions about the relationship between literary and theological issues have played a key role in the biblical interpretation of past ages. As such, looking at the historical interplay between the way that the psalms have been defined in genre terms and the way that they have been appropriated theologically allows one to put the whole question of their literary-theological relationship into a larger perspective.

In a somewhat narrower vein, an examination of the way the psalms have been defined in genre terms in the past allows one to gain some perspective on the form-critical consensus of the twentieth century. Particularly interesting in this respect is what it is that distinguished Gunkel's attempts at genre definition from those of his predecessors.

It is not, after all, that Gunkel was the first to categorize the psalms in terms of their genre. As will be seen throughout this book, genre definition has been a vital part of psalms interpretation from the earliest period. Nevertheless, Gunkel's approach differed from that of his predecessors in a number of respects, among them in his historical interests and in his concern for the ancient Israelite setting in life.

To the extent that scholars such as Westermann and Brueggemann have emphasized the theological implications of the form of the psalms, they have actually moved closer to the historical mainstream of psalms interpretation. While a post-Gunkel understanding of genre can never be the same as a pre-Gunkel understanding, looking at the differences between them seems likely to open up a number of perspectives on the state of genre definition at the present time.

Along these lines, looking at the history of psalms interpretation may help to clarify just what it is that we do when we define something as belonging to a particular genre. For all of the present century's concern with form and type, this basic question has only rarely been asked.[5]

---

5.   Perhaps the most searching analysis of the fundamental nature of form criticism is that of Rolf Knierem in his probing article, 'Old Testament Form Criticism Reconsidered', *Int* 27 (1973), pp. 435-68. See also his more recent work, 'Criticism of Literary Features, Form, Tradition, and Redaction', in D. Knight and

And yet, as has been seen, even Gunkel's influential formulation has not prevented a number of different interpretations of the task. Given the recent innovations of Westermann and Brueggemann, the time is clearly right for a full scale examination on the most basic level.

Using the Past to Understand the Present

It will, of course, be readily apparent that by using the history of interpretation as a means of raising such theoretical questions, this study is indebted to a number of critical developments, both within the field of biblical studies and in the humanities as a whole. Within the field, one thinks especially of the attempts of Brevard S. Childs to retrieve the heritage of earlier interpreters as a theological resource for modern interpretation. His masterful Exodus commentary serves as perhaps the classic example of a thoughtful attempt to interact with the larger tradition.[6]

The same tendency may be seen in the work of such recent Jewish scholars as James Kugel and Jon Levenson, both of whom are concerned to situate their work in the wider history of interpretation.[7] Finally, one might mention the work of such Catholic scholars as Raymond Brown and Roland Murphy who at various stages of their careers have attempted to incorporate an appreciation of the interpretive

G. Tucker (eds.), *The Hebrew Bible and its Modern Interpreters* (Chico, CA: Scholars Press, 1985), pp. 136-46.

6.   Childs, *The Book of Exodus: A Critical Theological Commentary* (Philadelphia: Westminster Press, 1974). Note Childs's assertion in the preface (p. ix) that 'an adequate interpretation of the Bible for the church must involve a continuous wrestling with the history of interpretation and theology'. Childs's work of retrieval has begun to make an impact on the field. See, for example, Brueggemann's statement of appreciation for the psalms' interpretive history in *Message of the Psalms*, pp. 16-17. One of the most insightful modern attempts to appropriate the psalms' interpretive history is that of J.L. Mays, *Psalms* (Louisville, KY: John Knox Press, 1994).

7.   Among Kugel's many works in this vein, see his *The Idea of Biblical Poetry: Parallelism and its History* (New Haven: Yale University Press, 1981); *In Potiphar's House: The Interpretive Life of Biblical Texts* (San Francisco: Harper & Row, 1990), and, most recently, *The Bible As It Was* (Cambridge, MA: Harvard University Press, 1997). For Levenson, see especially his *Sinai and Zion: An Entry into the Jewish Bible* (New York: Harper & Row, 1985) with its explicit defense of the relevance of the Jewish tradition for modern interpretation. His more recent work presents a number of fine examples of this sort of approach to the text.

tradition into their picture of biblical commentary.[8]

In the wider humanities, this approach is clearly indebted to the work of such critics as Hans Georg Gadamer and Hans Robert Jauss. It was, perhaps, Gadamer whose work was the most important in opening up a positive evaluation of tradition for modern interpretation.[9] The reception theory of Jauss is clearly indebted to Gadamer in its attention to the empirical realities of literary history and its recognition that such realities constitute a challenge to literary theory.[10]

Significantly, Jauss has devoted considerable attention to genre issues. As a result, his thought is often directly relevant to the present work.[11] This is also the case with Alastair Fowler, whose theoretical

8.   One of Brown's earliest works, *The Sensus Plenior of Sacred Scripture* (Baltimore: St Mary's, 1955) directly concerned the relationship between the history of interpretation and contemporary exegesis. In his recent article on hermeneutics ('Hermeneutics', in the *New Jerome Biblical Commentary* [Englewood Cliffs, NJ: Prentice–Hall, 1990], pp. 1146-65, he notes with approval that 'an element in modern literary criticism stresses that a text once written assumes a life of its own and may convey meaning or have significance beyond the original author's intention. Thus, there is a postwritten stage that cannot be neglected either.' (p. 1147).

Much of Murphy's recent work on the Song of Songs has shown a similar openness to the history of tradition. See, for example, his article, 'Patristic and Medieval Exegesis: Help or Hindrance?', *CBQ* 43 (1981), pp. 505-516, where he notes that 'positively, the traditional interpretation supports the view, widely accepted today, that a text acquires new meaning as it lives on within a community' (p. 515). See also his commentary on the same text, *The Song of Songs* (Hermeneia; Minneapolis: Augsburg–Fortress, 1990). For a similar interest in the different contexts of the psalms (though not without warnings against misuse), see his 'Reflections on the Contextual Interpretations of the Psalms', in J. Clinton McCann, Jr (ed.), *The Shape and Shaping of the Psalter* (JSOTSup, 159; Sheffield: Sheffield Academic Press, 1993), pp. 21-26, as well as his *The Psalms Are Yours* (New York: Paulist Press, 1993).

9.   See especially the section in Gadamer's *Truth and Method* (New York: Crossroad, 1975) which is entitled 'The Elevation of the Historicality of Understanding to the Status of Hermeneutical Principle' (pp. 235-75). Gadamer's interest in the effective-history (*Wirkungsgeschichte*) of a work of art is particularly relevant here.

10.   Thus, the English title of Jauss's classic methodological statement: 'Literary History as a Challenge to Literary Theory', in his *Toward an Aesthetic of Reception* (Minneapolis: University of Minnesota Press, 1982), pp. 3-45.

11.   See, for example, his essay, 'Theory of Genres and Medieval Literature', in *Toward an Aesthetic*, pp. 76-109. It is of interest for the present work that this essay

work on genre includes a consideration of the empirical realities of interpretive history.[12] These and similar literary critics help to place the current situation in biblical studies within a larger context of critical thought.

With this in mind, one may ask what exactly one is interested in when one looks at the history of a text's interpretation down through the ages. Because the mainstream of biblical studies in this century has seen most traditional criticism as fundamentally misguided, scholars have usually understood such criticism as providing more information about the age in which it was written than about the biblical text itself. As a result, biblical scholars have been less interested in such criticism than patristic, medieval or reformation scholars.

No one would deny that the exegetical works of Augustine, Rashi and Calvin are primary sources of insight into the theological issues of their times. The real question is whether such so-called 'pre-critical' biblical interpreters have anything to contribute to an understanding of the biblical text as well as to an understanding of their own periods. It is the recognition that these older critics, despite their methodological distance from the present, are capable of providing an insight into the *text* that constitutes the new direction of such critics as Childs.

Obviously, much discretion is called for in this matter, since one cannot simply pretend that one is in the same position as a pre-critical interpreter and take over such interpretation in an unquestioning way. To say this, however, is simply to say that the modern interpreter still has a task to do, no matter how much he or she becomes open to the interpretations of the past.

The modern interpreter cannot simply appropriate the past if for no other reason than the fact that the history of past interpretation is a very diverse history. As a result, the interpreter must at the very least either pick and choose from among his or her predecessors or learn selectively from each. Even more importantly, of course, the interpreter must be responsive to his or her own time in a way similar to the way that such past interpreters were responsive to their own times.

The questions raised by this new openness to past interpretations are many and complex, and the present book is clearly incapable of

includes both an examination of the relationship between form and function and a consideration of Gunkel and the form-critical method.

12. See A. Fowler, *Kinds of Literature: An Introduction to the Theory of Genres and Modes* (Cambridge, MA: Harvard University Press, 1982).

exploring all of them. Instead, the present work will consider a specific issue in this interplay between past and present, namely, the implications of past genre definitions for the current task of genre analysis. With this in mind, the book of Psalms is particularly fertile ground for a number of reasons.

First of all, the book of Psalms has a very full interpretive history, one in which genre considerations have always played a vital role. Moreover, it is a book where genre concerns are very much to the fore at present and where the modern study of genre has been felt to have been particularly successful. If there is any book of the Bible well suited to the sort of analysis envisioned here, it is the book of Psalms.[13]

With this in mind, the present work will examine some of the ways in which different genre definitions of the psalms have made a difference in their interpretation throughout history. It will also, however, attempt to draw the implications of this history for the nature of genre analysis at the present time. In such a way, the book uses the historical material as a springboard for a more theoretical reflection on the present act of interpretation.

It is only fair to caution the reader that no attempt at an exhaustive study of the psalms' interpretive history is contemplated here. Such a study would take a lifetime of research in the case of the psalms. Instead, this work will use representative studies from the past to illuminate issues that seem to be of some theoretical importance at the present time. A brief outline of the main concerns of the book may help to orient the reader.

The Present Work: Reflections on Genre and the Psalms

This work's analysis of genre begins in the next chapter with a concrete example of diversity in genre definition, namely the strange case of the 'seven penitential psalms'. In the definition of Psalms 6, 32, 38, 51, 102, 130 and 143 as penitential psalms, one meets with one of the most ancient and sustained genre classifications in biblical literature. For at least 1500 years, a great multitude of believers have read and prayed these psalms as a distinct genre grouping with a particular character.

---

13. For a recent overview of the interpretive history of the psalms, see William L. Holladay, *The Psalms through Three Thousand Years: Prayerbook of a Cloud of Witnesses* (Minneapolis: Fortress Press, 1993). Mays, *Psalms*, is also noteworthy for its attention to this history.

Such a phenomenon is clearly a significant datum for genre studies.

It is, however, the fact that this tradition of genre definition is not a unanimous one that makes these psalms of great theoretical interest for the present work. This tradition is not unanimous, on the one hand, because it is only to be found in western Christianity. Both eastern Christianity and Judaism appear to be largely unaffected by it, a circumstance which in itself raises questions about the relationship of genre definition and theological community.

It is, moreover, not unanimous because the classification of these seven psalms as penitential has been for the most part completely rejected by those who have adopted the modern form-critical approach to the psalms. Both Gunkel and Mowinckel explicitly reject this genre tradition for certain of these psalms, whereas most modern scholars simply pass over it in silence. Such a disparity between a 1500-year-old tradition and the modern methodological consensus raises exactly the kind of theoretical issues with which this book is concerned.

By focusing on the specific case of the seven penitential psalms, the second chapter hopes to raise at the most basic level the question of what is involved in the act of genre definition. How do different interpreters and their communities decide which texts should be grouped together as a common genre? What are the reasons for the differences between the genre definitions of these various interpretive communities?

Is it simply a matter of more and less perceptive readers, some of whom accurately read a text while others miss the point? Or is the act of genre definition one that allows or even demands that different readers come to different conclusions? In such a vein, one can even ask whether genre analysis is a descriptive or a constructive enterprise.

It is precisely this sort of far-reaching question that needs to be raised at the present moment of methodological searching in the field of biblical studies. It is, moreover, precisely this sort of question that is put in a larger perspective by engaging both pre-critical and critical interpretation in a constructive dialogue. The seven penitential psalms provide the perfect specific case with which to raise this sort of general question.

The chapter just described is concerned with how individual psalms are defined in genre terms. The task of psalms interpretation is, however, not finished once individual psalms are classified in this way. Indeed, recent scholars have been particularly interested in the relationship between the different types of psalms.

Along these lines, Westermann's study of praise and lament in the psalms has long been seen as a classic exploration of the relationship between psalm types. Brueggemann's conceptualization of the psalms in terms of orientation, disorientation and new orientation is more recent, though already quite influential. Clearly, in modern psalms scholarship, no psalm or psalm type is an island unto itself.

It should not, however, be imagined that this interest in the relationship between the psalms means that all of the psalms are conceived of in the same way or put on the same level. Particularly interesting in this respect is the recent tendency to emphasize the central importance of the lament. Many scholars of the last few years have seen the lament as the linchpin of the psalter, the prism through which the other types of psalms may be seen.[14]

The third chapter of the present work examines this recent tendency to highlight the lament with an eye towards understanding its implications for genre analysis as a whole. The wider perspective of the larger history of interpretation is particularly helpful in spelling out these implications. This wider view becomes especially significant once one realizes that ours is not the only age to have highlighted one particular psalm genre as of crucial importance for understanding the entire corpus. The fact that different ages have highlighted different psalm genres as the center of the psalms poses the issue in a particularly sharp way.

What one finds when one looks at the history of psalms interpretation is that genre definition always goes hand in hand with genre evaluation. Once again, it is the fact that both definitions and evaluations differ throughout this history that allows one to raise the most basic questions connected with the phenomenon of genre. The third chapter attempts to discern the reasons for such diversity and, in so doing, to further understand what one does when one engages in genre analysis.

As the second and third chapters imply, much of modern psalms scholarship has been devoted to the task of defining the genres of the psalms and coming to terms with how they relate to each other. Considerably less attention has been devoted to the actual way in which genre allows the different psalms to function in the lives of those who use them.

To say this does not mean that scholars have been uninterested in the way individual genres have been used, especially in their original

14. See especially Brueggemann, *Message of the Psalms*, and also his 'The Costly Loss of Lament', *JSOT* 36 (1986), pp. 57-71.

settings in ancient Israel. This was, of course, a major concern of Gunkel, and at least some of his form-critical successors devoted considerable energy to determining the exact settings of the various psalm types.

On the other hand, much less attention has been paid to the more basic question of the way that genres actually function in these settings. To say that certain psalms are at home in particular life settings does not necessarily illuminate the personal or communal dynamics by which genre allows the psalms to be appropriated in those settings. To understand this dynamic it is crucial to look at the nature of genre itself rather than simply the nature of individual genres.

Again, modern biblical scholars have been much less likely to pursue this basic theoretical task than to pursue the more concrete task of the historical placement of individual genres. The case of Sigmund Mowinckel, one of the few scholars who was interested in both tasks, is instructive in this regard.

In his series of works on the psalms, Mowinckel first of all continued Gunkel's basic form-critical agenda of defining psalm genres and searching for their life settings in ancient Israel.[15] To his great credit, he understood even more thoroughly than Gunkel the importance of the cult for understanding the role the psalms played in ancient Israel. Along these lines, he used information about other ancient Near Eastern cultures to describe what he considered to be the probable setting of many of the psalms in an Israelite new year's festival.

If this were all that Mowinckel had done, it would still have been an intellectual and scholarly achievement of considerable magnitude. Mowinckel, however, went beyond this sophisticated reconstruction of a new historical life setting for the psalms to investigate on a more basic level the personal and social dynamics involved in the cult itself. It is this more basic investigation which bears directly on the fundamental nature of genre.

As might be expected, Mowinckel's work has been much debated over the years. The debate, however, has focused mostly on the more historical question of whether Mowinckel's proposed life setting for the psalms was the correct one. In general, scholars have tended to accept

---

15. See S. Mowinckel, *Psalmenstudien*, especially volume two, *Das Thronbesteigungsfest Jahwäs und der Ursprung der Eschatologie* (Amsterdam: Schippers, 1961 [1922]). *The Psalms in Israel's Worship* (Nashville: Abingdon Press, 1962) is a useful English summary of Mowinckel's work on the psalms.

Mowinckel's cultic orientation but to be more suspicious of his proposed setting in an Israelite new year's festival. Alternate festivals have been proposed, with no clear consensus having been reached.[16]

What has received much less attention from the mainstream of biblical scholarship has been Mowinckel's more fundamental theoretical work on the nature of cult itself. With the possible exception of the myth and ritual school, few have been willing to entertain Mowinckel's far-reaching insights into the way that cult worked in ancient Israel. There are, however, signs that this aspect of Mowinckel's work is the focus of renewed interest at the present time.

Once again, it is the work of Walter Brueggemann that is indicative of these new directions in psalms research. In his 1988 book, *Israel's Praise: Doxology against Idolatry and Ideology*, Brueggemann has undertaken a vigorous retrieval of some of Mowinckel's more radical thoughts on cult. Coming on top of Brueggemann's earlier reformulations of genre, this work has clearly brought the fundamental nature of genre and cult into the center of the present debate.

The fourth chapter of this work uses the insights of the second and third chapters to address the question of the nature of genre in a direct way. The chapter is particularly concerned to discuss the ways in which a psalm's genre status makes possible that psalm's appropriation by individuals and communities, in both ancient Israel and the present. What, that is to ask, is it that gives genre its power, and how does this power help to define the different ways in which the psalms are able to function in the lives of individuals and communities?

In attempting to answer these questions, the work of such scholars as Mowinckel and Brueggemann is naturally of great importance. However, as in previous chapters, insights are also sought from the larger history of interpretation, which was in many ways even more concerned with such issues than most of recent scholarship. Along these lines, it will be seen that such treatises on the psalms as St

---

16. So Arthur Weiser has argued for the existence of a covenant renewal festival (*The Psalms: A Commentary* [Philadelphia: Westminster Press, 1962]), while Hans-Joachim Kraus has concentrated instead on the place of the psalms in the festivals of David and Zion (*Die Königsherrschaft Gottes im Alten Testament: Untersuchungen zu den Liedern von Jahwes Thronbesteigung* [Tübingen: J.C.B. Mohr, 1951]; *Worship in Israel* [Richmond, VA: John Knox, 1966]; *Psalms 1–59: A Commentary* [Minneapolis: Augsburg, 1988] and *Theology of the Psalms* [Minneapolis: Augsburg, 1986]).

Athanasius's *Letter to Marcellinus* have much to contribute to the present reassessment of the way we view the psalms.

The chapters considered so far all focus on the way that the genre of the psalms is related to questions of function and setting in the life of a community. Clearly, when one looks back over the history of the psalms, such questions may be seen to be of obvious importance. There are, however, other ways the psalms may be situated which have been influential in the past, some of which are of increasing significance at the present time.

It is, for example, possible to concentrate on the way that a psalm may be situated in the life of its author. This does not take away the need for genre analysis, since the reasons behind an author's choice of a particular genre are certainly a significant topic for critical inquiry.[17] Still, the inclusion of the author has an important effect on the way one both defines and evaluates genre.

This is particularly so in the case of the psalms. After all, the modern critical consensus is adamant that one cannot usually be sure about when and where a psalm was composed, much less about the identity of the individual responsible for it. Indeed, part of Gunkel's genius lay in shifting the emphasis from the specific author-centered questions which fragmented psalms scholarship in the nineteenth century to more general issues, such as form and life setting. In Gunkel's hands, genre became a way of bracketing the author in favor of larger yet more accessible concerns.

It is important to see that in moving to these larger concerns Gunkel not only broke with his immediate historical-critical predecessors of the nineteenth century. He also completed their break from the more traditional view which tended to accept David as the author of the psalms. These earlier readers also considered authorship to be an important aspect of psalms interpretation, though obviously not in the same way as their critical successors.

Given the differences between the traditional, early historical-critical, and form-critical views of authorship in the psalms, it is highly significant that such major scholars as Brevard S. Childs, Peter Ackroyd, and James Luther Mays have recently attempted to retrieve David's hermeneutical importance for our understanding of the

---

17. Indeed, some critics would see such authorial intentions as the crucial element in the definition of a text's genre. See, in particular, E.D. Hirsch, *Validity in Interpretation* (New Haven: Yale University Press, 1967), especially pp. 68-126.

Psalter.[18] None of these scholars, of course, are advocating a naive return to a pre-critical approach to the psalms. Nevertheless, they are concerned to move beyond a purely form-critical approach to include some conception of Davidic authorship.

The fifth chapter considers some of the different ways that questions about authorship affect the interpretation of the psalms. In keeping with the overall thrust of the book, the chapter is particularly interested in how such authorship questions intersect with the genre-related issues examined in previous chapters. How, for example, does attributing the psalms to David affect the way that one defines them in terms of genre? What are the differences between this sort of genre definition and the less author-oriented approach of form-criticism?

A consideration of the history of interpretation helps to place these important theoretical issues in a larger perspective. Once again, it will be seen that earlier ages were not unaware of the genre implications of their interpretations, even though they naturally did not express themselves on these matters in the same way as modern interpreters. A comparison of their approach with that of the form-critical consensus, as well as with the more recent post-critical approaches of Childs, Ackroyd and Mays will help in the fifth chapter's exploration of the relationship between authorship and genre in the psalms.

There remains to consider yet one more means of situating the psalms which is of some importance at the present time, namely, in the literary setting of the book of Psalms as a whole. First introduced by Brevard Childs, this 'canonical' approach to the psalms has been vigorously developed by Gerald Wilson and utilized by Walter Brueggemann and a number of other scholars.[19] Clearly, the fact that this approach to the psalms is, at least in some respects, much less speculative than other

18. B.S. Childs, 'Psalm Titles and Midrashic Exegesis', *JSS* 16 (1971), pp. 137-50, and *Introduction to the Old Testament as Scripture* (Philadelphia: Fortress Press, 1979), pp. 520-22. P.R. Ackroyd, *Doors of Perception: A Guide to Reading the Psalms* (London: SCM Press, 1983); J.L. Mays, 'The David of the Psalms', *Int* 40 (1986), pp. 143-55; *Psalms*.

19. Childs, *Introduction to the Old Testament*, pp. 504-525; G.H. Wilson, *The Editing of the Hebrew Psalter* (SBLDS, 76; Chico, CA: Scholars Press, 1985); W. Brueggemann, 'Bounded by Obedience and Praise: The Psalms as Canon', *JSOT* 50 (1991), pp. 63-92. Wilson has augmented his basic work with a series of articles along the same lines, one of which is part of an entire volume of *Interpretation* devoted to the canonical shape of the Psalter (*Int* 46 [1992]). The important work of J.L. Mays, J.C. McCann and G. Sheppard will also be discussed below.

means of situating the psalms makes it an attractive interpretive option at the present time.

Despite the rich potential of this canonical approach to the psalms, there remain a number of questions that have only begun to be explored. Perhaps primary among these questions, at least for the purposes of the present book, is the nature of genre definition in this new approach. Certainly, genre analysis is by no means absent from these recent attempts to come to grips with the canonical shape of Psalms. For Wilson and other similarly oriented scholars, an examination of the placement and interplay of the different genres in the book of Psalms is a major component of understanding the final form of that book.

Along these lines, it is significant that the genres that at least some of these scholars use to determine the canonical shape of the book of Psalms seem to be taken directly from the form-critical consensus of Gunkel and his followers. Such an approach is, of course, possible, and even attractive in that it allows for a connection between critical and post-critical methods. It is, however, not without difficulties that what is clearly a more 'literary' approach to the book should be dependent on such a 'historical' definition of genre.

Once again, bringing the history of interpretation into the discussion helps to illustrate the issues at stake here. After all, if different ages have defined and evaluated the genres of the psalms in different ways, it is clearly a major assertion to say that one can arrive at the definitive understanding of the psalter's final form by looking at the placement of genres as those genres have been defined by one particular age.

To put it even more pointedly, such an approach seems to assume a method of genre definition that is heavily descriptive in nature. That is to say, it sees genre definition as a largely objective historical enterprise rather than one that entails a certain amount of creative theological involvement. Such an approach is certainly possible. It must, however, be defended rather than assumed, especially in the light of recent developments in psalms research.[20]

One further question comes to mind when one considers issues of genre definition in connection with these canonical approaches to the psalms. It is clear that many of the genre issues considered in this book

---

20. Such an approach also assumes that the canonical approach to the biblical text is largely descriptive. As Childs's own appreciation of the history of interpretation might imply, it is more likely that the canonical approach has a considerable constructive dimension as well.

are intimately related to questions of how the psalms have functioned in the life and worship of believing individuals and communities. On the other hand, the canonical approach has tended to emphasize the fact that these texts which were once prayers have now become Scripture. What were once human words directed to God have now become the word of God directed to humanity.

Clearly, scholars such as Childs and Wilson are correct in their perception of a new dimension that has accompanied the canonical status of the book of Psalms. The question in need of further discussion is that of how this new dimension relates to the way one perceives the genre of the psalms. After all, the fact that the psalms have the canonical status of a divine word made available for theological reflection has certainly not meant that believing communities have stopped using these psalms as prayer.

This continued use as prayer has serious implications for both the canonical approach to the psalms and their ongoing genre definition. The sixth chapter examines these implications in some detail, focusing especially on the implications of this dual status for how one defines both the genres of the individual psalms and the genre of the Psalter as a whole. The chapter also examines how these two acts of genre definition relate to each other.

The book concludes with some final reflections on the methodological junction at which psalms scholarship finds itself at the present time. In addition, the last chapter attempts to make the case for a truly post-critical appropriation of the psalms, one which is respectful of the entire history of psalms reception down through the ages.

Such a post-critical appropriation would obviously be one that views tradition in a positive way. That there is considerable tension in this tradition goes without saying, particularly in light of the differences between the pre-critical and the critical approaches to the text. A truly successful post-critical approach will be one that is able to use this tension in a creative way.

There is a potential danger in this positive evaluation of tradition, one that has often been felt at various points in the history of biblical interpretation. The danger is, of course, that the tradition will in some way suffocate the text itself. It is in response to this danger that attention to the present canonical shape of the text is particularly important. As such, it is likely that an awareness of the implications of canon will be part of any effective post-critical appropriation of the text.

Finally, one needs to emphasize the important role of the interpretive community in a successful post-critical methodology. If the approach of the present work uncovers any feature worth emphasizing, it is that interpretation does not take place in a historical or theological vacuum. Similarly, any attempt to appropriate the tradition or come to terms with the canonical shape of the text does not take place in such a vacuum either. An awareness of and responsiveness to one's interpretive community would seem to be a vital element of any truly post-critical approach to the biblical text.

In terms of the specific focus of this book, such a post-critical view of the psalms would see genre definition as both a descriptive and a constructive task. Understanding a text's genre requires an appreciation of where that text has been throughout its interpretive history, as well as an awareness of where the interpreter is at the present. It is in such a dual context that one arrives at and evaluates one's own groupings of the psalms.

By its examination of the most basic aspects of genre definition, the present work hopes to make a contribution to the extremely vital discussion on the psalms that is taking place at the present time. Clearly, much more remains to be done, especially in terms of any serious retrieval of the past as a context for present interpretation. It is, however, hoped that this work will serve as an invitation to join that 'wide and glorious company' of past interpreters in an ongoing conversation about this most treasured of biblical books.

Chapter 2

THE ROLE OF GENRE IN BIBLICAL INTERPRETATION:
THE CASE OF THE SEVEN PENITENTIAL PSALMS

Ever since the ground-breaking work of Hermann Gunkel at the beginning of this century, one of the most basic principles of modern biblical
studies has been the need to read individual biblical texts in accord with
their genre. Indeed, it is no exaggeration to say that form-criticism has
defined the agenda for much of the twentieth century in the way that
source criticism dominated the previous century. While there have been
a number of calls to go beyond form-criticism in recent years, there is
almost no disagreement about the need to determine a text's genre in
order to interpret that text correctly. This is perhaps nowhere more true
than in the case of the psalms, where the lines of Gunkel's form-critical
analysis remain foundational.

The present chapter has no intention of challenging the necessity of
genre definition for biblical interpretation. It does, however, seek to
raise in a rather fundamental way the question of what the task of genre
definition actually involves. It also seeks to examine the functions such
genre definition is being asked to perform, especially in the interpretation of the psalms.

To accomplish this rather far-reaching theoretical task without
becoming overly abstract, the present chapter will focus on a concrete
group of biblical texts which raise many of the important issues. The
texts under consideration are a psalms grouping that have come to be
known throughout their long interpretive history as the 'seven penitential psalms'. The grouping together of Psalms 6, 32, 38, 51, 102, 130
and 143 as a distinct collection of penitential psalms began at least as
early as the sixth century, and it continues to the present day.[1] Through-

---

1. See, for example, Brueggemann, *Message of the Psalms*, pp. 94-106, and
B.W. Anderson, *Out of the Depths: The Psalms Speak for Us Today* (Philadelphia:
Westminster Press, 1983), pp. 93-98.

out their history as a separate group, these psalms have often either been the subject of their own commentaries or have had their special status noted in larger commentaries on the entire psalter.

This interpretive history testifies to a genre classification of extraordinary staying power. The problematic nature of this classification is, however, readily apparent when it is placed alongside the quite different genre classifications that stem from Gunkel and his form-critical successors. A brief examination of the form-critical approach to these psalms will illustrate some of the issues involved.

Two Different Genre Classifications

Gunkel considered the penitential psalm to be a subcategory of the larger genre of the lament.[2] For Gunkel, the penitential psalm is to be distinguished from the lament on the basis of whether a consciousness of sin has moved to the foreground of the psalm. While such a foregrounding of sinfulness is a normal part of collective laments, it is relatively infrequent in laments of the individual.[3] Where it is found in the latter, it is joined with a desire for absolution and forgiveness and an appeal for the remission of God's anger and the renewal of an inner life satisfactory to God. This appeal is grounded in an assurance of God's grace and loyalty, as well as in the divine readiness to forgive sins.[4]

In accord with his criterion, Gunkel saw Psalm 51 as the best example of the penitential psalm. He also included Psalm 130 in the genre, though only with some reservations.[5] Of the other psalms traditionally seen as penitential, Gunkel saw Psalms 6 and 38 as midway between the penitential psalms 51 and 130 and the standard lament psalms of the individual.[6] Psalm 143 was classed as a fairly normal individual lament, while Psalm 102 was seen to be a combination of that genre with certain hymnic and prophetic elements.[7] Psalm 32 was seen to be an

---

2.   Gunkel, *Einleitung in die Psalmen*, pp. 131-32, 251-52.

3.   Gunkel, *Einleitung in die Psalmen*, p. 131.

4.   Gunkel, *Einleitung in die Psalmen*, p. 252.

5.   These two psalms, together with the Prayer of Manasseh make up Gunkel's core group for this genre. Cf. *Einleitung in die Psalmen*, p. 251.

6.   A position they share with Psalm 69. So *Einleitung in die Psalmen*, p. 251, though see also his reservations about the penitential status of Psalm 6 in *Psalmen*, p. 21.

7.   Gunkel, *Psalmen*, pp. 602, 437.

individual psalm of thanksgiving with wisdom elements.[8]

In a number of places, Gunkel specifically objects to the tradition which sees all of these psalms as penitential psalms.[9] To be sure, a number of the psalms in this group have penitential motifs. However, since such motifs are a common feature of the individual lament genre, they do not mark these psalms as especially penitential.

Sigmund Mowinckel, the other early giant of the form-critical analysis of the psalms, follows Gunkel closely in distinguishing between the traditional group of penitential psalms and the penitential psalms which can be isolated by form-critical methods. As was the case for Gunkel, Mowinckel's penitential psalms of the individual include only Psalms 51, 130 and the Prayer of Manasseh.[10] Again, Mowinckel explicitly notes that most of the 'traditional group of "penitential psalms" of the church... are not typical penitential psalms'.[11]

This disjunction between the traditional grouping of the seven penitential psalms and the standard form-critical classification of that name raises a number of questions. The first of these is the historical question of how the traditional psalms came to be grouped together as a special group of penitential psalms when their penitential aspects are not sufficiently distinctive as to allow them to be grouped as penitential psalms according to modern form-critical criteria. Related to this question is the further question of how the special status of these psalms, once established, affected their subsequent interpretation within those circles that accepted this genre classification.

Such historical questions are interesting in their own right, but they are even more significant in terms of the theoretical issues that they raise. Among these are questions of how genre distinctions are made and how they function in the interpretation of biblical texts. In the

8. Gunkel, *Psalmen*, p. 135.

9. See, for example, his comment on Ps. 6 in *Psalmen*, p. 21: 'Man wird den Psalm demnach nicht unter die "Busspsalmen"—die anderen von der Kirche gezählten sind ψ 32. 38. 51. 102. 130. 143—rechnen können (Budde)'. Similarly, see his comments on Psalm 143 in *Psalmen*, p. 602: 'Zu den "Busspsalmen", unter die das Gedicht von der alten Kirche gerechnet worden ist, gehört es also nicht'.

10. Mowinckel, *Psalms*, p. 214 n. 47.

11. Mowinckel, *Psalms*, p. 214 n. 47. Mowinckel's comment that the work of Bernini, is 'more theological and doctrinal than literary' has some importance for the issues discussed in this essay. Giuseppe Bernini S.I., *Le preghiere penitenziale del salterio: Contributo alla teologia dell' A.T.* (Analecta Gregoriana, 62: Romae, Apud Aedes Universitas Gregorianae, 1953).

words of the literary theorist, Hans Robert Jauss, the literary history of these texts clearly functions as a challenge to any literary theory that attempts to interpret them.[12] It is to a consideration of both the historical questions and their theoretical implications that this chapter now turns.

The Question of Origins

The first unequivocal reference to the seven penitential psalms as a group is to be found in the *Expositio Psalmorum* of the sixth century Latin father, Cassiodorus.[13] In his introductory comments to Psalm 6, Cassiodorus urges his audience to 'remember' that this is the first of a group of psalms concerned with repentance. He then goes on to enumerate the seven psalms which constitute this group. Similarly, in his concluding comments on Psalm 143, Cassiodorus speaks of the 'course of tears' that has just been completed and once again specifies the individual psalms that make up this journey which begins in affliction but ends in joy.[14]

Cassiodorus's comments are worthy of note in a number of respects. First of all, it is clear that Cassiodorus is making a genre distinction between these psalms and the rest of the psalter. This genre distinction is clearly 'reader-oriented', in the sense that it flows from the use to which these psalms might be put by those faithful attempting to turn from their sins and avail themselves of God's grace.

The fact that these psalms are grouped together is also significant for how their individual details are interpreted. Cassiodorus's consistent interpretation of the individual elements of these psalms in a penitential light is clear testimony to the power of the genre designation he has made.

It is significant that Cassiodorus is able to remind his audience of an

---

12. Jauss, 'Literary History'.

13. There are, of course, a number of references among the earlier Fathers to the penitential nature of certain of the psalms, especially Ps. 51. Thus, for example, Tertullian specifically designates Ps. 51 as penitential, and Athanasius recommends the use of that psalm for penitential purposes. There is, however, no mention of a specific set of penitential psalms similar to what one finds in Cassiodorus. On the question of whether Cassiodorus is the originator of this grouping, see further below.

14. See also his concluding comments on Ps. 51 which bring in verses from each of the other penitential psalms. See Ps. 51, lines 690-704, in the Corpus Christianorum Series Latina edition.

already established tradition here.[15] This shows that the grouping together of these psalms apparently did not originate with Cassiodorus.[16] Given Cassiodorus's dependence on Augustine throughout his commentary, it is tempting to trace the origins of this tradition back to the latter father. There is, however, no direct evidence to support such an attribution. Augustine never distinguishes these psalms as a group in either his *Ennarationes* or his other writings, nor does Cassiodorus directly attribute this tradition to Augustine.[17]

What evidence there is to link Augustine with this genre distinction is circumstantial. Possidio, in his *Vita S. Augustini Episcopi*, notes that Augustine 'had ordered to be written for him those Psalms of David which are the fewest in number, concerning repentance'.[18] Even here, however, there is no indication of which psalms might have been included in this collection. Only in a late medieval manuscript from the fifteenth century do we find a direct attribution of these psalms to Augustine.[19] It is unclear how widespread this tradition was in the middle ages.

Despite the paucity of the evidence, there are good reasons to attribute this tradition to Augustine, if not directly to his own authorship, then at least to his influence in the West. These reasons become evident when one asks again the obvious but problematic question of why these psalms might have been grouped together as seven penitential psalms. The number seven is, of course, no problem, given its sacred quality in

15. 'Memento autem quod hic paenitentium primus est psalmus, sequitur tricesimus primus, tricesimus septimus, quinquagesimus, centesimus primus, centesimus uicesimus nonus, centesimus quadragesimus secundus'. Ps. 6, lines 43-47, in the Corpus Christianorum Series Latina edition.

16. Although it is possible that Cassiodorus is referring to a previous establishment of the tradition on his own initiative, this does not seem likely.

17. In the conclusion to his discussion of Ps. 6, Cassiodorus does, however, cite Augustine as one who has written especially well 'and briefly' on the subject of penitence. According to P.G. Walsh, *Explanation*, p. 50, the latter is apparently a reference to Augustine's Sermo 352: *de utilitate agendae poenitentiae*. See Migne, *PL* 39, cols. 1549–1560.

18. Migne, *PL* 32, col. 63.

19. Cf. H. Omont, *Catalogue des manuscrits français de la Bibliothèque Nationale* (Ancien Saint-Germain francais, 2; Paris: Leroux, 1898), p. 3. For this reference, I am indebted to Ruth Ringland Rains, *Les sept psalms allégorisés of Christine de Pisan: A Critical Edition from the Brussels and Paris Manuscripts* (Washington, D.C.: Catholic University of America Press, N.D.), p. 25.

both Judaism and Christianity.[20] On the other hand, the reasons why these seven psalms have been chosen are not at all clear, as may be seen from even the most cursory form-critical analysis.

To take only the most extreme example, one may look briefly at Psalm 102. In Gunkel's terms, this psalm combines some standard features of the lament of the individual with some more unusual hymnic and prophetic elements. It does not, however, have either the explicit confession of sinfulness or the thoroughgoing awareness of sin which would mark it as a penitential psalm according to Gunkel's definition of that genre. In fact, the only possible 'penitential' note is to be found in v. 11 (MT), where the psalmist's situation is seen to be a result of the wrath of God. There is, however, no development of the connection between the wrath of God and any sinfulness on the part of the psalmist.[21]

One may compare this with Psalm 25, in which the psalmist explicitly asks God to 'pardon my guilt, for it is great' and to 'forgive all my sins'. Yet Psalm 25 is not included among the seven penitential psalms, while Psalm 102 is. How is one to explain the grouping that is being made here?

Perhaps one clue is to be found in the fact that Psalm 102 specifically refers to the wrath (*orgē* in the LXX, *ira* in the Latin versions) of God, whereas Psalm 25 does not. This is suggestive in view of the fact that two of the other penitential psalms, Psalms 6 and 38, also refer to the wrath (*orgē/ira*) of God. In the case of Psalm 6, this is again possibly

---

20. Cassiodorus specifically links these psalms with the seven means of forgiving sins. (Ps. 6, lines 48-54, though note the additional comment which follows.) The tradition of seven means of forgiving sins seems to go back to Origen (*Homilies on Leviticus*), though there does not seem to be any connection between Origen and the seven penitential psalms.

21. The relationship between human sinfulness and divine wrath is not necessarily as simple as it has come to be seen in later theology. Thus, *TDNT* has correctly seen that such passages as Ps. 6.2, 38.2 and Jer. 10.24 see the divine wrath as something beyond simple chastisement for specific sins (Johannes Fichtener, 'The Wrath of God', *TDNT*, V, pp. 395-409 (408). *Mid. Teh.* also makes a distinction between divine wrath and divine chastisement in connection with Ps. 6. On this, see W.G. Braude, *The Midrash on Psalms* (2 vols.; New Haven: Yale University Press, 1959), I, pp. 95-99. In a somewhat different way, Augustine's view of God's wrath against general human sinfulness works against the simple equation of wrath with particular human sins.

the only penitential aspect of the psalm.[22] Psalm 38 is more specifically penitential with its explicit confession of iniquity and expression of sorrow for sin (v. 19 MT).

The possibility that it is the wrath of God that distinguishes these psalms as penitential receives some support from the fact that this reference to God's present wrath is fairly uncommon in psalms of the individual.[23] Such a possibility, however, raises two questions. Why, first of all, should it be the wrath of God that distinguishes these psalms as penitential? And secondly, if it is indeed the wrath of God that determines their penitential status, how is one to explain the inclusion

22.   Though in the LXX and the old Latin of v. 8, there is at least a possible confession of sinfulness, depending on whether one understands the *thymos* which disorders the eye as belonging to God or the speaker. This is not reflected in the MT.

23.   The Psalms contain a fair number of references to God's wrath against the nations or against Israel at some point in the past or present. There are also a number of references to God's anger against an individual in the past. The references to divine wrath against an individual in the present are much less common. Ps. 27.9 (MT *'ap*, LXX *orgē*), 88.8 (*ḥēmâ/thymos*), 17(*ḥārôn/orgai*), and 89.47 (*ḥēmâ/orgē*) are perhaps the closest parallels to the the usage found in the penitential psalms.

Of these texts, Ps. 88 would seem to be as capable of being seen as a penitential psalm as Pss. 6 and 102 in that all three are laments of the individual which mention the divine wrath. It is, however, likely that it is specifically the presence of the term *orgē* in the singular which distinguishes the penitential psalms. Such a usage, of course, conforms to the Pauline usage in Romans, something which will be seen to be of some importance below. It is perhaps significant in this respect that Augustine makes a distinction between *orgē* and *thymos*, as well as their Latin equivalents, in his comments on Ps. 88.8. (Compare his comments on Ps. 6.2.) Unfortunately, Augustine abbreviates his linguistic remarks here in favor of his dominant Christological interpretation of the psalm.

Ps. 27.9, on the other hand, does have the distinctive term *orgē*. As such, it would seem to be a good candidate for a penitential psalm, if the presence of that term is one of the criteria for such a designation. This psalm may, however, have been disqualified by its status as a psalm of trust in which the anger of God is more a hypothetical possibility than a present reality. In a similar way, the status of Ps. 89 as a royal psalm may have worked against its being considered as a penitential psalm.

Such considerations would indicate that it is not the mere presence of the term *orgē* which has resulted in the designation of Pss. 6, 38, and 102 as penitential psalms but rather the combination of this term and these psalms' overall content. Ps. 25 has the latter but is lacking the former, whereas Pss. 27 and 89 have the former but lack the latter.

in this group of those other four psalms that do not mention God's wrath—especially since some of these psalms are no more (and possibly less) 'penitential' than such psalms as Psalm 25?

The answer to both these questions would seem to be found in the same place, namely, in the connection between these texts and the Epistle of Paul to the Romans. Romans is, of course, the *locus classicus* of the wrath of God in Christian writings, and it is also a key text which specifically connects a lack of repentance with God's wrath (Rom. 2.5). Significantly, Augustine explicitly makes the connection between Paul's discussion of divine wrath and the wrath referred to in Psalms 6, 38 and 102. Such a connection is clearly crucial for his discussion of these psalms in penitential terms.[24]

The importance of this connection with Paul's letter becomes clear when one notes that Romans also specifically refers to the other four penitential psalms in the course of its argument about human sinfulness and divine wrath.[25] Once again, it seems to be this Pauline connection that has influenced how Augustine has interpreted these psalms.[26] In short, it may well be the presence of Romans as a hermeneutical key that unites the three psalms which refer to the divine wrath and the four other psalms that are alluded to in that letter.

This apparent connection between the seven penitential psalms and the Epistle to the Romans underlines the Augustinian nature of their genre classification. Even if Augustine himself was not responsible for this grouping, such a classification is only conceivable in the light of Augustine's retrieval of Romans and his anti-Pelagian emphasis on divine wrath and human sinfulness.

In such a way, it is readily apparent why it is specifically in western Christianity that one finds the tradition of the seven penitential psalms. If, as Krister Stendahl has contended, it is Augustine's interpretation of Romans that has been responsible for the introspective conscience of

---

24. Note, for example, Augustine's quotation of Rom. 2.5 in his consideration of Ps. 6.2 MT. Similarly, Augustine's treatment of the relevant verses in Pss. 38 and 102 makes the Pauline connection between the wrath of God and the sin of Adam.

25. Thus, Rom. 3.4 cites Ps. 51.4 (note the LXX and old Latin variant here); Rom. 4.7-8 cites Ps. 32.1-2; Rom. 3.24 refers to Ps. 130.7 and Rom. 3.20 refers to Ps. 143.2.

26. This is particularly apparent in Augustine's treatment of Ps. 32 which is almost completely Pauline in exposition. Augustine's treatments of the other psalms either cite Romans directly or assume its argument on sin and justification.

the West,[27] it is the seven penitential psalms which have been a consistent means for the actualizing of that Augustinian perspective in individual western consciences.[28] Since both eastern Christianity and, of course, Judaism have not been so influenced by Augustine's retrieval of Romans, they have likewise not been so inclined to read these psalms in an Augustinian manner. As a result, it is only in the interpretive community of western Christianity that one finds the seven penitential psalms as a distinct genre grouping.

The Effect of Genre Classification on Later Interpretive History

At least until the rise of modern biblical criticism, the western appropriation of these seven psalms has largely been determined by the genre classification of these early centuries. This is not to say that the interpretation of these psalms has been uniform throughout their history, for such is clearly not the case. As the western church's understanding of penitence changed over the years, so did its understanding of the role of the seven penitential psalms. Nevertheless, despite such variations in how their classification as penitential was understood, that genre classification itself has only rarely been either questioned or ignored.

One cannot hope to do justice to this rich history of interpretation here. Nevertheless, at least some attempt must be made to see the implications of the traditional genre classification. Such an attempt is necessary to set the historical parameters for the following theoretical discussion.

The Medieval and Reformation Periods

The middle ages undoubtedly was the time of the most intensive use of the seven penitential psalms. Commentaries that focused on these psalms were numerous in this period, and there is substantial evidence that the seven psalms (and their commentaries) played an important role

27. K. Stendahl, 'The Apostle Paul and the Introspective Conscience of the West', *HTR* 56 (1963), pp. 199-215.

28. For the correspondence between the penitential psalms and Pauline theology, see C. Westermann, 'The Role of the Lament in the Theology of the Old Testament', in his *Praise and Lament*, p. 274 n. 18. Westermann questions the prominence of the penitential psalms in western Christianity in view of the considerably larger number of non-penitential laments. He argues that the latter have an important theological contribution to make to the biblical view of suffering.

in popular devotion. To some extent, this widespread popularity may be tied to the growth of the medieval penitential system, since the psalms provided a means of actualizing that system in the spiritual lives of individual believers.[29]

In all of this, the middle ages accepted the 'Augustinian' classification of these psalms as penitential. It did not, however, fully accept the radical Paulinism that seems to have been responsible for this classification in the first place. This response was, of course, similar to the selective appropriation of Augustine which characterized the medieval period in general.

This selective appropriation may be seen in the way the medieval commentators dealt with the many details of these psalms that describe the psalmist's physical pain and social dislocation. For the modern critic, such descriptions clearly characterize these texts as examples of the genre of the individual lament. For the Fathers, especially Augustine, such descriptions refer instead to the torments of the guilty conscience that is oppressed by an awareness of one's sins. Even when such distress is understood in a more literally physical or social sense, it is seen almost exclusively either as the result of such inner spiritual turmoil or as a divine chastisement meant to move the person praying to penitence.

In like manner, the enemies that play such a large role in the lament psalms often are understood as the sins that oppress the psalmist. Alternately, they are seen as those human or supernatural agents who attempt to ensnare the psalmist into sinful acts. Gone, for the most part, are any historical enemies who are actually inflicting physical pain on the psalmist for reasons not necessarily connected with that person's sinfulness.

By virtue of such interpretations, these psalms no longer retained their ancient Israelite function as laments in which the psalmist appealed

---

29. The individual works on the seven penitential psalms were often directed to, and even written by, the laity. As such, they were often composed in the vernacular. See, for example, the commentaries on these psalms by Christine de Pisan, Pietro Aretino, John Fisher and Martin Luther. These psalms were also usually included in lay Primers and Books of Hours as a devotional sequence. On this, see R. Zim, *English Metrical Psalms: Poetry as Praise and Prayer 1535–1601* (Cambridge: Cambridge University Press, 1987), p. 70, and M.P. Kuczynski, *Prophetic Song: The Psalms as Moral Discourse in Late Medieval England* (Philadelphia: University of Pennsylvania Press, 1995), p. xix and *passim*.

to God for relief from physical suffering or historical enemies. Rather, these psalms all became penitential psalms similar to Psalm 51, in which sin itself was the cause of the lament and the problem in need of relief. If necessary, allegorical exegesis was used to bring the details of these psalms into line with their genre classification. By such means, even Psalm 102 became manifestly 'penitential'.[30]

In all of this, the medieval commentators closely followed the lines of interpretation laid out by the Fathers, especially Augustine. Where they differed from Augustine was in the way they saw the sins concerning which the person praying was to repent. For the medieval commentator, the penitential psalms provided a means of moral struggle against the actual sins that plague one's everyday life. The role of the psalms was to help foster a sense of contrition for one's past sins and to encourage a resistance to such sins in the future.

These psalms clearly have such a role in Augustine as well, but for Augustine they also function to remind the person praying of his or her inherently sinful nature and the need to rely on God's gratuitous offer of salvation. In other words, for Augustine these psalms also bring home the Pauline argument about human sinfulness, as that argument was interpreted by Augustine in the light of the Pelagian controversy.

For the medieval commentators, the penitential psalms were more a means by which the penitent could repent of his or her individual sins and be restored to God's grace. In this the psalms worked hand in hand with a sacramental system that had the same ends. They also tied in with the medieval paradigm of *imitatio Christi*, according to which the penitents were exhorted to imitate the humility and the charity of Christ.

For the most part, the Reformation did not affect either the genre classification of these psalms as a separate group or their popularity. Luther wrote a commentary on the penitential psalms, as did many of the later descendants of the Reformation, especially the Puritan commentators. As might be expected, however, the interpretation of these psalms shifted as the understanding of penitence shifted in accord with Reformation beliefs.

In general, the Reformation's use of the penitential psalms may be

---

30. In this, the penitential psalms may be seen as the most formal example of an interpretive tendency that affected how most of the laments in the psalter were seen. The significance of the fact that the latter were often given a penitential interpretation at variance with the modern understanding of their genre will be further explored in the following chapter.

characterized as a retrieval of the more Pauline side of Augustine's interpretation.[31] No longer were the psalms seen primarily as a means of moral struggle against one's individual sins, a struggle tied to a larger sacramental system. Instead, the psalms functioned to convict the person praying of his or her inescapably sinful nature. As such, they were seen to provide an example of the need to flee to and rely on God's grace.

As Preus has observed in his analysis of Luther's use of these psalms, the main thrust of their tropological appropriation has shifted from *imitatio* to faith.[32] In such a vein, contrition ceases to be a virtue to be increasingly perfected by the penitent. It is instead redefined in terms of the Reformation virtue of faith and the necessity of relying on God.

On the whole, the reformers continued to interpret the individual descriptions of physical pain and social dislocation in the spiritual way which was seen to characterize the medieval commentators. Since they saw allegorical interpretation as suspect, they did this by means of metaphor. Through such metaphorical interpretation, the presence of physical or social suffering recounted in these psalms was still routinely seen as related in some way to the terrified conscience of the person praying. The reformers, of course, saw the cause of such terror as humanity's inherently sinful nature rather than one's own individual sins.

Both the medieval and Reformation appropriations of the penitential psalms were dependent on Augustine, though each was dependent on a different side of Augustine. The medieval commentators saw the psalms as providing a means to journey toward greater virtue and an ever closer imitation of Christ.[33] The Reformation commentators focused instead on the inability of humanity to progress in this journey because of its basically sinful nature. Both of these moves were present in

31. Along these lines, it is significant that Luther called the penitential psalms the 'Pauline psalms'.

32. Alternately, no longer is Christ the model for imitation here, with the virtue to be imitated that of charity. Rather the model is that of David and the Jewish church who lived by their faith in the promises of God in much the same way that the contemporary Christian does. On this important hermeneutical shift, see J.S. Preus, *From Shadow to Promise: Old Testament Interpretation from Augustine to the Young Luther* (Cambridge, MA: Harvard University Press, 1969). That the medieval period did not neglect David as a model for imitation may be seen in Kuczynski, *Prophetic Song*.

33. As noted above, the view that these psalms involve a dramatic progression occurs as early as Cassiodorus.

Augustine and both lead in an introspective direction. For both the medieval and the Reformation periods, the penitential psalms remained a valued part of the spiritual life.

The Modern Period

It is only in the modern period that one finds a sustained questioning of the traditional genre classification of the seven penitential psalms. As was noted above, such influential modern scholars as Hermann Gunkel and Sigmund Mowinckel directly challenged the traditional classification of the seven penitential psalms by pointing to the difference between that classification and these psalms' different use in the life of ancient Israel.

Clearly the form-critical work of these scholars has been foundational for the modern consensus in psalms research. Nevertheless, even among these scholars' form-critical successors, the traditional genre classification of these psalms has continued to be influential to the present day.

This continued influence of the tradition takes a number of forms. There is, for example, sometimes a continued interpretation of these psalms within a Pauline context, especially among those with Neo-Orthodox tendencies. Such a Reformation reading of these psalms may be found in the Psalms commentary of Artur Weiser, as well as in Karl Barth's discussion of justification.[34]

Even more obviously indebted to the tradition are those modern scholars who explicitly deal with these psalms under their traditional status as the seven penitential psalms. Such a treatment may be found in the work of such important scholars as Bernard W. Anderson and Walter Brueggemann.[35] The fact that such links are to be found in these standard modern works is a striking testimony to the enduring nature of this ancient tradition. Nevertheless, where the dominant mode of interpretation follows the form-critical approach of Gunkel, the tradition can

---

34. See Weiser, *The Psalms*, and K. Barth, *Church Dogmatics* 4.1 (Grand Rapids: Eerdmans, 1987), pp. 577-81. See below for an analysis of the tension between Weiser's form-critical treatment of these psalms and his theological analysis of them. There is less of a tension in Barth, since he is more concerned with how these psalms (especially Pss. 32 and 51) illustrate his theological point than with how they fit Gunkel's form-critical categories.

35. See Brueggemann, *Message of the Psalms*, and Anderson, *Out of the Depths*. One may also mention here the work of Norman Snaith, *The Seven Psalms* (London: Epworth Press, 1964), which combines critical reflections on these psalms with theological observations in the Reformation tradition.

be maintained only at the cost of some consistency.

It seems, for example, quite clear that Weiser's discussion of these psalms in terms of the necessity of faith in the face of general human sinfulness is at odds with his form-critical concern to place these texts in the setting of ancient Israel.[36] Similarly, Brueggemann's discussion of the seven penitential psalms is possible only because he has emphasized the penitential aspects to be found in these psalms, while minimizing their non-penitential aspects, even when the latter are dominant in a particular psalm. He also has not dealt with those psalms which are the most difficult to define as 'penitential', such as Psalm 102.[37]

In the face of such tensions between the tradition and the form-critical consensus, it is not surprising that many modern scholars have been content to limit themselves to the role of these psalms in ancient Israel.[38] Still, the continued strength of the seven penitential psalms tradition seems to indicate an attempt to reach beyond such a historical analysis towards a contemporary appropriation of these psalms.[39] It is,

36. One sees this especially clearly in Weiser's treatment of Ps. 6, where the shift from lament to thanksgiving is explained in terms of a 'God-given assurance of faith' rather than on the basis of any salvation oracle that might have been given in its cultic setting (*The Psalms*, pp. 132-33). Weiser also seems to be indebted to the tradition in the way he sees the physical suffering of the psalmist as the physical effects of his inner battle (pp. 284, 773). On this, one may also take note of Weiser's many references to the Reformation use of these psalms. In such ways, Weiser shows himself to be linked to the penitential psalms tradition even though he is skeptical of the genre definition that underlies it.

Again, Weiser's comments on Ps. 6 are a good example of this interpretive tension. There he notes that despite the traditional designation of this psalm as one of the penitential psalms the theme of penitence is 'not particularly prominent'. The reason for this is that the psalm lacks the actual confession of sin which is central to Gunkel's form-critical definition of a penitential psalm. At the same time, however, Weiser's overall interpretation of Ps. 6 is entirely in accord with the Reformation's interpretation of the seven penitential psalms. As such, it emphasizes the justified nature of God's punishment, the terror-stricken conscience of the psalmist, and the need for the God-given assurance of faith. See *The Psalms*, pp. 129-33.

37. Brueggemann, in fact, deals only with four of the penitential psalms, claiming that these 'present the themes common to the entire group' (*Message of the Psalms*, p. 95). Again, a psalm like Ps. 102 would seem to raise some problems for such a statement.

38. For a rare attempt to take the interpretive history of these psalms into account, see Mays, *Psalms*.

39. Only recently have the theological implications of this recognition of genre

however, precisely in light of this tension that one needs to reflect further on the role of genre in biblical interpretation.

Theoretical Reflections on the Role of Genre in Biblical Interpretation

What then are the implications of this interpretive history for the role that genre plays in the interpretation of these and other biblical texts? The fact that the traditional classification of Psalms 6, 32, 38, 51, 102, 130 and 143 as the seven penitential psalms is clearly at odds with any standard form-critical classification of these psalms implies that different conceptions of genre are at work here. What are these different conceptions of genre and what is the role of each in modern biblical studies?

At the very least, it is clear that both the traditional and the form-critical classifications of these psalms may be seen as attempts to group together texts that are seen as in some way similar.[40] It is also clear, however, that traditional and form-critical classifications disagree as to what common elements these texts may be seen to share. As a result, they disagree as to whether these texts belong to the same genre.

The preceding historical analysis was to some extent an attempt to describe the different elements by which these psalms have been grouped, either with each other or with texts in other genre categories. Along these lines, it was suggested that the traditional grouping of the seven penitential psalms might have arisen as a result of the way the Augustinian tradition related them to the Epistle to the Romans. In the modern period, on the other hand, the individual psalms of this group were found to belong to a number of different genres with which they shared what were felt to be more compelling formal or thematic similarities.

The more theoretical question still needing to be addressed is that of

been dealt with as scholars have begun to move beyond descriptive studies of the use of the psalms in ancient Israel to how they might be appropriated. This has led to, or coincided with, a rediscovery of the lament as a resource for modern religious life and a minimizing of the penitential psalms. On this, see the following chapter.

40. The issue of what exactly constitutes the common aspect of texts of a certain genre is raised by Knierem in his article, 'Form Criticism'; see especially pp. 456-68. See also the theoretical discussions of A. Rosmarin, *The Power of Genre* (Minneapolis: University of Minnesota Press, 1985), pp. 3-51, and M. Gerhart, *Genre Choices, Gender Questions* (Norman: University of Oklahoma Press, 1992).

why the traditional and the form-critical interpreters chose these different elements to be the basis of their textual groupings. The answer to this question goes to the heart of the nature of genre itself.

The Importance of Setting

One may begin this more theoretical discussion of genre by taking a closer look at the definition of genre that has been normative for modern biblical studies, that of Hermann Gunkel. For the mature Gunkel, texts belong to a distinct genre if they may be seen to share certain thoughts and moods, a specific linguistic form and a common setting in life.[41] As has often been recognized, Gunkel's genius is most evident in the way he brought together literary and sociological elements in his definition of genre.[42] To the extent that form criticism is concerned solely with cataloguing morphological elements of literary structure, it falls short of the original vision of its founder.[43] It is form criticism's attention to setting that has distinguished it from more purely taxonomic 'literary' pursuits.

It is, however, precisely the issue of setting that has come to be at the center of a wide-ranging debate in recent years, as scholars have increasingly modified the type of setting in which biblical texts are to be viewed.[44] Nowhere has this development been more pronounced than in the study of the psalms.

41. See M.J. Buss, 'The Idea of Sitz im Leben—History and Critique', *ZAW* (1978), pp. 157-70 (159), which catalogues the places where Gunkel proposed this definition of genre. In this article, Buss also nicely describes the development of this view of genre in Gunkel and its relationship to the intellectual currents of his time.

42. Buss, 'Sitz im Leben', p. 157. Buss sees the term and concept of *Sitz im Leben* as Gunkel's most important contribution to methodology.

43. Knierem ('Form Criticism', p. 454 n. 84) notes that Gunkel himself often emphasized one or two of his three ideal elements in his own definitions of individual genres. Knierem's article is a detailed discussion of the question of which elements actually constitute a genre. He also notes the difficulties of relating morphological elements to social setting in any inevitable and/or consistent way.

44. Both Knierem ('Form Criticism', pp. 446-49) and Buss ('Sitz im Leben', pp. 166-70) have noted the different ways in which it is possible to understand the term setting. To a certain extent, these different understandings mirror the development in the understanding of psalms settings described in the text of this chapter. On this, see also W. Richter, *Exegese als Literaturwissenschaft* (Göttingen: Vandenhoeck und Ruprecht, 1971), pp. 145ff.

For Gunkel, part of the impetus behind the development of form criticism was a desire to go beyond the increasingly sterile concerns of the historical criticism of his own day. That historical criticism was characterized by its insistence on situating the text in a specific setting of individual historical events. As Gunkel saw, it was especially difficult to achieve this goal in the case of the psalms because of their stereotypical nature. While not turning his back on such historical matters altogether, Gunkel shifted the discussion of setting from particular historical settings to typical institutional settings in the ongoing life of the community.[45]

In the case of the psalms, this shift made possible an appreciation of their cultic setting, even though Gunkel himself saw many of the present psalms as imitations of cultic originals. Gunkel's concern for institutional setting was continued by such followers as Begrich and Mowinckel, the latter being especially known for his advocacy of a cultic setting of the psalms and his attempt to situate a number of the psalms in Israel's festival life.[46]

Viewed against the historical criticism of the nineteenth century with its concern for specific setting in individual historical events, Gunkel's move to typical institutional setting may be seen as a generalizing move. This move was, for the most part, extremely effective in liberating scholars from overly speculative efforts to reconstruct the historical background of psalm texts. Nevertheless, more recent scholars have felt a need to generalize the setting even further.

Thus, for example, Claus Westermann moved decisively away from a primary concern for institutional setting in his attempt to isolate the distinctively Israelite theological features of certain psalms.[47] For

---

45. For Gunkel, a history of literary form implied a related history of institutional settings. See his 'Fundamental Problems of Hebrew Literary History', in *idem, What Remains of the Old Testament* (New York: Macmillan, 1928).

46. Mowinckel continued this concern for institutional setting, even while he expanded the conception of such settings to further understand how individual psalms (and genres) relate to each other. See his *Psalms in Israel's Worship* for a convenient summary of his approach.

47. This is most apparent in his important collection, *Praise and Lament in the Psalms*. Note in particular Westermann's dominant interest in the different types of praise that may be found in the psalms, as well as his concern for isolating the distinctively Israelite aspects of such praise. Along these lines, Brueggemann's assessment of Westermann's more theological development of Gunkel is significant: 'The major contribution of Westermann for our study is the discernment of a literary

Westermann, the setting of the psalms has become that of Israel's overall relationship with God, especially as this theological stance may be distinguished from that of the ancient Near East. Needless to say, this generalization beyond institutional setting to a theological setting greatly facilitates Westermann's ability to appropriate these texts for Israel's religious successors in our own day.[48]

With the recent series of works by Walter Brueggemann, this progressive generalization of setting has reached its logical extension.[49] Brueggemann's classification of the psalms into texts of orientation, disorientation and new orientation clearly looks beyond their specific institutional settings and even their more general Israelite setting to a comprehensive existential setting in human life as a whole.[50] For

dynamic in the movement of the Psalms that corresponds to and gives voice to the dynamic of faith that we know in our experience with God' (*Message of the Psalms*, p. 18). Also see Brueggemann's comments on Westermann's lack of interest in specific life settings in his 'Costly Loss', pp. 57-58.

48. Similar to Westermann's approach is that of Mays who talks specifically about a theological setting for the psalms in his *The Lord Reigns: A Theological Handbook to the Psalms* (Louisville, KY: Westminster/John Knox Press, 1994), p. 27. For Mays, 'the historical setting of the psalms can be said to be the entire history of Israel's religion' (*Psalms*, p. 9.) For him, the psalms' story anticipates their later use in Judaism and Christianity (*Psalms*, p. 11.)

49. See, for example, Brueggemann's 1984 book, *Message of the Psalms*, as well as the series of articles which preceded it and anticipated it in part: 'From Hurt to Joy, from Death to Life', *Int* 28 (1974), pp. 3-19; 'The Formfulness of Grief', *Int* 31 (1977), pp. 263-75; 'Psalms and the Life of Faith: A Suggested Typology of Function', *JSOT* 17 (1980), pp. 3-32; see also John Goldingay's elaboration of the last article, 'The Dynamic Cycle of Praise and Prayer', *JSOT* 20 (1981), pp. 85-90 and Brueggemann's response, 'Response to John Goldingay's "The Dynamic Cycle of Praise and Prayer"', *JSOT* 22 (1982), pp. 141-42. Brueggemann's subsequent article, 'The Costly Loss of Lament', notes various institutional possibilities for the setting of the lament, though it also notes that 'more recently form-critical scholarship has moved away from a rigid and one-dimensional notion of *Sitz im Leben* to a much more comprehensive and dynamic notion which would be', Brueggemann suspects, 'more congenial to Westermann' (see pp. 58-59, especially n. 8.) His later work, *Israel's Praise: Doxology against Idolatry and Ideology* (Philadelphia: Fortress Press, 1988) aims at a recovery of Mowinckel's constitutive sense of liturgical action but also broadens the setting of that action to more general human social relationships.

50. As Buss has pointed out, this concern for what is universally human was not completely missing in the work of Gunkel, despite his dominant institutional emphasis. See his 'The Study of Forms', in J.H. Hayes (ed.), *Old Testament Form*

Brueggemann, the psalms are to be grouped according to the way they *function*, rather than according to any set literary or structural criteria.[51]

What is consistent throughout all of this is the way it is setting and function which have been determinative of which texts are grouped together.[52] This emphasis on setting and function is not meant to imply that Gunkel's other criteria—thoughts, moods and literary formulas— have been absent in the modern classification of texts. It does, however, suggest that the way scholars see such elements is to a large part determined by the way they see the setting and function of the texts under consideration.[53]

When setting and function, rather than purely literary elements, are seen to be the major factors in the definition of genre categories, the traditional grouping of the seven penitential psalms ceases to be as puzzling as it seemed at the beginning of this chapter. After all, the historical analysis of the first section of this chapter indicated that the traditional classification arose precisely because these texts were being read in a setting marked by a certain theological perspective. The

Criticism (San Antonio, TX: Trinity University Press, 1974), pp. 53-56. See also Buss's own argument that this be the ultimate concern of form criticism ('Sitz im Leben', p. 167).

51. For Brueggemann, setting has largely become synonymous with function, though this does not negate a connection with a specific social setting, especially in *Israel's Praise*. On this, see his 'Psalms and the Life', together with the subsequent exchange with Goldingay, and his *Message of the Psalms*.

52. Cf. the significant comment of Knierem: 'The conclusion seems inevitable that form criticism is heading towards a typology of setting', 'Form Criticism', p. 465. In the area of the psalms, Brueggemann has clearly played a major role in moving the field in this direction. Note his approval of the work of Knierem and Buss in 'Costly Loss', p. 58 n. 8. On the importance of function for genre, see also C.L. Broyles, *The Conflict of Faith and Experience in the Psalms: A Form-Critical and Theological Study* (JSOTSup, 52; Sheffield: JSOT Press, 1989), p. 22.

Along similar lines, other recent scholars have argued that certain psalms have taken on different functions in different settings even in the biblical period. See, for example, J.L. Mays, 'Past, Present, and Prospect in Psalm Study', in J.L. Mays, D.L. Petersen and K.H. Richards (eds.), *Old Testament Interpretation: Past, Present, and Future* (Nashville: Abingdon Press, 1995), and F. Stolz, *Psalmen im nachkultischen Raum* (Zürich: Theologischer Verlag, 1983).

53. It is only in rare cases that strictly literary or morphological elements actually determine a genre. (The sonnet might be such an example.) Usually, such elements play a supportive role to classifications established on the basis of how and in what setting one sees these texts at work.

modern classifications see different connections here because they are reading these texts in different historical and /or theological settings.

The implications of this are clear. Once one shifts the setting in which these texts are to be seen, one shifts the way one sees the features that these texts have in common. That is to say, once one shifts the setting, one shifts the genre. In the case of the seven penitential psalms, once one moves to a setting marked by an Augustinian reading of Romans, one is able to group these texts according to a common element that was not present in the historical setting of ancient Israel.

The case of the seven penitential psalms helps us to see that setting is not a given for a text. Texts may be situated in any number of settings, and these different settings will result in a similar number of genre possibilities. There is no natural or universal setting for any text. There are only historical settings, either in the past or in the present. In short, to engage in genre analysis is to engage in a historical enterprise.

Determining Genre: A Descriptive or a Constructive Task?

The view that genre analysis is a historical enterprise would have come as no surprise to Gunkel and his immediate successors. After all, these scholars saw themselves basically as historians of ancient Israel, interested in the role of certain groups of texts within specific institutional settings in particular times and places. Gunkel saw his method as enabling him to describe the way certain texts functioned in ancient Israel.[54]

What more recent scholars like Westermann and Brueggemann have done is to move from this descriptive historical task to more theological claims about the role of these texts for the modern day. Nevertheless, to the extent that they advocate a function for these texts in the modern period similar to that which they played in ancient Israel, they have moved from a descriptive to a constructive enterprise.[55]

---

54. Whether such a descriptive historical task is ever completely objective or free from the constructive demands of the present is a much larger epistemological problem. It is, nevertheless, certain that such a scientifically descriptive task is what these early form-critics saw themselves as doing.

55. This move is perhaps most forcefully seen in Brueggemann's work on the lament. Brueggemann's argument in this work is not only the descriptive historical point that the lament was central for ancient Israel but also the prescriptive theo-

While asserting an identity of ancient and modern function is in many respects a 'natural' move for those with a modern historical consciousness, it is neither an inevitable move nor a purely 'descriptive' move. It is a prescriptive move since, as the case of the seven penitential psalms shows, there are clearly other genre possibilities.

The point is that such genre classifications are not 'intrinsic' to the text itself.[56] They are instead dependent on the way texts function in various historical settings. Thus, what were in Israel originally unremarkable psalms of lament became penitential psalms in later settings shaped by different historical forces.[57]

What also needs to be seen here is that to prescribe a genre is, at least to some extent, to prescribe a setting, since the highlighting of common features that is constitutive of genres is intimately related to one's setting. In such a way, the assumption that the contemporary reader will appropriate the psalms in much the same way as the ancient Israelite is essential to the work of both Westermann and Brueggemann.

There are two parts to this assumption. The first is that the ancient and modern settings of these texts are either essentially the same or at least sufficiently analogous as to allow the psalms to be grouped (and to function) now according to much the same genre categories that they would have had in ancient Israel. In such a way, both Westermann and Brueggemann talk about the universal human situations of suffering and relief which lead to an appropriation of such psalm genres as the lament and the psalm of thanksgiving.[58] The need for such universal

logical point that the lament's loss in the modern church is a 'costly' loss. See especially Brueggemann's 'Costly Loss'.

56. Cf. the work of E.D. Hirsch (*Validity in Interpretation* [New Haven: Yale University Press, 1967], pp. 78-89) who defines intrinsic genre in terms of the author's intentionality. The present work is obviously at odds with Hirsch in its emphasis on the way that texts *function* in various settings. Still, Hirsch's insight that genre is defined by 'purpose' is clearly relevant here. The question is whether it is the purpose of the author or the interpreter that is determinative. It is this distinction that Westermann and Brueggemann have blurred by their assumption of a common human setting.

57. Mays also talks of these psalms 'becoming' penitential psalms. (So on Ps. 6 in *Psalms*, p. 62.) For him, this is a move to 'a different hermeneutical situation'. Considering the present argument about the nature of genre definition, it is significant that Mays sees this move as a 'shift in the function of the psalm'.

58. It is important to note that this immediate identification of setting would not

situations is clear, for without them these genres will not be able to continue to function in the way they did in the past.

The second assumption is that these psalms' historical genres not only *can* be seen as their present genres by the modern reader but that they *should* be seen as such. This is clearly a prescriptive move, and one which is rooted in the Neo-Orthodox and existential nature of both Westermann's and Brueggemann's analyses. Thus, while their Neo-Orthodoxy leads these authors to assert the distinctiveness of Israel's insights, their existential leanings lead them to assert the universal applicability of such insights to all of humanity.[59]

The case of the seven penitential psalms challenges both of these assumptions, and especially the second. The question is, first of all, whether such universal or analogous situations do indeed exist, or whether the various settings of these psalms throughout history are sufficiently distinctive so as to require a much more individual analysis. Clearly, those communities that saw Psalm 102 as a penitential psalm rather than a psalm of lament saw suffering in a different way than these scholars are contending is natural. The physical fact of suffering may remain the same throughout history, but the way this suffering is seen clearly has changed.

Even granting, however, the possibility of settings that are sufficiently analogous to allow for similar genre classifications, one may wonder whether such classifications are to be seen as inevitable. Again, the case of the seven penitential psalms would seem to indicate that other genre definitions have been seen as both possible and preferable. The presence of such alternatives underlines the prescriptive nature of the move made by scholars such as Westermann and Brueggemann. Such a prescriptive move is not necessarily wrong. It must, however, be defended against

be possible in the case of the more institutional settings of Gunkel, Begrich and Mowinckel, though it would still be possible to argue that they are sufficiently analogous to present settings that their application is appropriate. This means, however, that a historical argument would have to be made. It is only with the assertion of a universal human situation that the more immediate applications of Westermann and Brueggemann are possible.

59. There are obviously similarities to the theological approach of Rudolf Bultmann here. The twin claims of distinctiveness and universality sometimes come into conflict in these authors' own work. See, for example, Brueggemann's 'Formfulness of Grief', where the pattern of the lament psalms does not exactly match the pattern of modern grief as isolated by Kubler-Ross.

other equally possible prescriptive moves as more adequate to the
community for whom these authors are writing.

Toward a Constructive View of Genre: Possibilities and Controls

All would agree that texts are defined as belonging to a certain genre
because such texts are seen to share certain features in common. What
is less acknowledged, however, is that the question of genre is really a
question of *which* elements a reader is brought to see as common to
certain texts.[60] To see this is to see that texts are grouped according to
some criterion external to themselves.

This is the case even when texts are grouped because they share similar morphological elements (such as in the case of a sonnet), since other
groupings (for example, according to subject matter) are quite possible.
The question of which external criteria are chosen depends at least in
part on the setting in which the reader places the text and the use to
which the reader wishes to put the text.[61]

To view genre in such a way is to see it as essentially a means by
which certain texts are read together as mutually informative. That is to
say, it is to see genre as a reading convention rather than as a property
of the text itself.[62] It is also to acknowledge the importance of genre in
the production of meaning, since it is only through association with

60. On this, see again Rosmarin, *Power of Genre*, pp. 3-51, and Gerhart, *Genre
Choices*. See also E. Schauber and E. Spolsky, *The Bounds of Interpretation:
Linguistic Theory and Literary Text* (Stanford: Stanford University Press, 1986) and
R. Cohen, 'History and Genre', *New Literary History* 17 (1986), pp. 203-217.

61. Again see Cohen, 'History and Genre', p. 210: 'Genres are open categories;
they are groupings of texts by critics to fulfill certain ends'. Cohen sees such genre
choices as historical in nature, involving the critic in certain ideological, social, and
literary commitments (p. 214).

Once the genre of the psalms has been established according to setting and function, the details of these psalms may be interpreted according to that genre. Those
details most helpful to the setting and function will be highlighted and others will
drop into the background. If complete consistency is desired, one may resort to such
techniques as allegory or metaphor to bring one's reading into line with the genre.

62. On genre as a reading convention and on reading conventions in general, see
J. Culler, *Structuralist Poetics: Structuralism, Linguistics, and the Study of
Literature* (Ithaca, NY: Cornell University Press, 1975), especially pp. 136-37. Also
important here is the work of Jauss, *Toward an Aesthetic*, especially Chapters one
and three. On this, compare Hirsch (*Validity*) as someone whose view of genre is
author-centered rather than reception-centered.

other texts that one knows how to approach any particular text.[63]

In the present case, the traditional genre classification of the peniten-tial psalms enables the reader to approach these psalms in a way that is different from that allowed by other genre classifications. It also allows the reader to enter into a certain attitude towards life as defined by that genre.[64]

This is not meant to imply that this attitude towards life is necessarily better than other attitudes made possible by other genre classifications. Such a determination can only be made according to how a person is situated historically. To say this, however, is to affirm once again that it is setting that is a major factor in the determination of genre. This is never more evident than when one is aware of different genre possibilities for the same text.

According to this view, genre analysis is both an historical task and an act of self-definition. It is both a way of describing others' interactions with a text and a way of interacting with that text oneself. By reading a text in a certain way, one makes a statement about who one is and the historical community to which one belongs. In such a way, the divergence between the traditional classification of the seven penitential psalms and the more recent form-critical classification of these texts challenges the reader not only to say how he or she is to read these texts but also to say who he or she is.

Does this mean that one's definition of genre is completely free, or more accurately, that there are no constraints on that definition other than one's present historical circumstances? To argue in such a way would be to misunderstand both the above analysis and the nature of biblical texts. What the case of the seven penitential psalms shows is that there are a number of constraints upon the way a biblical text

63. It is, nevertheless, through such reading conventions that the power of the text is unleashed. Through such reading conventions the text is brought into relationship with the rest of existence. In such a way, genre produces the meaning of the text, as David Tracy has put it. See his *The Analogical Imagination: Christian Theology and the Culture of Pluralism* (New York: Crossroad, 1981), p. 129. See also the work of M. Gerhart and Chapter 4 of the present work.

64. To a certain extent, these texts may be seen as performative. This implies that certain texts make possible the entrance into a setting that is not the current setting of the reader. This is certainly the case with the penitential psalms. Such a view is similar to Ricoeur's concept of the world in front of the text, though it is a world that is mediated by a certain community in a particular historical time. Again, this will be discussed further in Chapter 4.

functions, constraints that often decisively influence a person's definition of genre in a certain direction.

The first of these constraints is the fact of the canon itself. Because a
particular biblical text already exists in a larger body of texts defined by
the canon, biblical interpreters have tended to privilege texts from
elsewhere in the canon in their definition of that text's genre. That is to
say, one usually tends to locate one's similar texts from within the
canon of Scripture or at least to place these texts on a special level.

This canonical definition of genre is especially likely when the genre
classification is seen to have theological significance. In such cases,
there may even be a certain tendency to see the biblical texts as consti-
tuting a distinctive genre and to argue for the theological importance of
such distinctiveness.[65] There is less concern along these lines when the
grouping is for the purposes of historical reconstruction.[66]

Another constraint on genre definition in the case of biblical texts is
the tendency to group texts within the canon according to a certain
tradition of genre conventions. Such traditions of interpretation help to
distinguish those who follow them as members of a distinct historical
community. This traditional reading may be either conscious or uncon-
scious, depending on whether the choice of genre is a deliberate interpretive move or one which is 'natural'.[67] It may also be regulative, if
such a move is dictated by a community for its members. Again, such
genre traditions are an element in the maintenance of community identity. As such, a reformulation of such traditions may sometimes mark a
shift in a community's historical self-understanding over against other
communities.

The traditional grouping of Psalms 6, 32, 38, 51, 102, 130 and 143 as

65. One sees this attempt at linking the distinctiveness of the biblical form to the
distinctiveness of biblical revelation in the claims made for the distinctiveness of
the gospel form or in Westermann's arguments for the distinctiveness of Israel's
lament form. One also sees it in a different way in the critical discomfort felt in
those cases where biblical texts are dependent on non-biblical examples.

66. Because their task was primarily historical rather than theological, the early
form critics felt quite free to bring in parallels from the ancient Near East and
beyond to support their views of how biblical texts functioned in the institutions of
ancient Israel. The same historical goals and willingness to bring in extra-biblical
parallels is to be found among more recent sociological critics as well.

67. On the different ways in which a community affirms a particular view of a
text, see S. Mailloux, *Interpretive Conventions: The Reader in the Study of
American Fiction* (Ithaca, NY: Cornell University Press, 1982).

the seven penitential psalms is a good example of the way that genre definition helps to maintain community identity. By identifying these psalms as 'penitential psalms' and placing them in the context of an Augustinian reading of Paul, the western church has appropriated these psalms in a different way than that which would arise from an alternate genre classification. Such a classification has functioned as a means of actualizing the epistle to the Romans (as seen in an Augustinian light) in the lives of the faithful. This interpretive tradition is distinctive to western Christianity, as it is to be found in neither Judaism nor the eastern church.[68]

A third constraint on genre definition is the fact that such definition is not usually an individual activity but rather one that takes place in a living interpretive community. Such a community might well have considerable diversity in terms of how it views its texts. If, however, it is a viable community, it will at the very least be marked by a conversation about those texts which informs its interpretation, including its genre definitions.

It is, of course, possible to shake free of these constraints of canon, tradition, and community by simply stepping outside their authority and approaching the text from another perspective. In different ways, a purely literary or a strictly historical approach to the text does precisely that. Nevertheless, for those who see themselves as involved in a more specifically theological enterprise, canon, tradition and community function as powerful guides to interpretation in general and genre definition in particular.

Conclusions

This chapter has used the case of the seven penitential psalms to illustrate the complexities of genre and genre definition. In particular, these texts have helped to show the ways in which genre analysis is both a descriptive and a constructive task. The descriptive task of genre anal-

---

68. Such identity definition is also accomplished through a shift in the way the genre is seen, even when the texts are still seen as belonging to the same genre. Thus, the reformers accepted the medieval genre definition of the seven penitential psalms, but they shifted the way in which such psalms were to be seen as penitential. In so doing, they established an interpretive tradition different from the medieval and ongoing Catholic tradition, one which effectively functioned to define—and engender—a more distinctively Protestant identity.

ysis is to bring to light the different ways in which texts have been grouped with other texts throughout their history, from their origins to the present. The constructive task of genre analysis is to make a case for the way such texts should be grouped in the present historical moment. The two tasks seem to be distinct, yet they are ultimately related.

To understand a text fully is to be as aware of its genre possibilities as one is able.[69] An overview of that text's genre history is a first step towards such an awareness. Nevertheless, one cannot rest with such a historical overview. One must make a genre definition for the present interpretation of the text. Such a genre definition will necessarily be influenced by one's historical situation and the functions that one wishes the text to perform. It also, however, may be influenced by a retrieval of those genre possibilities that are brought to light by an analysis of the text's interpretive history.

All of this suggests an ongoing dialectic between the descriptive and constructive aspects of genre analysis. To fully define a text's genre is not only to study the history of that text's interpretation but also to become involved in that history. The succeeding chapters of this work will further investigate the mode of this involvement.

69. There is no need to deny that the author of a text may have intended that text to be read as an example of a certain genre and that that author's intentions may be reconstructed with varying degrees of probability. Still, as Jauss has shown, an audience's perception of a text's genre is seldom static throughout history. See also Tracy here, *Analogical Imagination*, p. 128.

Chapter 3

THE SHIFTING CENTER OF THE PSALMS: GENRE DEFINITION AND EVALUATION

The previous chapter's argument concerning the constructive aspect of genre analysis has a number of important implications. Primary among these is perhaps the recognition that genre analysis is at least in part an evaluative enterprise. The fact that the act of defining a text's genre is a choice among a number of real possibilities means that genre definition is an indication of what the person involved considers significant. Indeed, the evaluation of what is significant in a text is perhaps the most basic step in defining that text's genre.

There is, however, another evaluative aspect of genre analysis, one that occurs after the basic genre definitions have been made. This other aspect is the task of determining how different genres relate to each other. This task is evaluative in that it invariably involves some judgment as to these genres' relative importance. As with the initial act of genre definition, this task is, to some extent, a historical enterprise in that it involves a description of how different genres have related to each other in the past. Once again, however, it is also a constructive task of present interpretation, one which very much depends on the interpreter's own perception of what is central.

The case of the biblical psalms provides a particularly instructive example of this second evaluative step in genre analysis. In fact, a look at recent scholarship on the psalms shows this to be an especially important issue at the present time. Once again, one thinks especially of the attempts of Claus Westermann and Walter Brueggemann to move beyond the form-critical consensus that has dominated the field since the work of Hermann Gunkel. Such scholars assume the great literary and historical gains of Gunkel's method but seek to sharpen the theological and existential implications of his work. It is precisely this sharpening that brings in the evaluative dimension.

Genre Relationships in Contemporary Psalms Scholarship

In their attempt to highlight the distinctive theological and existential aspects of the psalms, both Westermann and Brueggemann are distinguished by the attention they pay to the dynamic relationship that exists between the psalm genres established by Gunkel. For Westermann, the psalms are characterized by the interplay between lament and praise.[1] Ancient Israel lamented its misfortunes before God and then declared its praise of God's salvific mercy and activity. These divine actions served in turn as the assurance by which Israel was able to bring its laments before God.

Brueggemann's work builds on that of Westermann. For Brueggemann, the psalms may be arranged according to a dynamic schema of orientation, disorientation and new orientation.[2] Psalms of orientation praise the stability of the cosmic and moral order established by a trustworthy God. Psalms of disorientation protest the seeming failure of that order in the face of individual or communal suffering. Psalms of new orientation reflect the surprise and joy that result from God's new salvific activity on behalf of those who are suffering.[3]

Clearly, these scholars have broken significant new ground in the way the psalms may be seen. Where Gunkel brought order to the Psalter by grouping together similar psalms in genres defined by their common mood, literary features and social settings, Westermann and Brueggemann have attempted to construct a new, more inclusive order

---

1.   See his *Praise and Lament*. For Westermann, praise and lament are not entirely to be assigned to distinct psalm genres. The genre of the lament often ends in praise, while psalms of praise (especially declarative praise) often look back to the situation of the lament.

2.   It is important to note that Brueggemann himself cautions against using this schema as a 'straightjacket' in which to place the psalms. It is instead a 'paradigm' or a 'heuristic' means of allowing us to see things in the psalms which we might otherwise have missed. Cf. his *Message of the Psalms*, pp. 9-10. See also 'Psalms and the Life', p. 23 n. 19, where he defends his use of Ricouer's interpretation theory in terms of its 'heuristic value' for relating his psalms schema to 'actual human experience'.

3.   This dynamic schema is not a circle in which one simply returns to the state previous to the disruption. Rather there is a transformation to a new state of being quite different from what went before. Goldingay sees this as a spiral rather than a circle in his 'Dynamic Cycle', a usage of which Brueggemann approves in his 'Response', p. 141.

by relating these genres to each other in wider theological and existential categories. Such a means of relating the psalms to each other is obviously very different from Mowinckel's alternate attempt to relate different genres by situating them in a common cultic setting.[4]

It is the combination of inclusivity and dynamism that makes these new approaches so attractive. Both Westermann and Brueggemann make it possible to conceive of the psalms as a whole, bringing a cohesiveness to the psalms which was not always to be found when these texts were grouped according to their different institutional settings.[5] At the same time, they avoid simply reducing the psalms to a monolithic theological statement that would undervalue their inherent diversity.

This is clearly an achievement of some magnitude. Nevertheless, despite the impressive nature of this work, these new approaches raise a number of questions that have only begun to be considered. This chapter is particularly interested in the questions that arise from a more precise awareness of what is involved in genre definition.

Setting and Function

Perhaps the most important aspect of Gunkel's work was his bringing together the classification of literary form with the discernment of that form's social setting. Gunkel's definition of genre included both the aesthetic features of a text (its 'mood' and literary aspects) and its social

---

4.   Brueggemann finds Mowinckel's attempts to relate the psalms in such an institutional way to be 'highly speculative'. So 'Psalms and the Life', p. 23 n. 19. Despite his reservations about Mowinckel in this respect, Brueggemann acknowledges his indebtedness to Mowinckel's larger insights about the creative role of the cult. See 'Psalms and the Life', p. 18 (where he interprets Mowinckel in the light of Ricoeur's language theory), *Message of the Psalms*, p. 26, and *Israel's Praise*, esp. pp. 1-28.

5.   Brueggemann explicitly argues that form criticism by itself cannot deal with the relationship of the psalms to each other. As a result, he sees the need to move beyond form criticism to a schema based on the 'unarguable' dynamics of human life. As noted above, he finds Ricoeur's interpretation theory to be helpful in establishing this schema. So 'Psalms and the Life', p. 23 n. 19.

This attempt to come to terms with the psalms as a whole has obvious 'canonical' implications, an approach to which Brueggemann is obviously sympathetic. See, for example, his comment that 'to value fully any psalm, it must be used in the context of all of them' (*Message of the Psalms*, p. 16). Brueggemann's later attempts to address the canonical setting of the psalms in a more direct way will be considered in Chapter 6 of this work.

setting in the life of ancient Israel. This combination holds together two main elements of biblical research.[6]

According to Brueggemann, Westermann has broken with more traditional form-critics in his lack of interest in the question of institutional setting.[7] As Brueggemann sees it, Westermann's importance lies instead in his concern for the larger sphere of the human–divine relationship which is mirrored in the psalms.[8] Brueggemann follows Westermann in moving beyond institutional settings to the different aspects of human experience which lie behind these genres. It is this move which allows Brueggemann to establish a dynamic relationship between the genres and to make an existential connection with the modern situation.[9]

For Brueggemann, a psalm's significance is directly dependent on its 'function', a term which for him seems to have a wider human reference.[10] To determine a psalm's function, one must look beyond its institutional setting (of the sort that concerned Gunkel and Mowinckel) to its role in the life of the individual or community.

This different emphasis has important implications for how Brueggemann is able to group the psalms. For him, different types of psalms

6.   For a discussion of Gunkel's joining of form and setting, see Buss, 'Sitz im Leben'. Contemporary biblical scholarship is still dominated by literary and social concerns, though the two are no longer always connected in the way that Gunkel connected them.

7.   'Psalms and the Life', pp. 3-4. In fact, Brueggemann claims that Westermann 'has largely dissolved the question of *Sitz im Leben* so that it is meaningless'. In another place, he says that Westermann has 'largely begged the question of life setting for the laments. He is most reluctant to use the category of cult and when that category is denied, it is most difficult to discuss "Sitz im Leben" in any formal sense', 'Costly Loss', p. 58.

8.   'The major contribution of Westermann for our study is the discernment of a literary dynamic in the movement of the Psalms that corresponds to and gives voice to the dynamic of faith that we know in our experience of God'. *Message of the Psalms*, p. 18.

9.   Thus, 'Psalms and the Life', p. 5: 'In this discussion, we hazard the provisional presupposition that the modern use of the Psalms and ancient use shared a common intent and function, even though other matters such as setting and institution may be different... The hermeneutical possibility of moving back and forth between ancient function and contemporary intentionality exists because the use of the Psalms in every age is for times when the most elemental and raw human issues are in play'.

10.   Brueggemann, 'Psalms and the Life', p. 5.

may have the same function, while psalms of the same type may have different functions. Thus, the declarative hymn may be seen as sharing a similar function with the formally different category of the thanksgiving song. Conversely, the declarative hymn is radically different in function from the descriptive hymn whose form it shares.[11]

Indeed, the same psalm may even have different functions, depending on how (and by whom) it is used.[12] Thus, for example, descriptive hymns may function to support the present social order if they are used by those who benefit from that social order. On the other hand, they may be a radical challenge to that order, an 'evangelical nevertheless', when used in hope by those who have been left out.[13] Depending on their use, such psalms would occupy a different place in Brueggemann's orientation, disorientation, new orientation schema.[14]

This usage clearly loosens the link between literary form and sociological setting that Gunkel tried to fashion.[15] Now psalms with the same combination of literary features and content may have different functions, depending on their different 'settings'.[16] These settings no longer refer to institutional settings within ancient Israel but rather to

11. 'Psalms and the Life', pp. 9-10. Also note his comments on pp. 15-16: 'While declarative and descriptive hymns may be grouped together form-critically, they stand at the opposite extremes of Israel's experience of life and of God'. See also his later comments on the psalms of orientation in *Message of the Psalms*, p. 25: 'It will be clear that we are not following any strict form analysis, but are paying primary attention to the content and the mode of articulation'.

12. This capacity of a psalm to bear different functions depending on the situation of its use is especially clear in Goldingay's interpretation of 'Psalms and the Life', an interpretation later confirmed in Brueggemann's 'Response', p. 141. According to Goldingay, 'At each point, everything depends on what those who use the psalms bring to them and mean by them' ('Dynamic Cycle', p. 89). In his later *Message of the Psalms*, Brueggemann again agrees with Goldingay and notes that 'one's hermeneutical stance toward the psalm might determine how it is to be classified in terms of function. This classification of function is much less stable and much more dynamic than the usual classification of form, which tends to be stable and even static', p. 125.

13. Brueggemann, *Message of the Psalms*, pp. 26-28.

14. Similarly, the same psalm could indicate a situation of either old orientation or new orientation, depending on how and by whom it is used. Cf. *Message of the Psalms*, p. 125.

15. Such a loosening was already anticipated by Knierem in his 'Form Criticism'.

16. Again, see Knierem, 'Form Criticism'. Cf. also Buss, 'Sitz im Leben'.

various possibilities of more general human experience which continue to the present.[17] For Brueggemann, this general human experience is 'unarguable'.[18]

With this shift from specific institutional settings to general human experience, form takes on new meaning. In such a way, Brueggemann sees the literary form of the lament as mirroring the anatomy of the human soul.[19] Such a form brings to expression the various trials and triumphs of human life. By focusing on how form relates to the existential, rather than the institutional, setting, Brueggemann has clearly broken new ground in psalms scholarship in a way that promises great theological fruitfulness.

Defining the Center of the Psalms: Historical and Universal Arguments

Brueggemann's formulation is obviously one of much power. Still, there is a curious ambiguity that runs throughout the argument. On the one hand, Brueggemann stresses the universality of the psalms which makes them accessible to repeated generations down through history. More specifically, it is this tie to 'unarguable' human experience that allows the psalms to give expression and provide form to such experience.[20] On the other hand, Brueggemann also argues that the way these

17. For another example of this move to incorporate modern setting in the concept of *Sitz im Leben*, see E.S. Gerstenberger, 'Canon Criticism and the Meaning of *Sitz im Leben*', in G. Tucker, D. Peterson, and R. Wilson (eds.), *Canon, Theology, and Old Testament Interpretation* (Philadelphia: Fortress Press, 1988), pp. 20-31. In a somewhat different vein, see also the reluctance of Mays to 'bind the interpretation of a psalm to a defining setting' as determined by form criticism' (*Psalms*, p. 20). For Mays, the psalms 'are to be interpreted in the service of their use' (p. 34).

18. The term is used with reference to situations of new orientation in 'Psalms and the Life', p. 10, and with reference to the schema as a whole on p. 23 n. 19.

19. Thus Calvin, as quoted by Brueggemann in *Message of the Psalms*, p. 17, spoke of the psalms as the 'anatomy of the soul'. Brueggemann himself has argued the correspondence of form to experience, especially in the case of the lament. See his 'Formfulness of Grief', pp. 263-75, as well as *Message of the Psalms*, p. 54. He also notes in his analysis of the psalms of new orientation that 'human experience strangely corresponds to the flow and form of these texts' (*Message of the Psalms*, p. 125). In this case, however, he couples his discussion of form with a further discussion of how the psalms are used. The methodological importance of this juxtaposition will be discussed further below.

20. It is important to note that Brueggemann also sees these texts as *evoking* such experience in the sense that such experience cannot be said to exist prior to its

psalms function depends on the specific situations in which they are used. This is most graphically shown by the fact that the same psalm may have entirely different functions when used in different situations.

Thus, when Brueggemann is discussing the psalms' ability to give expression to human experience, the power to determine how these texts function seems to be located in the texts themselves. In such cases, these texts seem to be a paradigm of human experience in such a way as to allow those undergoing similar experiences to recognize and give expression to such experiences.

When, on the other hand, Brueggemann is discussing the way that the psalms function in specific social and political situations, the power to determine how these texts function seems to rest in particular individuals and communities. That is to say, it is the individuals and communities themselves that define the function of these texts according to their particular situations.

The underlying question here is that of the nature and power of texts. Do texts have immediate access to a universal human experience in such a way that they have real power to express and give shape to that experience? Or is such access inevitably filtered through the varied historicity and intentionality of either individual or communal experience in such a way that the individuals or communities involved have the power to determine how such texts are used?

In other words, do texts have the power to define human experience or does human experience have the power to define the way texts are used? To some extent, Brueggemann's answer depends on which texts he is talking about.

Brueggemann is most likely to speak of a shift in function in the case of his psalms of orientation. As noted above, such psalms may either be a defense of the established order or a protest against that order, depending on who is praying those psalms.[21] To some extent, the psalms

being given form by the use of these texts. Cf. 'Psalms and the Life', pp. 17-19; also *Message of the Psalms*, p. 53. Brueggemann has especially developed his thoughts on the ability of the psalms to 'create a world' in *Israel's Praise*. This issue will be discussed at length in the next chapter of this book.

21. Thus, when such psalms are in the mouth of the 'economically secure and politically significant', they may 'serve as a form of social control'. On the other hand, in the mouth of 'those who share in none of the present "goodies"', such psalms are an expression of an eschatological hope. 'Thus, the very psalms that may serve as "social control" may also function as "social anticipation", which becomes

of new orientation also share this twofold possibility.[22]

On the other hand, the psalms of disorientation, especially the lament psalms, seem to speak directly to what Brueggemann sees as the universal human experience of suffering.[23] Such suffering is, to be sure, manifested in various historical circumstances.[24] Nevertheless, Bruegge-

"social criticism". But that requires that we be aware and intentional in our usage and the orientation that we articulate through them' (*Message of the Psalms*, pp. 26-28). See also 'Psalms and the Life', p. 11, where Brueggemann notes that such psalms 'at times may assert the new and at times stand in need of the radical criticism of suspicion'. As noted above, this insight is sharpened in the subsequent exchange with Goldingay.

22. That the psalms of new orientation are similar to the psalms of orientation in their being open to different functions according to the hermeneutical stances of the individual or community praying them may be seen in *Message of the Psalms*, pp. 125; 196 n. 7. Cf. also Goldingay, 'Dynamic Cycle', and Brueggemann, 'Response'.

23. On this, note Brueggemann's correlation of the form of the lament to the movement of human grief ('Formfulness of Grief'), a correlation echoed in *Message of the Psalms*, p. 19, where he likens the 'anatomy of the lament psalm' to the 'anatomy of the soul'.

Also note his argument against the theories of such scholars as Mowinckel, Johnson, Schmidt, Delekat and Beyerlin ('Costly Loss', pp. 58-59) which would have the effect of disrupting the direct connection he sees between the laments and immediate human experience. His preference for the alternate theories of Albertz and Gerstenberger is a natural corollary to his larger views. While many of his evaluations seem quite plausible, one does wonder whether Brueggemann's preference in this respect is at root a historical judgment about the role of such psalms in ancient Israel or a theological judgment about the most effective way of appropriating these psalms for the present. Thus, for example, Brueggemann comments that Mowinckel's theory connecting the 'evildoers' with sympathetic magic is 'an attempt to distance the laments from actual social processes'. This seems to suggest that Brueggemann's problems with Mowinckel's theory are not with its historical accuracy in ancient Israel but rather with its hermeneutical implications and effects.

Similarly, one may note the different evaluation of Schmidt, Delekat and Beyerlin ('Costly Loss', p. 62), where Brueggemann wants to emphasize the connection of the lament to questions of justice. Again, this seems to suggest that such theories are being evaluated less in terms of how accurately they describe the way the psalms functioned in ancient Israel and more in terms of whether they provide a hermeneutically significant reference for the present day.

24. 'The enduring authority of this language [in the laments and the songs which celebrate new orientation] is in the combination that it bears witness to common human experience, but it is at the same time practiced in this concrete community with specific memories and hopes. Thus the openness to the universal and the passion for the concrete come together in these poems', 'Psalms and the

mann does not seem to allow for any shift in function for these psalms depending on who is using them.[25]

One finds a similar turn in Brueggemann's use of Ricoeur's hermeneutics. For Brueggemann, the psalms of disorientation correspond to Ricoeur's hermeneutics of suspicion, functioning as a challenge to the stable world affirmed in the psalms of orientation.[26] On the other hand, the psalms of new orientation correspond to Ricoeur's hermeneutics of representation, a hermeneutics which is only possible after the suspicious questioning and complete rejection of the old orientation.[27]

Brueggemann's suspicions of the psalms of orientation derive, at least in part, from their social situation, a social situation which he identifies as primarily that of the economically and politically secure.[28] On the other hand, the social and political matrix of the psalms of disorientation never seems to be open to the same sort of suspicious critical assessment. These texts are the means of challenging the unchallenged order, but they themselves do not appear to be open to suspicion.

Accordingly, the psalms of disorientation have a clear and immediately recognizable function in a way that the psalms of orientation do not. Indeed, Brueggemann sees these psalms as having been neglected precisely because that distinctive function could not be incorporated into the polite hermeneutic of standard church practice. The only recourse was to banish these psalms from the formal life of the church,

---

Life', p. 17. Also note *Message of the Psalms*, p. 175: 'That is, the spirituality of the Psalms is shaped, defined, and characterized in specific historical, experiential categories and shuns universals'.

25. Thus, for example, Brueggemann can speak of their 'specific social function', a function that has been lost to the church by their neglect throughout the church's history ('Costly Loss', p. 57). The function of such psalms does not change depending on the situation or intention of the individual or community praying them. According to Brueggemann, they have been neglected by those uncomfortable with their implications. On the question of their neglect, see further below.

26. 'Psalms and the Life', pp. 11-14. Note that it is only at those times when the psalms of orientation do not assert the new that they 'stand in need of the radical criticism of suspicion'.

27. 'Psalms and the Life', p. 4.

28. *Message of the Palms*, pp. 26-28. In view of the Ricoeurian background of much of his analysis, it is significant that Brueggemann describes his critical assessment of the social situation of these psalms as a 'suspicious possibility'.

a move which Brueggemann has consistently opposed throughout his writings.[29]

Following Westermann, Brueggemann sees the anatomy of the psalms of lament as structurally central for the entire Psalter.[30] Indeed, in their move from 'wretchedness to joy' or 'plea to praise', these psalms lie at the heart of Brueggemann's entire schema.[31] In such a way, Brueggemann may be said to see the lament as the interpretive key to the Psalter as a whole.[32]

It is important to note that this central status is to some extent based upon the hermeneutical immediacy that Brueggemann has granted to the lament and denied to the other types of psalms.[33] Whereas the function of the psalms of orientation and (to some extent) new orientation can only be ascertained by examining their setting, the psalms of disorientation are assumed to have only one possible setting. In much the same way, these psalms are assumed to be above Ricoeur's hermeneutical suspicions.

The question that needs to be raised is that of whether the psalms of disorientation really have the hermeneutical immediacy that Brueggemann claims for them. Are they indeed immune from the need for their own suspicious examination, as Brueggemann seems to feel?

As Brueggemann notes, Ricoeur's hermeneutical process is 'inherently dialectical' in its linking of suspicion and representation.[34] It is, however, doubtful whether Ricoeur would apportion his hermeneutical functions to different texts the way that Brueggemann does.[35] Rather,

29. See, especially, 'Costly Loss', which argues forcefully for the retrieval of the vital function of the lament in contemporary church practice.

30. *Message of the Psalms*, pp. 18-19.

31. See *Message of the Psalms*, pp. 124, 194 nn. 3-4.

32. See *Israel's Praise*, p. 133, where he refers to the 'pain at the center of praise'. Also note p. 140, where he notes that 'the possibility of genuinely liberated praise depends upon lament as its point of origin'.

33. Note his comment in 'Psalms and the Life', p. 6, that the psalms of orientation are 'not the most interesting'.

34. 'Psalms and the Life', p. 16.

35. The question of whether the psalms of orientation require a third hermeneutics is relevant at this point. See 'Psalms and the Life', p. 19, where Brueggemann tentatively suggests the phrase, 'hermeneutic of convention'. Goldingay correctly notes that no third hermeneutic is needed ('Dynamic Cycle', p. 89), but, like Brueggemann, he also seeks to match the remaining two hermeneutics to the different psalms depending on how they are used. The point of the present work is that

Ricoeur's point would seem to be that *every* text is subject to both suspicion and representation.[36] As such, the latter are more properly seen as successive aspects of the interpretation of every text than as hermeneutical stances that may be assigned to different texts.

Brueggemann's exemption of the psalms of disorientation from questions about the way they function in different settings enables him to use these psalms as the still point around which other psalms revolve and from which they take their significance. What needs to be explored further here is whether the function of these psalms is so obviously beyond question or suspicion. The answer to this question is not philosophical as much as it is empirical. That is to say, the answer lies less in assertions about the links of such psalms with universal human experience and more in the actual historical data of how such psalms have been interpreted down through their history.

The Different Faces of Disorientation

It is, first of all, necessary to look a bit more closely at those psalms that make up Brueggemann's category of disorientation, a category that Brueggemann himself notes includes 'a great variety' of psalms.[37] The most important of these psalms for Brueggemann are the psalms of lament, especially the laments of the individual.[38] Also included, however, are certain prophetic psalms, the seven penitential psalms, and finally those wisdom psalms that reflect on disorientation from a little distance.

Brueggemann is able to include these diverse elements together because of the way that he defines disorientation—namely, in relational terms. Psalms of disorientation 'reflect the awareness that things between Yahweh and Israel are messed up... In the broadest sense, they have one partner or the other speak about the "disarray" into which the

both hermeneutical moments are a necessary part of the post-critical interpretation of any psalm.

36. Thus, it is only by subjecting one's first 'naive' reading of a text to the hermeneutics of suspicion that one can come to a genuinely post-critical 'second naiveté'.

37. *Message of the Psalms*, p. 58.

38. For Brueggemann, the personal lament is the 'clearest and most simple example' of the speech of disorientation, a 'nearly pure type'. Some of the other psalms which reflect disorientation range 'far afield' from the 'classic shape' of the lament psalm. *Message of the Psalms*, p. 58.

relationship has fallen. It is a disarray that concerns both partners in various ways.'[39]

One may contrast this with the way Brueggemann has defined the psalms of orientation. The latter psalms describe life not so much in relational terms as in cosmological, or even ontological, terms. Here the emphasis is on the trustworthiness of both God and the cosmic and moral order God has created. It is the system that is celebrated along with the God who stands behind that system.[40]

It is important to note that whereas some of the psalms of disorientation challenge the system celebrated in the psalms of orientation, this is in fact not true for all of them. The prophetic psalms, for example, reaffirm the moral order and indict Israel for its violations of that order.[41] Similarly, the penitential psalms uphold the moral order by ascribing the suffering of the one praying to the latter's violation of that order.[42]

These different types of disorientation seem to suggest that there are two separate issues here. The first is whether the system has a coherent order and a trustworthy God. The second is whether, given a coherent system and a trustworthy God, there are still problems in the relationship. If the latter is the case, the problems must then be the fault of the person praying.[43]

39. *Message of the Psalms*, p. 58.
40. So 'Psalms and the Life', pp. 6-7; *Message of the Psalms*, pp. 25-26.
41. *Message of the Psalms*, pp. 88-94. Note especially p. 94, where Brueggemann seems to imply the similarity between the 'second opinion' of these psalms and the stance of the psalms of orientation.
42. *Message of the Psalms*, pp. 94-106. Note also p. 20 of that work, where Brueggemann argues that the psalms of the innocent sufferer more directly apply to Jesus than the psalms of penitence. Since Jesus' suffering is a major embodiment of the disorientation aspect of his schema, this would seem to imply that the penitential psalms are less appropriate to such disorientation than the laments. This is also suggested by 'Costly Loss', p. 61, where the acceptance of guilt is a response to disorientation that is at odds with the response of the lament for which Brueggemann is arguing in the article. Since an acceptance of guilt is certainly present in the penitential psalms, this would seem to raise some questions as to how these particular psalms of disorientation fit into Brueggemann's overall schema. This is perhaps most explicitly affirmed by the final chapter of *Message of the Psalms*, where Brueggemann sees the penitential psalms as a 'yearning for a return to the orientation' (p. 174).
43. For this possibility and certain problems that Brueggemann has with it, cf. *Israel's Praise*, p. 133. Note that the seven penitential psalms are absent from this

It is only when the blame for the 'mess in the relationship' is seen to be on the part of God that any unexpected cosmological or theological possibility is being raised—namely, that the system is not working properly or that God is untrustworthy. When the blame for the mess is on the human side, this does not shake the foundations of the world in quite the same way.[44]

The truly radical psalms are those which, like the book of Job, challenge the coherence of the cosmic and moral order and the trustworthiness of that order's God. This challenge is to be found pre-eminently, if not exclusively, in the psalms of lament.[45] More specifically, it is to be found in those laments that have an accusatory question or declarative accusation directed against God.[46] It is these psalms which dare to sug-

later book, though Brueggemann does not entirely rule out the possibility that God's anger might be appropriate (cf. p. 146).

44. For Brueggemann, these questions are not only, or even primarily, abstract philosophical questions about the nature of the universe or theological questions about the nature of God. They are concrete questions of justice that arise from the social realities of everyday life ('Costly Loss', p. 62). On some occasions, however, 'not only is the social system awry, but the God who legitimates the system seems also to have failed. Not only the *nomos*, but the "guarantor of *nomos*" is in question' (*Message of the Psalms*, p. 174; see also 'Costly Loss', pp. 62-63). In these cases, it is the lament that comes to the fore.

On the other hand, Brueggemann sees other types of disorientation speech, such as the penitential psalms, as a 'yearning for a return to orientation'. The implication would seem to be that the person praying is not contesting the system as unjust but rather admitting his or her own unrighteousness within a just system. This is the case even if, as Brueggemann asserts, 'the righteousness of God becomes a point of appeal that lies outside the standard explanations' (*Message of the Psalms*, p. 174).

There is a larger question here, namely that of whether the penitential psalms actually imply that the suffering of the person praying is just and accepted. The answer to this question depends on whether one highlights the penitential parts of these psalms or the parts which are more similar to the lament.

45. In this respect, Brueggemann's 'in any case' on p. 174 of *Message of the Psalms* is somewhat misleading, since it implies that the penitential psalms are as 'revolutionary' as the laments in their 'violation of the conventions of the fully ordered world'. The problem lies again in the two different ways that disorientation functions in Brueggemann's schema. While the prophetic and the penitential psalms clearly manifest 'a relationship in disarray', they do not challenge the underlying order or the justice of God in the same 'revolutionary' way that the laments do.

46. As Brueggemann notes in *Message of the Psalms*, p. 173, and 'Costly Loss', p. 62, there are a number of laments that assume the justice of God and appeal to that against those who have perverted the way that justice should be manifested in

gest that the person praying has lived up to the system but that God has not. Such a claim is especially present in those psalms that specifically affirm that person's innocence.

In other words, those psalms that contend that the problem with the relationship is on God's part raise the unsettling possibility that the system itself has broken down. In contrast, Brueggemann's other psalms of disorientation may see trouble in the relationship (on the human side), but they do not question the system. Indeed, in pointing to human responsibility for the problem, they seem to reaffirm their belief in the system.

This distinction is important for a number of reasons. First of all, it helps one to understand better the truly radical nature of the challenge of the lament. Secondly, it helps to clarify the way in which the psalms of disorientation have been interpreted down through history. Those psalms which do not challenge the coherence of the system or the trustworthiness of God have been far from neglected throughout this history. Indeed, such examples as the penitential psalms have often enjoyed a central status during that history comparable to that which Brueggemann now seems to accord the psalms of lament.

The real significance of Brueggemann's attempt to see the lament as central is that it reflects a *change* as to which psalm genre is to be seen as the prism through which to approach the entire Psalter. Unless the case can be made that this privileged status of the lament is self-evident from the nature of the Psalter itself,[47] it can only be seen as a historical act of interpretation done in particular circumstances for particular purposes. This brings the context of interpretation to the fore.

---

the social system. These do not pose the same radical questions that are posed by the laments which question or accuse God directly, although at times the question of why God allows these human agents to continue (and thrive) in their unjust ways seems to lurk just below the surface. One should note that the accusatory question is to be found more often in the communal lament than in the lament of the individual. See Westermann, *Praise and Lament*, pp. 176-78, 183-86.

47. It is not clear whether Brueggemann intends to make this particular argument in his earlier works. On the one hand, he does point to the large number of laments in the Psalter and cites Westermann in defense of the centrality of the lament. On the other hand, he admits the 'subjective' nature of the schema that sees the lament as central. In his later work, Brueggemann is more explicitly 'canonical' in his analysis. On this, see the detailed discussion in Chapter 6 of the present work.

The Context of Interpretation

Brueggemann is not alone in decrying what he sees as the minimal role that the lament has played in the community of faith. Indeed, it is almost a commonplace of modern psalms scholarship that the laments are the neglected stepchild of Christian prayer.[48] To be completely accurate, however, one must qualify this statement somewhat. Certainly, whatever is the case in personal devotion and community worship,[49] this charge of neglect is not completely accurate in terms of what it implies for the role of the lament in the scholarly literature of the past. Anyone who has written a commentary on the psalms has by necessity paid considerable attention to the lament.

The real issue is not whether these psalms have been neglected but whether they have been understood and valued in the way that their modern advocates understand and value them. Here Westermann comes closer to the mark when he remarks upon the Pauline context in which the laments have been used in the western church:

> From the standpoint of the Pauline doctrine there can be no lament without a confession of sin; a lamenter appears before God as one who is guilty. But the lament is not a constituent part of Christian prayer, and we can say that in a certain sense the confession of sin has become the Christianized form of the lament: 'Mea culpa, mea culpa, mea maxima culpa'.[50]

For Israel, of course, it was quite possible to have a lament without a confession of guilt, at least at one point in its history. Indeed, certain lament psalms assert the innocence of the lamenter in quite vigorous terms. Nevertheless, as Westermann himself has noted, there was a distinct move away from the accusatory question even within the history

---

48. See, for example, the remarks of O. Fuchs, *Die Klage als Gebet: Eine theologische Besinnung am Beispiel des Psalms 22* (Munich: Kösel, 1982), p. 9. See also Westermann, *Praise and Lament*, where it is asserted that 'in Western Christendom the lament has been totally excluded from human relationship with God, with the result that it has completely disappeared above all from prayer and worship' (pp. 264-65).

49. Even in these areas, it is difficult to justify such a sweeping charge of 'neglect' or 'loss', particularly in those churches that have either a lectionary system or a tradition of reciting the divine office. One could, of course, attempt to argue that even here the lament is underrepresented in terms of their numbers in the Psalter. To my knowledge, such a case has not been made by these authors.

50. Westermann, *Praise and Lament*, p. 274.

of ancient Israel itself.[51] Thus, even according to Westermann's own analysis, it may not be entirely accurate to attribute the neglect of the lament to Pauline influence alone.

The true insight of Westermann's comments is not that the lament has dropped out of use in Christianity but rather that it has become something else because of its Christian context. Once again, it is only the lament *as defined by modern scholars* that can be said to have been neglected in Christian circles.[52] As laments that have been transformed into other genre categories, these 'neglected' texts have in fact received considerable attention in both the scholarly literature and popular devotion of these circles.

One sees this transformation in the way the traditional commentaries deal with the distinctive details of the lament. Thus, for example, the lament's graphic descriptions of social dislocation and physical suffering are frequently interpreted as the pain that comes from one's own sinfulness. This pain is sometimes seen as a divine chastisement meant to prompt one to repent. At other times, it is seen as the anguish of the terrified conscience aware of its own guilty status before God. Such anguish may cause actual physical pain, but the significance of such pain is to be found in its underlying spiritual causes.

The enemies that seem to dominate whole sections of the lament are reinterpreted as well. In this new context, they often become supernatural enemies, such as the devil, who inflict pain upon the person praying by tempting that person to sin. Alternately, the enemies may be the human counterparts of these supernatural beings who again torment the person praying by tempting that person to sin. Less frequently perhaps, the enemies are seen as the human agents of God's chastisement, though the suffering involved is again seen as a means to prompt the repentance of the person praying.[53]

51. Westermann, *Praise and Lament*, pp. 165-213.

52. One sees this, for example, in Brueggemann's relating the psalms of lament to those parts of life 'for which the human person or community is not responsible and therefore not blamed' (*Message of the Psalms*, p. 52). Such a description clearly rules out the formal connection that Gunkel made between the penitential psalms and the lament. It also denies that the lament psalms as interpreted in the Pauline context described by Westermann are truly laments.

53. Such interpretations of these psalms are by no means restricted to the allegorical interpretation of the early church and the middle ages. Even a modern critical commentator such as Weiser may be seen to relate the lamenter's sufferings

Quite clearly, there has been a change in the way the laments are used by those who advocate their importance for the modern age. However, it would be a mistake to see this change as simply stemming from our being able to see these elements as referring to real pain and this-worldly enemies. Obviously, Gunkel and the historical critics before him were quite able to do this. The real change lies in a new willingness to understand the psalms in this way in a context other than that of ancient Israel. In other words, the real change lies in taking these elements seriously for modern theology, as Westermann, Brueggemann and other recent commentators have done.[54]

What such authors have done is to argue for a retrieval of what they see as the ancient function of the lament in the practice of the modern church. Such a combination of historical argument and pastoral significance is often quite compelling. What is clear from the history of interpretation, however, is that, given a different context of interpretation, the texts themselves are quite capable of being understood in a very different light.

It would be wrong to see the modern shift in the way the laments are understood as simply the result of methodological developments. Again, Gunkel and the other early historical critics certainly understood the broad meaning of the lament in the way their more recent successors have. What they did not do was reclaim these laments as theological resources for the modern community of faith.

The recent movement to reclaim the lament would seem to owe its impetus less to a shift in the methods of interpretation than to a shift in the context of interpretation.[55] More specifically, certain historical

to the need to come to terms with his or her own guilt. See, for example, Weiser's comments on Ps. 31 in *Psalms*, pp. 278-79.

54. The more literal view of suffering was not entirely absent from the reformers' theological reflections on the lament, as may be seen by their view of their troubles as analogous to those of the Jewish synagogue. Nevertheless, as in the case of such modern critics as Weiser, the reformers still tended to interpret these literal sufferings in the context of the lamenter's own sinfulness. It is only comparatively recently that the sufferings of the lament have been understood both literally and apart from the issue of human sinfulness which is not to be found in the text.

55. This is not to say that the methodological shift from allegorical interpretation to a more historical approach to the text does not support the recent shift in interpretation. It does, however, mean that one should not attribute the latter shift to

developments of the recent past seem to have helped form a new context in which the psalms of lament are now able to function in a different way.[56]

Two recent historical factors seem particularly important in this respect. The first is the Holocaust, an event that has forced much searching theological reflection among both Jews and Christians. The second is the increasingly desperate situation of the world's oppressed, a situation that has come to the fore of theological thought in the various theologies of liberation.

Both the Holocaust and the desperate plight of much of the world's population are examples of suffering that are extremely difficult (one might better say impossible) to understand in any conceivable framework of sin and punishment. As such, it is not surprising that those who have attempted to deal with this suffering theologically have availed themselves of the lament as a means of coming to terms with a God who is difficult to understand in view of such situations.[57]

It is within the historical context of these situations that the lament has come to be read in the way modern scholars are suggesting. In other words, the lament is not some immediately accessible paradigm of human suffering that is brought to bear on various human situations of suffering, as Brueggemann seems to suggest. Rather, it is in the context of such specific historical situations of suffering that the psalms function in such a way. In different situations, such psalms will function— and have functioned—in other ways.[58]

---

methodological causes alone. Rather, one should also look for factors in the historical context that contribute to the new way such methods are used.

56. So C. Westermann, *The Living Psalms* (trans. J.R. Porter; Edinburgh: T. & T. Clark, 1989), p. 67.

57. For an account of the role of these psalms in Jewish attempts to come to terms with the Holocaust, see H.J. Levine, *Sing unto God a New Song: A Contemporary Reading of the Psalms* (Bloomington: Indiana University Press, 1995), pp. 204-228. Fuchs also sees the memory of Auschwitz as a primary reason why the modern age needs to pay more attention to the lament genre. (*Die Klage als Gebet*, p. 9.) For examples of the use of the lament to frame the issues of liberation theology, see, among others, Ee Kon Kim, '"Outcry": Its Context in Biblical Theology', *Int* 42 (1988), pp. 229-39, and J.D. Pleins, *The Psalms: Songs of Tragedy, Hope, and Justice* (Maryknoll, NY: Orbis Books, 1993). Most of these works directly address the question of the suffering of the innocent that these situations raise.

58. One sees similar tendencies in the case of some of the reformers who saw

It is clear that both the Holocaust and the situation of the oppressed have played an important part in Brueggemann's thinking about the role of the lament in his schema of psalms interpretation.[59] Indeed, one might say that it is precisely because Brueggemann allows these factors to enter his field of vision that he is open to certain ways of appropriating the lament that were not considered relevant before.

Brueggemann, however, seems more inclined to see his interpretive schema as arising directly from the texts themselves.[60] This is the significance of his reliance on the hermeneutical immediacy of the lament. Brueggemann's argument is that this particular psalm genre is so reflective of human experience that it has only one possible function. While the function of the psalms of orientation and new orientation are dependent on their settings, the function of the lament is never in doubt because it is assumed to have only one possible setting, the universal situation of human pain. This allows Brueggemann to read these texts without suspicion and to give them a hermeneutical centrality which undergirds his entire schema.

What the history of interpretation makes clear is that the lament has no such hermeneutical immediacy. How the lament functions is affected by its historical context in much the same way that the functions of the psalms of orientation and new orientation depend on their settings.

Rather than simply hearing the psalms themselves, what Brueggemann is really asking us to do is to evaluate the roles of the different psalm genres in the light of our particular circumstances in the modern world. As such, Brueggemann's schema is indeed, as he admits, 'subjective'.[61] However, this 'subjectivity' lies not so much in terms of his own status as an individual interpreter as in terms of his challenge to a particular historical moment. It is, in fact, this address to a particular

themselves as the true church and the victims of oppression. Even in such cases, however, the reformers' emphasis was on the need for faith and repentance.

59. Thus, Brueggemann notes that the dismantling move of disorientation is a 'characteristically Jewish move', as is the related question of theodicy (*Message of the Psalms*, pp. 20, 168-69). With respect to the latter, Brueggemann further notes that 'it is especially the Holocaust that has made the question of theodicy both unavoidable and insoluble' (p. 202 n. 7). Brueggemann's interest in liberation theology is equally clear throughout, as his concern with social justice and the Miranda quote at the beginning of the book demonstrate.

60. Note, for example, his claim to be 'committed to no goal but to hear the Psalms', *Message of the Psalms*, pp. 12-13.

61. Brueggemann, 'Psalms and the Life', p. 20.

shared historical moment that makes his work of such theoretical and existential significance.

The Shifting Center of the Psalms

It is important to note that Brueggemann's attempt to define a central genre for the psalms is only the latest in a series of such attempts.[62] One sees this particularly clearly when one looks at another group of Brueggemann's disorientation psalms, the seven penitential psalms.

In his comments on the neglect of the lament, Westermann contrasts this neglect with the privileged place of the seven penitential psalms throughout the western tradition. Westermann thinks it 'extremely odd that preference for these Psalms has lasted for centuries without anyone having ever asked why, among such a large number of Psalms, there are in fact so few Psalms of repentance'.[63] The reason why these psalms have been so preferred is, of course, precisely because they are much more in tune with the Pauline tradition which Westermann claims has ruled out the authentic lament psalms.

One of the effects of this preference for the penitential psalms may be seen in the way that earlier ages appropriated the lament along penitential lines, something which was noted earlier in this chapter. Similarly, the psalms of orientation and new orientation often came to focus on the praise of God's gracious forgiveness of the sins confessed in the penitential psalms. By centering the Psalter around these particular psalms, the interpreters of earlier ages defined the rest of the Psalter in relationship to them, at least to a certain extent.

This does not mean that the interpreters of earlier ages neglected suffering in its use of the laments. Rather, those interpreters placed such

---

62. Both Brueggemann and Westermann attempt to privilege their psalms center in the name of that which is distinctively Israelite. For Brueggemann, that which is not distinctively Israelite falls under suspicion, while that which he judges to be distinctive is not called into question in a similar way. This is, of course, not to say that the former category is incapable of retrieval for Brueggemann, once it is brought into relationship with what is distinctive.

Other times appear to have been less concerned about what was distinctively Israelite and more concerned about which psalms could best serve to actualize some particular theological or religious purpose. Some may have even been interested in those psalms which would best harmonize with non-Israelite elements of either philosophy or other religions.

63. Westermann, *Praise and Lament*, p. 274 n. 18.

suffering in a different context, one which centered on sin and penitence. The modern world may not be comfortable with this different
context, but it would be wrong to argue that the earlier interpreters were
ignoring human suffering simply because they did not treat such suffering the way we do now.

When the Pauline view of human nature came under siege in the
Enlightenment, the seven penitential psalms lost their central status as
well, at least among those circles most affected by Enlightenment
thought. Conversely, with the Neo-Orthodox revival of the Pauline
tradition has come a revival of interest in these psalms.[64] Not surprisingly, Barth's treatment of these psalms has a distinctly Pauline flavor.[65]

Other times considered other psalms as their interpretive center. The
early church, for example, focused on those psalms which it saw as
having Christological significance, especially those that could serve
apologetic purposes.[66] The Enlightenment church, on the other hand,
seems to have been most involved with descriptive hymns that stressed
God's role as Creator and the stability of the universe.[67]

In other words, the history of psalms interpretation is a dynamic history in which the center of interpretation shifts according to changing
historical and theological concerns. The perspective one gains from
taking this history into account is helpful in determining how one
should view the genre issues considered in this chapter.

The Dynamic History of Psalms Interpretation

What are the theoretical implications of all this for the interpretation of
the psalms? The first and most obvious implication is the historical

---

64. See the treatment of such psalms in Weiser's commentary, the work of
Snaith, the special sections for these psalms in Anderson and, of course, Brueggemann's own treatment. These modern treatments have the problem discussed in the
previous chapter, namely that these psalms are not always penitential in the way
that form criticism defines its penitential psalms.

65. Barth, *Church Dogmatics*, 4.1, pp. 577-81.

66. On this period, see O. Linton, 'Interpretation of the Psalms in the Early
Church', *Studia Patristica* IV, TU 79, (1961), pp. 143-56.

67. So Westermann, *Praise and Lament*, p. 33 n. 20, who notes that the hymns
of that period are descriptive praise of a very reflective type, nearer to the psalms of
the Apocrypha than to those of the Psalter. In contrast, the praise of the Middle
Ages is much closer to the descriptive praise of the biblical psalms, while the praise
of the Reformation is more declarative in character.

nature of psalms interpretation. How the psalms function depends, at
least to some degree, on the historical circumstances in which they are
functioning.

Brueggemann clearly saw this in the case of the psalms of orientation. Nevertheless, he still attempted to ground his overall interpretive
schema in what he saw as the unarguably clear and central role of the
lament. What the above attention to the lament's interpretive history
has shown is that neither Brueggemann's interpretation of the lament
nor his seeing it as central is 'unarguable'. Rather, both are historical
arguments arising from and addressed to the modern world.

It is obviously appropriate to address the concerns of one's own age
and situation. Still, the fact that the same biblical texts may be used to
address other concerns in other contexts raises a number of theoretical
questions. How, for example, does one evaluate whether one's approach
to the text is appropriate to one's particular context? Furthermore, what
does one do with previous understandings of the text now that the
contexts which called forth those understandings are in the past?

The answer to the first of these questions cannot be simply a textual
answer. That is to say, it cannot be an answer based solely on whether
one's understanding of the words of the text are in some way 'accurate'.
As Brueggemann's own analysis of the psalms of orientation makes
clear, the same words, even the same words understood 'literally', are
capable of radically different interpretations in different contexts. What
needs to be evaluated is not one's understanding of the text as much as
one's understanding of the relationship between text and context.

Clearly, one part of the evaluation process is to be found in the
context itself, namely in the community in which the interpreter stands
and to which that interpreter is addressing his or her interpretation. How
one defines this community is obviously a crucial question. In Brueggemann's case, a community of the economically and politically secure is
much less likely to accept his analysis of the correct setting for the
psalms of orientation than is a community in the midst of pain and
sorrow. It is Brueggemann's appropriation of the viewpoint of these
latter communities that makes it possible for him to understand the
psalms in the way he does.

Underlying Brueggemann's analysis is an analogical dialectic. On the
one hand, it is the modern historical situation that has allowed Brueggemann to focus on each individual's experience of human suffering as

the context out of which to approach the psalms. Conversely, however, it is each individual's experience of such suffering that allows that individual to make the connection with the suffering of other communities. Such an analogical dialectic makes it possible to enlarge the context out of which one reads the text.

Attention to the role of the community in interpretation helps to answer the second question raised above, that of the significance of past relationships of text and context. What is clear is that it is not only the text that has a past history. The interpretive community has a past history as well, part of which is the attempt to relate to the text. As such, cultivating an awareness of that community's past and its interpretive traditions is another means of enlarging the context out of which one reads a text.[68] This is particularly the case if one is attentive to the diversity of a text's reception, even within a particular historical tradition.

Such attention to the tradition does not dictate present interpretation. It does, however, form part of the context for that interpretation. As such, it provides a link with a wider community in time whose voice should not be lost. Such a conversation with one's predecessors results in a certain humility before the text even as one moves beyond such previous interpretations in an attempt to interpret the text correctly out of one's own historical context.

It might well be asked whether such attention to historical context and previous interpretation has the effect of shifting the focus away from the text itself. The argument of this chapter is, of course, that the text is a somewhat flexible thing whose interpretation depends precisely on such matters as historical context. If one is to begin to understand the text in its full scope, one needs to understand its relationships with a variety of contexts.

One safeguard against such a neglect of the text is the need to see the text in its canonical context. The fact of the canon means that every biblical text has a given literary context. Historical interpreters who accept the fact of the canon wrestle with individual biblical texts in this given literary context.

In the case of the psalms, this means that individual psalms are interpreted primarily in the context of other psalms. As argued in the

---

68. This is one of the most important functions of the historical-critical method.

previous chapter, this means that one tends to make one's genre classifications by grouping certain psalms together with other psalms that are perceived as similar in some way. The larger canon, especially its Davidic traditions, also provides a certain literary context which must be taken into account. Both of these canonical contexts will be considered further below.

Conclusions

One may conclude this chapter by affirming once again the force and persuasiveness of the arguments of Westermann and Brueggemann in favor of the primacy of the lament as the interpretive key to the psalms. One makes this affirmation, however, without necessarily accepting such authors' claims that such a genre preference is a more 'accurate' reading of the psalms than other genre preferences in some objective or universal sense.

What one affirms is rather that this genre preference is particularly appropriate to our modern historical moment. Other historical moments have had, and will have, other genre preferences. Indeed, other historical moments have had, and will have, other ways of defining the genres that are to be found in the Psalter. Because of this, one never reaches a definitive interpretation of the psalms.

This does not mean, however, that the interpretation or evaluation of psalm genres is arbitrary. Such factors as community, tradition and canon work against both the whims of individual interpretation and a complete reduction to the concerns of the historical moment. It is, however, only when one is aware of how these factors enter into the way the biblical text functions that one avoids the danger of universalizing one's particular genre preferences as inevitable.

An awareness of how the 'central genre' of the psalms has shifted down through history underlines once again the fact that neither the definition of individual psalm genres nor the analysis of how these genres relate to each other is a purely descriptive enterprise. Rather, both of these tasks are also constructive dialogues between historically situated interpreters and the biblical text. At its best, this dialogue is informed by as full a knowledge as possible of one's community and its interpretive traditions, as well as of the text's canonical context. Seen in such a way, genre definition goes right to the heart of both textual interpretation and theological reflection.[69]

69. One should not leave this discussion of the center of the psalms without taking note of the similarly titled study of J.L. Mays, 'The Center of the Psalms: "The LORD Reigns" as Root Metaphor', in *idem*, *The Lord Reigns*, pp. 12-22. In this article, Mays proposes the reign of God as the central organizing principle for a theological appropriation of the Psalter. Although the actual phrase *YHWH malak* is found only in Pss. 93, 96, 97 and 99 (with Pss. 47, 95 and 98 clearly related) Mays sees images of God's royal activity scattered throughout the entire Psalter. As a result, Mays also sees this image as of crucial importance for how one understands that book.

Mays's work is fundamentally different from that of Brueggemann in that his center is a 'metaphor' rather than a genre. It is, moreover, a fairly broad metaphor that can incorporate much of the Psalter. Along these lines, one might note the fact that Mays specifically rejects any 'neat separation of Yahweh's roles into the categories of creator and savior' (p. 16). This argument obviously cuts against Brueggemann's different view of the psalms of orientation on the one side and disorientation on the other. I suspect that few interpreters would want to deny the centrality of Mays's metaphor. Many might, however, want to emphasize one aspect of it over another, as seems to have happened throughout the psalms' interpretive history. In such situations, particular genres will continue to be valued more than others.

Chapter 4

THE POWER OF GENRE: FORM AND FUNCTION IN THE PSALMS

In some ways, the argument of the preceding chapters has remained remarkably true to Gunkel's classic definition of genre. After all, what has been said above agrees with Gunkel's most basic insight that genre is both a literary and a social phenomenon. More specifically, both Gunkel and the argument so far see the act of genre definition as a grouping of similar texts that have a definite setting in the life of the community.

Despite this essential similarity, however, there are a number of significant differences between Gunkel's view of genre and that of the present argument. The most crucial of these is how life setting is to be understood. As a historian of ancient Israel, Gunkel was primarily interested in the relationship between texts and institutional settings throughout Israelite history. In contrast, the present work has broadened the scope of genre analysis to include other social settings in which such texts have functioned. These other settings include the many post-biblical generations that constitute the history of interpretation down to the present.

This broadening of genre analysis to include a wider range of social settings has had two effects. First of all, it has led to the recognition that the possible groupings of texts are much more varied than one might suspect from an overview of the form-critical literature. What an awareness of the history of interpretation has shown is that the same text can be seen to have belonged to different genres at various times in its history. That is to say, depending on the function a text has been asked to perform, different aspects of that text have been highlighted, thus causing it to be included in different groupings of other texts.

The second effect of looking at the different social settings of a text throughout its interpretive history has been to highlight the important role of the community in both the definition and evaluation of genre. Again, the way communities group texts together is very much dependent on the function such texts have in those communities. The same is true of the different values assigned to each genre in those communities. Once again, function has been seen as a key element in genre definition, and function exists primarily in a community setting.

With this in mind, the present chapter will take a closer look at the relationship between genre and function. Of particular interest is the way that genre enables texts to function differently in different communities. More generally, one might ask how seeing texts as in some way connected to each other as a particular genre allows those texts to function in a particular way? In other words, what is it that gives genre its power?

The Power of Genre: Preliminary Questions

One may begin by recalling the example of the seven penitential psalms considered in Chapter 2. Grouped together, possibly because of their connection with St Paul's Epistle to the Romans, these psalms came to function in a certain way in western Christianity. More precisely, one may say that these psalms came to function in a variety of ways throughout the history of western Christianity, depending on the theological concerns of different communities of western Christians.

This same interplay of genre and function was also seen in the work of Brueggemann, particularly at the level of his schema of orientation, disorientation, and new orientation. In such a vein, Brueggemann's classification of a particular psalm as a psalm of either orientation or new orientation was seen to be dependent on how that psalm functioned in a particular community. The flexibility of these different types of psalms in Brueggemann's system only underscores the crucial role of function in genre definition.

It is important to note the complexity of the interplay between genre and function here. Clearly, texts may be grouped together on the basis of their functioning in certain ways—as Brueggemann's treatment of the psalms of orientation and disorientation demonstrates so well. It is, however, also true that texts function in certain ways because they have been grouped together—as may be seen in the case of the seven penitential psalms. The relationship is intriguingly double edged. Even once one sees the close relationship between function and genre classification, there are many interesting questions that need to be asked about the dynamics of this relationship.

One may begin to examine this relationship further by inquiring about the nature of the function that the different genre definitions of the psalms perform. What does it mean that we can isolate hymns, thanksgiving psalms, penitential psalms or laments? Obviously, at the most superficial level this means that it is through these psalms that people have praised, thanked, confessed and complained to God. However, this does not even begin to answer the question, either in the sense of what it meant to do these things in ancient Israel or in terms of what function these classifications have today. Even Westermann's penetrating theological analysis of praise and lament in ancient Israel needs to be taken further in a basic but as of yet unexamined direction.

The crucial question is not so much what functions the psalms perform as that of how they actually perform such functions. *How* do the hymns function as texts of praise, especially for those communities who have been given such texts as examples of canonical or community-authorized prayer? The fact that we tend to assume the answer to such a question shows just how basic this question is.

It is to Brueggemann's great credit that he has reopened this more basic question in a fundamental way, especially in his 1988 book, *Israel's Praise*, which is an analysis of the way praise intersects with ideology. Nevertheless, more needs to be said here. In keeping with the overall approach of this book, this chapter hopes to deepen the analysis of this topic by situating such modern insights as that of Brueggemann in the context of those provided by the larger history of interpretation.

How Genres Function: Another Look at Brueggemann's Different Functions

How the psalms function has clearly been a major question for Brueggemann throughout his recent writings. Much of what the present work has examined so far has constituted an attempt to unpack the implications of this emphasis on function. In particular, Brueggemann's insight that certain psalms take on different functions in different settings may be seen as central. In a real way, this insight is crucial for many of the new directions pursued in this book, even if one may argue that Brueggemann did not completely follow up on its implications.

Brueggemann, however, does more than simply point to the diverse functions a text may have in different settings. He also examines the nature of these functions in a more fundamental way, focusing not only on the social ends texts were meant to serve but also on the way such texts served those ends. To be more specific, Brueggemann raises the whole question of the basic dynamics that take place between a text and an individual or a community.

The Expressive Function of the Psalms

On this point, there are a number of tendencies to be found throughout Brueggemann's writings. First of all, Brueggemann sees the psalms as functioning in what might be termed an 'expressive' manner. On the most basic level, the psalms may be used to express the conscious sentiments of the person praying. Thus, a person who is suffering might use the lament psalms to express his or her feelings of pain and to bring his or her complaint before God.[1] Alternately, a psalm of praise may be used to express one's joy in God's mercy.[2] Such cases illustrate the simplest of the ways in which a psalm can function—as a mirror of a person's clearly understood thoughts and feelings. It is also, I suspect, the way many moderns usually assume that the psalms work.

Brueggemann is, however, aware of another, deeper way the psalms function in an expressive manner. As he has shown so well, the psalms may also work to 'bring to speech' that which is felt but which does not become fully real without the assistance of these texts.[3] In such a way, the psalms help a person to understand his or her feelings better. In both this and the former, more self-conscious manner, the psalms are expressive of what is in the human soul.[4]

Brueggemann's analysis, however, goes deeper still. For Brueggemann, at least some of the psalms have the additional function of bringing to expression how life really is.[5] Such psalms, particularly the psalms of disorientation, have the ability to uncover the truth even in those cases when the one praying is engaged in an act of self-

---

1. One sees the expressive aspect of the lament from Brueggemann's earliest works on the Psalms. Thus, he notes that 'the lament manifests Israel at her best, giving authentic expression to *the real experiences of life*' ('From Hurt to Joy', p. 3).

2. One will remember Brueggemann's agreement with Goldingay that we may find the same psalms 'expressing' either orientation or new orientation 'depending on the context and intention of the speaker' (*Message of the Psalms*, p. 22).

3. So Brueggemann, *Message of the Psalms*, p. 52.

4. One will remember that for Brueggemann the lament in particular mirrors the anatomy of the human soul.

5. Brueggemann, *Message of the Psalms*, p. 53.

deception.[6] In this case, 'language leads experience so that the speaker speaks what is unknown and unexperienced until it is finally brought to speech. It is not this way until it is said to be this way'.[7] In these psalms, the very form may be seen to mirror experience.[8]

Taking note of these three roles helps to explain what Brueggemann means when he talks about the psalms 'articulating, illuminating and evoking' experience.[9] In all of this, the psalms may be seen to have what might be called an expressive function.[10] As such, they give a person words to verbalize one's feelings or state of being; they help one to come to a better understanding of one's feelings; and they even work to strip away those acts of self-deception which keep one from coming to grips with reality.

Particularly in the last two functions, Brueggemann has understood in a dynamic and vital fashion the way that the psalms work in an illuminative or evocative manner. They are not simply set texts that one picks up when they fit one's state of being. Rather, one is led to understand that state of being in a way which would not be possible without the help of the psalms themselves. They are in this sense 'expressive', but in a most active way.

The Creative Function of the Psalms

Brueggemann's understanding of the evocative power of the psalms is itself an advance over many of the older approaches to the psalms which focused rather exclusively on their more strictly conscious usage. To his great credit, however, Brueggemann has recognized the creative potential of the psalms in an even deeper way, especially in his later work, *Israel's Praise*.[11] Significantly, his vehicle for this deeper under-

---

6.   'To evoke reality' for someone who has engaged in self-deception (and still imagines and pretends life is well ordered, when in fact it is not). Cf. Brueggemann, *Message of the Psalms*, p. 53.

7.   Brueggemann, *Message of the Psalms*, p. 53.

8.   So Brueggemann, *Message of the Psalms*, p. 54: 'As the speech has form, so it is discerned that the experience has form too. The form of experience is known in the form of speech'.

9.   Brueggemann, *Message of the Psalms*, p. 53.

10.   Brueggemann himself uses this terminology when he speaks of the psalms of disorientation as 'a means of *expressing* that tries to match *experience*' (italics Brueggemann's), *Message of the Psalms*, p. 53.

11.   This important move is anticipated in 'Psams and the Life', p. 18, and

standing is a retrieval of Mowinckel's cultic analysis of the psalms.

In this retrieval, Brueggemann is, as one might expect, not primarily interested in Mowinckel's conclusions about how the psalms were situated in the institutional setting of the New Year's Festival. Rather, he has focused on what are perhaps the more radical aspects of Mowinckel's analysis, namely, his view that the central feature of what is usually called cult is an act of 'world-making'.[12]

For Mowinckel, cult is an 'effective and reality generating drama, a drama which actualizes with real power the dramatic event, a reality which shows forth real power, or in other words, a sacrament'.[13] In this view, the cult sustains the world; it effects something.[14] The cult is not simply the expression of a subjective state of mind already present in the worshiper or even a better apprehension of denied reality. Rather, it brings about something which did not exist before. The cult makes God a reality in the community and brings about God's world.[15]

To be sure, Brueggemann has philosophical reservations about the ontological (and theological) status of Mowinckel's sacramental act.[16] Nevertheless, he still wants to affirm that more is at stake than what is in the mind of the worshiper. His emphasis is instead on the social world through which people experience all reality. Indeed, Brueggemann wants to break down what he sees as a false subject–object distinction and to understand Mowinckel in terms of 'praxis'.[17]

One especially sees this emphasis on world making in Brueggemann's discussion of praise. For Brueggemann, the human vocation of praise involves a maintaining and transforming of the world and the obtaining of a blessing 'that would not be obtained, maintained, or transformed, except through this routinized and most serious activity

briefly detailed in *Message of the Psalms*, pp. 26-27, 174. Its full discussion is found in *Israel's Praise*.

12. This first shows up in *Message of the Psalms*, p. 26, but it is especially to be found in *Israel's Praise*.

13. So Brueggemann, *Israel's Praise*, p. 8, quoting Mowinckel, *Psalmenstudien*, II, p. 21.

14. Brueggemann, *Israel's Praise*, p. 8.

15. Brueggemann, *Israel's Praise*, p. 10.

16. Thus, he notes that 'there are of course problems if [Mowinckel's] argument be taken as an ontological statement' (*Israel's Praise*, p. 11). Brueggemann instead opts for 'bracketing' the ontological implications of Mowinckel's language. Cf. also his comments about ontology and 'life world' on p. 25 of *Israel's Praise*.

17. Brueggemann, *Israel's Praise*, p. 9.

authorized by God and enacted by human agents'.[18] Praise is more than a remembering of God's past deeds. Rather, it is a means of bringing about a world that would not otherwise exist.

By his retrieval of Mowinckel's understanding of cult, Brueggemann has clearly seen a dynamic usage of the psalms that goes well beyond the expressive usage discussed above. It is, however, important to see that Brueggemann is also aware that the cult and the psalms can be misused, both in the time of ancient Israel and today. Thus, he notes that certain of the psalms of praise could easily be used in the service of a state that tries to construct a world undisturbed by the pains of ordinary life.

Such psalms tend towards pious generalities that are distant from the actions of God on behalf of God's people. Such actions are embarrassing, inconvenient and disturbing for those in power who prefer a more predictable world free from divine irruption.[19] More general praise brings about just this kind of world. As such, it can easily serve the interests of the status quo and those in power.

For Brueggemann, authentic Israelite praise is always close to the reasons for such praise—namely, God's actions on behalf of those in pain. The awareness of pain provides the context for authentic praise. Thus, Brueggemann sees the credo, the lament and the thanksgiving song as more authentic praise, since all of these point to just such divine action in times of actual pain.[20]

Much of what Brueggemann has done in *Israel's Praise* is consistent with his previous work on the psalms, particularly his synthetic treatment in *The Message of the Psalms*. As such, some of what was said in the previous chapters of this book might well be recalled here. One might note especially Brueggemann's preference for certain genres as being more authentic than others. In this, of course, he is following Westermann, who also sees genres containing concrete declarative praise as more distinctively Israelite (and therefore of greater significance) than those dominated by more general descriptive praise.[21] Brueggemann does, however, go further than Westermann in that he

18. Brueggemann, *Israel's Praise*, p. 11.
19. Brueggemann, *Israel's Praise*, pp. 96-100.
20. Brueggemann, *Israel's Praise*, pp. 137-48.
21. So Westermann, *Praise and Lament*, pp. 36-51, even though he does find a few examples of declarative praise among Israel's neighbors.

situates descriptive praise in a social context that he views as suspicious and in need of correction.

Once again, Brueggemann makes a prescriptive choice of genres according to which type of world he sees as authentically Israelite. This move has obvious canonical implications that will need to be discussed further at another point. What need to be considered here are the implications of Brueggemann's analysis for how one sees the *function* of the psalms.

Crucial in this respect is Brueggemann's linkage of Mowinckel's insistence on the power of the cult to a social analysis of the ideological substructure that underlies that cult. In this, Brueggemann is indebted to the seminal work of Peter Berger and Thomas Luckmann on the sociology of knowledge.[22] These authors also use the language of world making in their discussion of the social construction of reality, and they also see such worlds as 'externalizations' of an underlying substructure.

Brueggemann is certainly correct in his assertion that these worlds may be challenged, and it may be that such genres as the lament have precisely that function. Once again, this fits with his previous categorization of the lament psalms as the means of calling one's world into suspicion, a function that has much to do with his assertion that such psalms are at the heart of the Psalter. One will, of course, remember that despite Brueggemann's universal claims, this is a historical argument that is not valid for every period of the interpretive history of these texts. Beyond this, however, there are some implications of the world-making potential of the psalms which need to be explored further.

Expressive and Creative Functions in Brueggemann's Psalm Genres
According to Brueggemann's analysis, the psalms may be seen to have two functions, the expressive and the creative.[23] It is clear that

22. P. Berger and T. Luckmann, *The Social Construction of Reality* (Garden City, NY: Doubleday, 1966).

23. Brueggemann refers to what is done in the cult as both creative and constitutive. (So *Israel's Praise*, p. 6: 'If the cult is creative, then what was done in the cult is constitutive'.) While his usage is to some degree interchangeable, it is possible that there is a subtle difference between these two terms, with the term constitutive referring more to the imposition of a social world on others. The emphasis in Mowinckel is more on the creative function of cult, as may be seen from the subheading of the part of the chapter where Brueggemann introduces Mowinckel's theories: 'The Psalms as Creative Acts'. Nevertheless, the title of Brueggemann's chapter on this subject is 'Praise as a Constitutive Act'. While both terms are

Brueggemann in no way sees these functions as mutually exclusive, since one of his main points is that *every* psalm creates a world with a particular view of God and social reality. Nevertheless, how these different functions relate to each other is an extremely significant question, especially given what this book has argued is the close relationship between function and genre definition. A closer analysis of how the psalms function in expressive and creative ways will also contribute to an understanding of the source of the power of genre.

One may begin this analysis by taking note of which psalms Brueggemann treats as primarily expressive and which he sees as primarily creative. One will remember that the previous chapters have argued that a certain division of labor may be seen in Brueggemann's consideration of the psalms. The fact that one finds a similar division of labor here is suggestive for understanding how genre is able to function in different ways.

When one asks which psalms function for Brueggemann in an expressive way, the lament psalms immediately come to the fore. Throughout his work, Brueggemann sees the lament as giving voice to some of the most vital human experiences, bringing those experiences to expression where they belong, before God.[24] Similarly, it is with regard to these psalms that Brueggemann talks about the text as allowing a person to give expression to what does not become real until it is verbalized.

To say that the lament psalms are Brueggemann's primary example of the expressive use of the psalms is not, however, to say that other psalms do not have an expressive function. Clearly, Brueggemann sees the psalms of thanksgiving as facilitating the expression of feelings of gratitude, particularly when there is an immediacy between the memory of the pain and the thankful narration of deliverance. For Brueggemann, such psalms of declarative praise are directly rooted in the experiences of the person praying, which have resulted in the expression of thanksgiving.

Does Brueggemann also see the psalms of descriptive praise as expressive? In *Message of the Psalms*, the answer seems to be yes. One will remember that Brueggemann locates the primary setting of these

appropriate descriptions of what goes on in the cult, it may be that Brueggemann emphasizes the constitutive aspect more than the creative, something which will be seen to be significant in the following analysis.

24. So, for example, 'From Hurt to Joy', p. 3; 'Palms and the Life', p. 12, cf. pp. 17-18; *Message of the Psalms*, pp. 53-54.

psalms among the secure and powerful.[25] As such, these psalms express feelings of order and security precisely because those who pray such psalms experience the world in such a way. Even when these psalms function as a form of 'evangelical nevertheless' among those who do not have access to such power, they still seem to be expressive of a feeling of confidence in the ultimate trustworthiness of the God who is being praised.[26] As such, these psalms may be seen to have an expressive function in *Message of the Psalms*.

The answer is somewhat more complicated in *Israel's Praise*. One will remember that it is especially with regards to praise that Brueggemann is able to discuss the world-making function of the psalms. Through its painting of a particular portrait of God, praise implies a particular type of world. In both ancient Israel and the present, theological confession is inevitably intertwined with political implications.

What is significant here is that for Brueggemann different types of praise imply different types of worlds. On the one hand, declarative praise emphasizes God's actions on behalf of either Israel or an individual. This type of praise has concrete reasons for praise in what God has done at some point in the past. Such praise creates a world in keeping with Israel's central tradition of liberation and its recognition of a God of mercy.

Descriptive praise, on the other hand, tends to emphasize summons rather than reasons. Even when reasons are given, they are usually more general and abstract.[27] Similarly, God's actions are no longer specific, pointing back to a concrete point in the past. Such praise tends instead to be general, using participial forms rather than finite verbs.[28] It also tends to emphasize God's majesty rather than God's mercy, a feature which links Israel with the rest of the Near East rather than accentuating its distinctive traditions.

In such a way, different types of praise imply different worlds. Considering the discussion of the previous chapter, it is not surprising that Brueggemann evaluates these different worlds in different ways. It is declarative praise which creates a world more in keeping with what Brueggemann sees as the central Israelite tradition. In this tradition,

25. Brueggemann, *Message of the Psalms*, pp. 26-27.
26. Brueggemann, *Message of the Psalms*, p. 28.
27. Brueggemann, *Israel's Praise*, pp. 96-100.
28. Brueggemann, *Israel's Praise*, p. 99.

God's mercy is manifest in vital and surprising activity on behalf of the powerless.

In contrast, the psalms of descriptive praise create a world that is more fixed and stable. For Brueggemann, it is a status quo world, where the order of the universe—and the socio-political system—is fixed, where God does not act and where nothing changes.[29] Once again, it is majesty rather than mercy that is God's dominant attribute here, some-thing which, for Brueggemann, is more in keeping with the dominant ideology of the larger ancient Near East than with the authentically Israelite tradition. As a result, the world that these psalms create needs to be challenged by the more specifically Israelite perspective seen in the psalms of declarative praise.

The crucial point here is that most people do not experience the world in the way that is described in the psalms of descriptive praise. As a result, these psalms really do not express the feelings of anyone beyond a privileged few. Nevertheless, since Brueggemann sees the cult as being in the hands of this privileged few, he argues that it is the psalms of descriptive praise which have tended to dominate. This means, however, that for most people these psalms do not function in an expressive way as much as in a creative or, even more exactly, a constitutive way. That is to say, such psalms impose on their audience a world that does not arise out of their own experience.

A Closer Look at the Relationship of Setting and Function
To understand the importance of Brueggemann's argument that declar-ative and descriptive praise function in different ways, it is useful to compare his treatment of these types of praise to that of Westermann on which it is based. For Westermann, as for Brueggemann, declarative praise is the more fundamental, and more distinctively Israelite, type of praise. Declarative praise arises out of concrete situations in which God has acted on behalf of either the community or an individual. In con-trast, descriptive praise is derivative for both authors.

For Westermann, descriptive praise comes about as a result of abstracting a general principle from the specific acts that underlie declarative praise.[30] Because God has been shown to be merciful in a

29. Brueggemann characterizes this world as an 'absolute', *Israel's Praise*, p. 90.
30. Westermann, *Praise and Lament*, p. 32. Cf. Brueggemann, *Israel's Praise*, p. 83.

number of concrete instances, God may be described as merciful in general. However, even though Westermann sees declarative praise as more authentically Israelite, he, unlike Brueggemann, does not see descriptive praise as necessarily suspect in itself. Descriptive praise is rather a natural outgrowth of Israel's declarative praise. The latter is temporally and logically prior. Nevertheless, it leads directly on to the former.[31]

In contrast, Brueggemann tends to present descriptive praise as prior to declarative praise. This is clearly seen in his orientation—disorientation—new orientation schema, where these three stages are represented by psalms of descriptive praise, laments and psalms of declarative praise, respectively. For Westermann, the order is instead lament, declarative praise and descriptive praise.[32]

The reason for the difference between Westermann's and Brueggemann's evaluations of descriptive praise is to be found in the way they see the social setting of such praise. For Westermann, descriptive praise has the same setting as declarative praise, namely, that of Israel as a whole. As such, it is simply another expression of Israel's fundamental attitude towards God. Like declarative praise, it is rooted in the basic relationship between Israel and its God.

In some ways, this would seem to be the case for Brueggemann as well, especially when he talks about a circle or spiral of experience.[33] In such a schema, those who at one time sing the psalms of orientation can under different circumstances make use of the psalms of new orientation.[34] Conversely, the same person or group can move from declarative praise to descriptive praise as the experience of God's saving act becomes less immediate.[35]

Once, however, Brueggemann emphasizes the existence of different social settings, as he does in *Israel's Praise*, he no longer seems to be

31. Along these lines, it is significant that for Westermann 'the conclusion of the declarative Psalm of praise is a descriptive Psalm of praise', *Praise and Lament*, p. 117.

32. See again Westermann, *Praise and Lament*, p. 117.

33. See especially his 'Response', where he accepts Goldingay's suggestion of a spiral of experience.

34. Cf. 'Psalms and the Life', p. 12, where Brueggemann notes that 'it is likely that the speakers of harsh laments are the same voices as the singers of hymns, but in radically new circumstance'. This then leads on directly to thanksgiving if and when God acts to answer the lament.

35. Cf. Brueggemann, 'Response', p. 141; *Message of the Psalms*, p. 22.

referring to experiences that happen to the same group or individual as much as to the experiences of two completely separate social circles. In this latter case, descriptive praise is the preferred genre of those groups in control of society who look to maintain the status quo by projecting a world of order. Because declarative praise arises out of God's activity on behalf of those in need, it is inappropriate and even dangerous for such establishment groups. Instead, such praise has a different social setting entirely, among those who are at the other end of the social order.

The connection between Brueggemann's two books is to be found in the fact that psalms of descriptive praise are consistently associated with a social setting of well being and the status quo. The difference between them lies in the fact that in the later book the people who occupy this social setting no longer seem to be the same as those who at another time occupy the social setting connected with declarative praise. In other words, the connection between descriptive and declarative praise seems to be less a circle or spiral and more a set of parallel lines.

This shift is even more significant because of the latter book's emphasis on world making. Now such psalms are seen not simply as expressive of an outlook on the world. They are also seen as helping to *create* such a world—especially in the sense of establishing a particular view of the universe as normative. Because the different social circles in which these types of praise are at home have different degrees of social power, their world creating potential has real political implications.

Once again, Brueggemann sees the psalms of descriptive praise as the prayers of those who are well off and who have a vested interest in the status quo. Since, however, such social circles tend to have control of the cult, they also have the power to impose their static world on the rest of society. By doing so, they seek to safeguard the status quo and choke off any world view that allows for God's surprising action on behalf of the have-nots.[36]

Brueggemann's situating of the different psalms of praise raises some interesting questions on both the historical and the theoretical levels. On the historical level, one may ask how Brueggemann knows which psalms were used by certain groups in ancient Israel. His division of the

---

36. According to Brueggemann, these circles see such a world view as 'politically awkward, liturgically offensive, and intellectually embarrassing' (*Israel's Praise*, p. 98).

different types of praise is indeed quite plausible in many ways. It does, after all, seem to make sense that those interested in preserving the status quo would not be eager to perpetuate a world in which God acts freely on behalf of the powerless.

Nevertheless, one needs to ask what evidence there is that ancient Israel actually used its psalms in such a way. After all, if Mowinckel is to be believed, certain individual laments are actually national laments spoken by the king himself.[37] The myth and ritual school is, of course, even more inclusive in tying the king to the individual laments.[38] One might also note the canonical witness of the superscriptions that attribute many of the personal laments to David, something which may well indicate an original royal provenance. Such superscriptions are, in any case, an indication that much of Israel's interpretive history saw little problem in the connection between the king and this particular genre.

Similarly, one might ask whether declarative and descriptive praise are as easily definable as Brueggemann claims. For the most part, Brueggemann's argument is one which moves from the psalms themselves to the social setting. In such a way, psalms without reasons are held to be attempts by the establishment to control the cult in favor of the status quo. Again, such a social setting is certainly possible, even plausible. Is it, however, necessary or proven?

One may re-enforce this point by looking at a particular psalm that is somewhat suspect in Brueggemann's analysis, namely, Psalm 117. This psalm grounds its summons in God's *ḥesed*. It does so, however, in what Brueggemann calls a 'programmatic' way that moves away from specificity.[39] As such, 'the characteristic words to portray Yahweh are used without any substance and so have become a conventional slogan'.[40]

Once again, however, a look at this psalms's interpretive history helps to provide some perspective. Psalm 117 is, after all, one of the psalms of the Egyptian Hallel found in the standard Passover Haggadah. In such a context, the psalm is anything but a 'conventional slogan' lacking in specificity. It is instead a classic celebration of victory over slavery and oppression.

37. Mowinckel, *Psalms*, pp. 225-46.
38. So, for example I. Engnell, *Studies in Divine Kingship in the Ancient Near East* (Uppsala: Almqvist and Wiksells, 1943), p. 176.
39. Brueggemann, *Israel's Praise*, pp. 79, 104.
40. Brueggemann, *Israel's Praise*, p. 104.

The point of this example should be obvious by this stage of the present work. It is the context of a psalm that makes all the difference in terms of how it functions. Accordingly, it is not possible to determine how a psalm functioned from that psalm's text alone without further information about its setting.[41] A historical argument that a particular psalm or psalm genre functioned in a certain way in ancient Israel remains to a large extent dependent on external evidence that shows that psalm or genre actually functioning in that way.

Even though Brueggemann talks throughout of these genres' settings in ancient Israel, one wonders whether Brueggemann's argument is not in reality based more on how he sees these genres functioning in modern settings. One can, of course, argue that such modern usage is indicative of their ancient usage. However, the history of interpretation clearly shows that such a fixed function is not necessarily the case. Indeed, a more inclusive look at these genres' modern usage would show that there is no such uniformity of function even at the present time. Once again, function depends on the setting.

The earlier chapters of the present book argued that Brueggemann saw this connection of function and setting in his earlier writing, even though he did not follow his argument through consistently. Such a connection is, of course, the implication of his argument that the same psalms may be psalms of either orientation or new orientation, depending on their setting. While this argument is not entirely absent in his later work, it is certainly much less prominent, in part because of his largely unsupported historical speculations about the use of the psalms in the socio-economic divisions of ancient Israel.

The historical question leads directly to more theoretical problems with Brueggemann's argument. Brueggemann is, I would agree, correct when he asserts that the psalms create a world. Do they, however, necessarily create the sort of world that Brueggemann claims? Do the psalms of descriptive praise, for example, necessarily imply a status quo world? Once again, the history of interpretation helps to provide a certain perspective on this issue.

One may take, for example, Psalm 46, a psalm which Brueggemann sees as a psalm of the establishment. For Brueggemann, this psalm celebrated the then contemporary social arrangement of king and society.[42]

---

41. It was because Mowinckel saw this that he tried to locate the exact setting of the psalms.

42. Brueggemann, *Israel's Praise*, p. 110.

More specifically, Brueggemann sees this psalm celebrating king and Zion as a text that had 'silenced the hard tales of hurt, bondage, and injustice' in favor of a world 'good, lovely, ordered and under control'.[43]

It is, however, this very psalm that provided the inspiration for Luther's 'Mighty Fortress' hymn. In Luther's usage, what Brueggemann sees as an 'establishment' hymn of descriptive praise became a thundering anthem of religious protest and social change. Such a history seems difficult to reconcile with Brueggemann's argument that that psalm's descriptive praise indicates a function in support of the status quo.

This difficulty exists to some extent on the level of ancient Israelite history, since one should not, at the very least, rule out the possibility that what was used in a critical way in Luther's time might have had a similar function in ancient Israel. It is, however, even more of a difficulty in terms of the modern usage of the psalm. To repeat yet again one of this book's central arguments: how a psalm functions depends very much on its setting.

What this implies is that the type of world created by a particular psalm depends at least somewhat on the social setting. In other words, Brueggemann's argument concerning the psalms of descriptive praise in *Message of the Psalms* still holds true. The same psalm may be used in different ways in different settings. Conversely, unless one has independent information about a psalm's setting, one cannot necessarily infer that setting from the psalm itself.

Again, to a certain extent, Brueggemann sees how crucial setting is, especially in *Message of the Psalms*. Nevertheless, his appreciation of the important role of setting remains in some ways incomplete, precisely because it remains very much tied to what he sees as the psalms' original settings in ancient Israel. As seen in the previous chapters, Brueggemann's argument implies that the original function of a psalm remains prescriptive for its later usage. In the present case, however, there are two problems with this mode of operation.

First of all, as noted above, it is not at all clear that the psalms actually functioned in the way that Brueggemann claims. As so often happens in historical-critical studies, Brueggemann's only evidence for his setting comes from the text itself. While his settings are plausible, there are other plausible explanations that have been put forward by

---

43. Brueggemann, *Israel's Praise*, pp. 110-11.

other critics, as noted above. Without supporting evidence from other sources, one must always face the possibility that certain historical settings seem plausible not because they actually existed 'back then' but because they fit with our experience in the present. Thus, Brueggemann may well be right that some contemporary churches use descriptive psalms as a way of maintaining a stable world that keeps God at a distance. This does not, however, prove that the psalms were used that way in ancient Israel.

Secondly, even if the psalms were used in a certain way at a particular period in ancient Israel, this does not mean that they necessarily continued to be used in that way in other periods or settings. The examples of Psalms 46 and 117 obviously prove otherwise. Psalms may change their function according to their setting in various communities at different historical periods. As has been seen, such a change in function has clear implications for their genre definition as well.

What is so striking about such cases as Psalms 46 and 117 is that Brueggemann's historical speculations have led him to see these psalms as suspect, even though these very psalms are used in a very different way in the larger Jewish and Christian traditions. Indeed, the latter traditions often use these psalms in support of the very theological emphasis on an active saving God of which Brueggemann himself would heartily approve. The reason such traditions are able to do this is because they have not been bound to a supposed original setting.

Brueggemann thus would seem to find himself in a rather peculiar situation. He is forced by his method into seeing certain psalms as suspect because they are not authentically Israelite in their view of how God relates to the world. At the same time, these very psalms are central to major strands of the Jewish and Christian traditions, precisely because these traditions have read them in the way that Brueggemann has ruled out for them. One cannot help but wonder whether it would be better not to follow Brueggemann into such an impasse.

Eschatology and Transformation

These difficulties in Brueggemann's position do not mean that the psalms should not be seen as world making. On the contrary, the problem lies precisely in Brueggemann's inability to see the full implications of Mowinckel's emphasis on the world making potential of the cult. Where Brueggemann's retrieval has fallen short is perhaps best illustrated by an examination of the different ways that he and Mowinckel see the relationship between cult and eschatology.

As Brueggemann himself notes, Mowinckel saw the issue of cult as directly related to questions of eschatology.[44] For Mowinckel, the cult makes present—and helps to create—an alternate world in tension with the everyday world in which we live most of our lives. What Mowinckel saw as ancient Israel's central cultic celebration had a future dimension in that it looked forward to the beneficial effects of Yahweh's present accession in the coming year. When the cult no longer succeeded in presenting an adequate alternate world, this future vision was projected in a more eschatological dimension towards the end of time.

It is the cult's temporal dimensions that are important here, especially the way it incorporates both present and future.[45] According to Mowinckel, the cult makes an alternate reality available to the worshiper in the present. Cult is a holy, sacramental act which establishes a bond both among the worshipers themselves and between them and God. It is a present *experience* of the Deity, through which the worshiper is filled with divine strength and becomes another person. This strength is what the worshiper lives on between feasts.

At the same time that the cult brings about these experiences for the worshiper in the present, it also effects a new future reality by its ability to shape the world in a certain way.[46] Because of what has taken place in the cult, the new year is very different from what it might otherwise have been. As a result, the participants in the cult can look forward in confidence to what God will do in the coming year.

In keeping with standard scholarly usage, one may profitably describe what one sees here in terms of two different types of eschatology. First of all, one can recognize a realized eschatology that is a present reality for the individual worshiper. This present reality is a powerful experience of the divine, an experience on which one lives until the next feast. This reality also includes an experience of communion with one's fellow worshipers.

44. Brueggemann, *Israel's Praise*, p. 5. One may see this connection in the title of Mowinckel's seminal work *Psalmenstudien. II. Das Thronbesteigungsfest Jahwäs und der Ursprung der Eschatologie*.

45. Mowinckel also sees the cult as interacting with the past, in either its mythical or historical form.

46. Mowinckel, *Psalmenstudien*, II, p. 25.

Secondly, one can speak of a future eschatology that has to do with the future shape of the world in the coming year. Although the cult helps to bring this future reality about, the latter is not completely present at the time of the cultic event itself. What one experiences in the cult is only a foretaste of what is to become actualized during the coming year as a result of what has taken place there.

Brueggemann follows Mowinckel a long way in his insights concerning eschatology. He does not, however, follow him completely, and the difference between them is significant for how one sees the cult—and the psalms—functioning. The differences become apparent when one examines the temporal status of the world that Brueggemann sees as created by the psalms.

For Brueggemann, Israel's distinctive doxology is eschatological in that 'it promises something not yet visible, but the hope is certain and settled'. This doxology 'is an act of hope' that 'promises and anticipates a hoped-for world that is beyond present reality'.[47] In singing this doxology, Israelites 'commit themselves again to that hoped-for world that is sketched in the liturgy before their very eyes'.[48]

Clearly prominent in Brueggemann's comments is the role of hope. This is, however, very different from Mowinckel's own account of the worshiper's participation in the cult. For Mowinckel, the world created in the cult is not so much hoped for as *experienced*. Indeed, it is the *later* development from cult to eschatology that Mowinckel describes as a movement 'from experience to hope'.[49] To be sure, the cult looked forward to the imminent actualization of that which was experienced in the cult in the world outside the cult. Nevertheless, in the case of the cult, this expectation was based in the present experience of that which was expected.[50]

What is missing in Brueggemann's retrieval of Mowinckel is a sufficient appropriation of what has been described above as the cult's 'realized eschatology'. For Mowinckel, the cult is not just the place where one 'commits oneself' to a new world. It is much more the place

47. Brueggemann, *Israel's Praise,* pp. 51-52.

48. Brueggemann, *Israel's Praise,* p. 52.

49. This ('Vom Erlebnis zur Hoffnung') is the title of the concluding chapter of Mowinckel's *Psalmenstudien,* II, p. 315.

50. Significantly, Mowinckel seems to use the word *Erwartung* to refer to what was looked forward to in the cult. *Hoffnung* is used more in connection with more long range eschatological thought. So *Psalmenstudien,* II, pp. 315-25.

where one has an actual *experience* of that new world, an experience which then informs one's life between cultic occasions.

There are places in *Israel's Praise* where Brueggemann appears to come close to seeing cult as a present experiencing of a world different from that which one usually inhabits. Thus, for example, he talks of the king's being 'shaped by' the liturgy, an expression which would seem ....⌐ the cult something of the experiential power that it has for

more closely, however, one finds that for Bruegge-
ⁿo a large extent the master of his own experience.
ⁿann talks of the need for the king to 'submit',
ʰe world acted out before him.[51] Whether or
ˡiturgy still seems very much up to him.
his own liturgical experience is also
⸴ueggemann makes between such
⸴ for by the laws in Deut. 17.14-20.[52]
⸴ubmission to the torah is closely related
⸴rgy which is an enactment of the central
⸴vision that the king should regularly read the
⸴o mean that he should 'submit' to it and 'be

⸴ne problem lies in the pairing of 'being shaped' with the
⸴ve 'submit'. It is certainly the case that the king is expected to submit to and obey the laws specified in Deuteronomy. The modification of future behavior may, after all, be said to be the primary purpose of the genre of law. The dynamics of liturgy are, however, not necessarily the same as those of law. In law, character is molded through obedience to commands.[53] In liturgy, the goal may be, at least in part, the same, but the means are different.

As Mowinckel has seen, the cult has a more direct effect on the worshiper. The latter undergoes a powerful 'shaping' experience which

51. Brueggemann, *Israel's Praise*, p. 63.

52. Brueggemann, *Israel's Praise*, p. 175 n. 21.

53. Thus, Deut. 17.19-20 stipulates that the king learns to fear the LORD by keeping and doing all the words of the law and that this will prevent his heart from being lifted over that of his fellow Israelites. For an account of the way law leads to character formation, see Nasuti, 'Identity, Identification, and Imitation: The Narrative Hermeneutics of Biblical Law', *The Journal of Law and Religion* 4 (1986), pp. 9-23.

is more the cause than the result of obedience. By focusing so much on the king's responsibility, Brueggemann has minimized what Mowinckel has described as the sacramental aspect of the cult. The result is that the realized eschatology that animates much of Mowinckel's distinctive view of the cult has not been sufficiently recognized.[54]

Brueggemann's underestimating of the role of realized eschatology in the cult is accompanied by some important differences from Mowinckel in the area of future eschatology. For Brueggemann, both cult and eschatology 'mediate an alternative which critiques the present world and invites liberation from it'. Liturgic activity, especially praise, is 'an act of embracing an alternative future'. As such, it provides a basis for hope.[55]

Here again, one wonders whether Mowinckel would accept Brueggemann's emphasis on hope as something that cult engenders in the worshiper. It is perhaps more in keeping with Mowinckel's views to say that in the cult the worshiper 'experiences' a reality that he or she then 'expects' to be effected outside the cult in the near future.[56] In any event, Mowinckel certainly does not collapse cult and eschatology in the way that Brueggemann seems to suggest. While Mowinckel sees the roots of eschatology in cultic experience, he also sees eschatology as a development from that experience, one that is necessitated to a certain extent by the latter's inadequacies.

It is significant that despite his connection of cult and eschatology Brueggemann makes a distinction as to how certain types of psalms relate to the future. Not surprisingly, his distinction is between those psalms that incorporate descriptive praise and those that incorporate declarative praise. According to Brueggemann, such psalms present two radically different views of the future.

One will recall that for Brueggemann the psalms of descriptive praise create a static world in which God is not expected to act and nothing

54. Indeed, Brueggemann appears to be in some ways hostile to the very idea of realized eschatology, at least to the extent that he identifies it with a claim of privileged society to definitive status. So *Israel's Praise*, p. 71. The problem is that what has been described as Mowinckel's realized eschatology exists only in the cult itself, not in the world outside the cult. The effects of the cult on the world outside are to be looked for in the near future.

55. Brueggemann, *Israel's Praise*, p. 5.

56. Again, one may recall Mowinckel's references to *Erlebnis*, as well as his distinction between cultic *Erwartung* and long range eschatological *Hoffnung*.

changes. As a result, such psalms do not look toward the future except as a continuation of the present. There is no future eschatology here, no divine in-breaking, except in terms of maintaining the status quo. Such psalms are instead oriented towards the present, in service of the socio-political status quo. In fact, as noted above, Brueggemann sees these psalms as ruling out change.

It is, however, striking that some of the psalms that Brueggemann sees as most static (such as Psalm 46) are seen by Mowinckel as part of his world making festival. Perhaps one should expect this, since it is the king who both controls the festival and (at least according to Brueggemann) is interested in the preservation of the status quo. It is, nevertheless, crucial to recall that while Mowinckel certainly sees this festival as creating a world, he does not present this as a world that is already in existence. It is instead a world that comes into existence in the cult itself and which is then to be actualized in the coming year.

In contrast to the psalms of descriptive praise, Brueggemann sees the psalms of declarative praise as celebrating rather than avoiding change. On the one hand, such psalms point to a transformation that has already taken place and for which thanks need to be given. On the other hand, future change is not denied. Such psalms imply future change in that the God who has acted once on behalf of the individual or the community can be expected to act again.

It is significant that Brueggemann connects the *form* of declarative praise with its eschatological function. The relevant passage is instructive and may be quoted at length:

> The concreteness of the *credo recital*, the remembered pain of the *lament*, and the inscrutable transformation of the *song of thanksgiving* all move from remembered hurt and trouble to celebrated well-being and resolution. The speech form in each case carries that move. The rhetoric reenacts the transformation and makes the remembered transformation available again each time the psalm is recited. Indeed these modes of speech present a community whose characteristic mode of life is to be transformed, to have been transformed, and to still be transformed in time to come. This community is under transformation in its past, its present, and its future. It is being transformed as long as it uses this transformative speech.[57]

For Brueggemann, it is the term transformation that seems to be the key to how eschatology works in the psalms.

57. *Israel's Praise*, pp. 148-49.

By celebrating God's past transformative actions, psalms that include declarative praise create a world in which the future is open to God's transforming actions. Indeed, according to Brueggemann, such psalms themselves transform those who use them. At first sight, this looks like exactly the sort of realized eschatology that Brueggemann was said not to have adequately appropriated from Mowinckel. Upon closer analysis, however, one wonders whether this is necessarily the case.

The crucial question is that of how exactly Brueggemann sees these psalms as transformative in the present. If he means that such psalms change a community that did not accept the possibility of God's transformative actions into a community whose world now includes such an active God, then such psalms are certainly transformative agents in the fullest sacramental sense. Even the re-enforcement of such beliefs in a community that is beset by other possibilities in a contrary world would be at least in part a transformative action.

If, on the other hand, these psalms are used by those already convinced of such a world, they are more expressive than transformative in function. That is to say, such psalms do not effect a change in the person praying. At best, they help that person to better express a change that has already taken place. Thus, in the case of the thanksgiving psalm, the person praying is already convinced of the transforming power of God because of what God has done on his or her behalf.[58]

For Brueggemann, the world created by the cult is really one which is already in existence before the cult. It is a world which, as he says, becomes real in the cult in the sense of being announced to the participants there. It does not, however, actually become real in the cult in the sense of being brought about through cultic actions.[59] Brueggemann's

58. It is the community which is exhorted to praise that such psalms might invite to inhabit a different world. How, however, would this community express their acceptance of and participate in this world? One does not often find psalms in which God is praised because of actions done on behalf of a specific individual other than oneself. The closest one comes is perhaps a psalm like Ps. 146 which talks of God's actions on behalf of those that need divine assistance. It is, however, worth noting that despite Brueggemann's approval of the reasons given for praise in this psalm, such reasons are general and participial. They are, in fact, descriptive praise. It seems that Brueggemann is not so much opposed to descriptive praise *per se* as he is to certain types of descriptive praise. It is perhaps less the form that is the problem here than the content.

59. One sees this reluctance to attribute 'reality' to the cult in Brueggemann's ontological reservations which are found throughout his book.

cult may re-enforce a world in which its participants already believe, but it does not appear to bring about anything really new.

For Mowinckel, the cult makes available an alternative reality that its participants appropriate at the time of their participation. The world created in the cult is not the way the participants' world already *is*. It is, instead, the way the world should be and to a certain extent will be in the coming year. By participating in the cult, the worshiper experiences something that was not present before.

In the case of declarative praise, there are in fact two types of transformation which are at issue. The first is the historical transformation that is being remembered in the declarative praise.[60] In a situation of pain God acted in a surprising way which transformed darkness to light. God is now praised by retelling the story—by re-enacting it for the present community.

The second transformation is the transformation of other worshipers, which takes place through the psalm's recounting (and once again making present) the original historical transformation. When these worshipers are called upon to praise the God who has acted on behalf of the suffering individual, they are being called upon either to reaffirm an already existing belief in a world that includes a God who acts in history or to adopt such a belief in place of a more static world view.

Because Brueggemann has emphasized the world-creating function of the psalms, he has tended to focus on the first of these transformations, that which has happened in the life of the one praising. By affirming the possibility of God's surprising activity in the life of God's people, the psalms of declarative praise 'work against absolutizing the present and excessively legitimizing present arrangements'.[61] Brueggemann seems to assume that the world created in the cult is one in which the worshiping community already believes. Once again, such a picture reduces the psalms to an expressive rather than a truly creative function.[62]

If, however, one takes the second transformation into account, the

---

60. For Brueggemann, this is an 'evangelical reality' rather than 'simply a literary phenomenon'. *Message of the Psalms*, p. 125.

61. Brueggemann, *Israel's Praise*, p. 149

62. It is instructive that the one area in which Brueggemann does emphasize the ability of the cult to transform its audience to a different worldview is in the case of those who have the power to impose their views on those who do not. Significantly, Brueggemann does not use the term transformation to refer to this process.

psalms take on a somewhat different aspect. It is, in fact, through this second transformation that the world created by the psalms is actually inhabited by the worshiping community. Indeed, in this second transformation, the psalms themselves are the *agents* of transformation. That is to say, they not only construct a world where transformation is possible, they also help to bring about a transformation in the present.

One may illustrate this in another way by a further consideration of the work of Peter Berger and Thomas Luckmann on the social construction of reality, work which Brueggemann has used to describe the process of world making.[63] In their work, Berger and Luckmann discuss the process of externalization and objectification by which the underlying social substructure becomes a self-standing world that is seen as reality with a capital 'R'.[64] Obviously, such a conception fits nicely with the way Brueggemann sees the social concerns of the status quo projected into the psalms of descriptive praise with their stable world. It also works, at least in part, with Brueggemann's view of the psalms of declarative praise.

Berger and Luckmann, however, also talk at length about the process of internalization by which the externalized world becomes a social reality in individual lives.[65] Brueggemann is not unaware of this function by any means. He knows that language leads reality.[66] He knows that the psalms of praise have the power to 'invite and evoke genuine covenanted persons'.[67] He also sees that the king needs to be 'shaped' by the authentically Israelite liturgy.[68] Above all, he knows that the forms of the psalms can be transformative.[69]

Nevertheless, Brueggemann's main emphasis remains not on the internalization process but on that of world making—that is to say, the externalization part of the equation. In such a way, the psalms of orientation remain for the most part tied to what Brueggemann sees as their historical origins in the social elite of ancient Israel. Indeed, for all of his comments about flexible functions and contemporary settings,

---

63. Brueggemann, *Israel's Praise*, p. 14.
64. See, for example, Berger and Luckmann, *Social Construction*, p. 61.
65. See the sections on 'internalization of reality' and 'internalization and social structure', in Berger and Luckmann, *Social Construction*, pp. 129-73.
66. Brueggemann, *Israel's Praise*, p. 150.
67. Brueggemann, *Israel's Praise*, p. 159.
68. Brueggemann, *Israel's Praise*, p. 62.
69. Brueggemann, *Israel's Praise*, p. 149.

Brueggemann remains very much a historical critic whose view of the way the psalms function remains tied to their supposed historical setting.[70]

This continued desire to limit the psalms' functions to those that are at least analogous to those of a reconstructed historical setting also limits Brueggemann's ability to come to terms with the further evocative or internalization function of the psalms. This is especially so in the case of those psalms with whose supposed origins Brueggemann does not sympathize. As a result, Brueggemann's discussion of the function of the psalms remains compartmentalized.

Indeed, the important retrieval of world making developed in Brueggemann's later work only compartmentalizes the psalms more strongly by separating them out according to different socio-economic groups, in contrast to his earlier more flexible categorization according to different social situations. This compartmentalization has a somewhat ironic effect. Thus, while Brueggemann clearly sees the psalms of declarative praise as transformative in the first sense discussed above, he does not see them as transformative in the second sense, since he does not really see them as effecting any change in those in power. On the other hand, it is the latter group that is able through its control of the cult to impose its will on those who otherwise might hold a different view of the world. Because of this, the psalms of declarative praise are less able to function in a transformative way than their descriptive counterparts.

What is missing here is a full sense of the cult as a present *experience* which has a decisive effect on its participants. For Mowinckel, this experiential aspect of the cult was a key element in its ability to function as a reality-generating 'sacrament'. Similarly, it is the process of internalization that completes Berger and Luckmann's social construction of reality. There is, in short, a need to augment Brueggemann's analysis of the psalms' world making function with a greater appreciation of their transformative possibilities.

Function and Genre: The Perspective of the Interpretive Tradition

As always, it is helpful to compare the modern appropriation of the psalms with earlier appropriations to be found in the history of interpre-

---

70. Again, the fact that Brueggemann must determine the setting from the psalms themselves show the difficulties connected with this approach.

tation. Here too the psalms may be found to perform a variety of functions, including the expressive and creative. As might be expected,
however, the perspective is very different from what we are used to in
the modern period. This different perspective is quite useful in providing an insight into the way that genre works.

One may, for example, look carefully at one of the earliest theoretical
discussions of the psalms, St Athanasius's *Letter to Marcellinus*.[71] This
ancient work is striking in a number of respects. It is, first of all, quite
conscious of the fact that certain psalms belong together in certain
ways. Athanasius, in fact, provides detailed lists of psalms that belong
to certain types or perform certain functions.

Some of Athanasius's psalm groupings mirror standard form-critical
designations. In such a vein, one finds groups of psalms which
Athanasius explicitly defines as petition, praise or thanksgiving.[72] Some
of Athanasius's other categories bear different names but are still
recognizable in form-critical terms. Thus, Athanasius speaks of psalms
'proclaiming words that boast in the Lord', a category that overlaps to
some degree (though not entirely) with psalms of trust or confidence.

Athanasius is also sensitive to more general literary aspects of the
psalms. Along these lines, he characterizes certain psalms by their
narrative shape, while grouping others together because they contain
prophetic elements. Athanasius also distinguishes psalms of moral
admonition, prayer and confession.

Athanasius's general categorization of the psalms according to genre
is complemented by an extended discussion of the settings in which
such psalms are to be used. This is, of course, no form-critical investigation of these texts' settings in the life of ancient Israel. It is instead a
guide to how the psalms may be appropriated by contemporary believers
such as Marcellinus, the addressee of the letter.

In terms of the focus of the present chapter, it is this account of how
the psalms function that is of particular significance. Athanasius's
comments in this regard may be seen as falling into two general categories. The first are those that begin with such phrases as 'if you wish',

---

71. Migne, *PG* 27, pp. 1-46. For a modern English version with a useful commentary, see St Athanasius, 'A Letter of Athanasius, Our Holy Father, Archbishop
of Alexandria, to Marcellinus on the Interpretation of the Psalms', in *The Life of
Antony and the Letter to Marcellinus* (trans. R.C. Gregg; New York: Paulist Press,
1980). The English translations that follow are from this version.

72. Athanasius, 'Letter', ch. 14.

or 'when you want'. Typical is Athanasius's comment on Psalm 65 (MT): 'Whenever you want to celebrate God in song, recite the things in Psalm 64.'[73]

This type of injunction may easily be seen as a classic example of the expressive use of the psalms. One uses the psalm in question to express an already existent feeling or desire. The purpose of using the psalm is to provide the words which allow such a feeling or desire to be expressed in the best possible manner.[74]

The second way in which Athanasius counsels the praying of certain psalms makes use of such phrases as 'When you stand in need'. Along these lines, he writes: 'Let us say you stand in need of a prayer because of those who have oppressed you and encompass your soul; sing Psalms 16, 85, 87, and 140'.[75] Also, 'when you stand in need of confession of your sins, sing Psalms 9, 74, 91, 104, 105, 106, 107, 110, 117, 135, and 137'.[76]

This type of injunction does not serve an expressive function in the way that injunctions introduced by phrases such as 'Should you wish' do. Here the reason for recommending the psalm is not the desire of the person praying but rather that person's internal or external situation. In such a vein, Athanasius sees the suggested psalms as those that are best able to furnish what *needs* to be expressed in the situation.

It is not, in other words, assumed that the person already has the sentiments given words in the psalm or even that person knows what sentiments are appropriate to the situation. Rather, it is Athanasius who is recommending certain psalms for specific situations. By praying the

---

73. Athanasius, 'Letter', ch. 21. The key term here is *boulē*.

74. One should be aware that there is a difference between the possible reasons for the 'wish' that Athanasius describes in this case. One may already have the feeling or emotional state which lends itself readily to the words of the psalm in question. On the other hand, one may simply desire to have such a state, whatever one's present attitudes might be, because one recognizes that praising God is something that one should do.

Athanasius does not seem to distinguish between these two reasons for choosing a psalm, and both may be seen as expressive of something already present in the individual, either a disposition to praise or a recognition that one should praise. This difference does, however, point to something in the way the psalms work which emerges even more clearly in Athanasius's second type of comments on the use of the psalms.

75. Athanasius, 'Letter', ch. 17. The key term here is *chreia*.

76. Athanasius, 'Letter', ch. 21.

recommended psalms, an individual is able to deal with these situations in a more spiritually appropriate manner.

What needs to be seen here is Athanasius's confidence that the psalms are able to provide the person praying with *more* than simply appropriate words. This is shown quite clearly by Athanasius's comments on Psalm 73 (MT): 'When you perceive the godless flourishing in peace and yet the righteous who suffer affliction living in complete dejection, say what is in the seventy-second psalm, lest you be caused to stumble and be shaken to the foundation.'[77] In other words, this particular psalm is able to have a significant effect on the attitude of the person praying in that it helps to keep that person from 'stumbling' and 'being shaken'.

One sees this ability of the psalms to affect the person praying in other comments as well. Thus, Athanasius continues: 'And whenever God's wrath is stirred against the people, you have for consolation in this circumstance the prudent words in Psalm 73.'[78] The situation is such that one feels God's wrath in the circumstances of a national (or ecclesiastical) affliction. In such a situation, the suggested psalm is able to provide a 'consolation' that would not be present without the psalm.

In these and other comments, Athanasius clearly implies that the psalms have the power to affect individuals in a decisive way. It is, in fact, this power that he feels is the peculiar grace and marvel of the psalms, that which sets them apart from all the rest of Scripture.[79] Happily, Athanasius also discusses this distinctive aspect of the psalms in a more expansive theoretical way throughout his letter. As such, his work is particularly valuable for this chapter's discussion concerning the power of genre.

According to Athanasius, the Psalter 'contains even the emotions of each soul, and it has the changes and rectifications of these delineated and regulated in itself'.[80] While the first part of this statement might imply the standard modern view of the psalms as texts that are able to express human emotions in a perceptive and appropriate fashion, the second part moves in a somewhat different direction. Athanasius continues,

77. Athanasius, 'Letter', ch. 21.
78. Athanasius, 'Letter', ch. 21.
79. Athanasius, 'Letter', ch. 10.
80. Athanasius, 'Letter', ch. 10.

Therefore anyone who wishes boundlessly to receive and understand from it, so as to mold himself, it is written there. For in the other books one hears only what one must do and what one must not do ... But in the Book of Psalms, the one who hears, in addition to learning these things, also comprehends and is taught in it the emotions of the soul, and, consequently, on the basis of that which affects him and by which he is constrained, he also is enabled by this book to possess the image deriving from the words.

In such a way, the psalms not only express emotion already present but also allow the person praying to 'comprehend' and learn the 'emotions of the soul'. This is, of course, quite similar to Brueggemann's insight that the psalms allow the expression of certain feelings and perceptions that would not have been possible without their aid. As noted earlier in this chapter, this is still the expressive use of the psalms, but in a most active sense.

Athanasius, however, goes an important step further. The psalms do more than simply express the state of one's soul or allow one to recognize that soul's true state. They also are a means of 'molding' a person in a certain way. They 'affect' a person. They even 'constrain' a person. As a result, they 'enable' that person to be conformed to the text in a special way ('to possess the image deriving from the words'). In the words of R.C. Gregg, 'the comprehension of the image produced by the phrases in a psalm...uniquely involves the hearer as the psalm's speaker and actor'.[81]

In other words, Athanasius sees the psalms as *doing* something to the person praying, something that happens specifically through the agency of these texts. For Athanasius, the psalms have a 'sacramental' function. They are the means of divine activity on behalf of the person praying.

It is with this idea of the psalms' power to effect change that one can profitably bring Athanasius into dialogue with such modern critics as Mowinckel and Brueggemann. Along these lines, one may well recall that Mowinckel's radical edge was to be found in his belief that the cult had a truly sacramental quality. In his view, the cult is able to effect a reality, to create a different world.

Given the purposes of his letter, Athanasius is more concerned with how the psalms function on an individual rather than a social level. Despite this difference, Athanasius's view of the psalms is similar to

81. Gregg, 'Letter', p. 145.

Mowinckel's view of the cult in that both are manifestly sacramental in nature. Again, for Athanasius, the psalms are causative agents that effect a change in the individual reality of the person praying.

What is it that allows the psalms to act in such a sacramental or effective way? According to Athanasius, it is the unique ability of the psalms to be seen as the actual words of the person praying. Those who listen to the rest of Scripture 'consider themselves to be other than those about whom the passage speaks, so that they only come to the imitation of the deeds that are told to the extent that they marvel at them and desire to emulate them'. This is also true in the case of the 'prophecies about the Savior' that one finds in some of the psalms. In contrast, one recognizes the rest of the psalms as 'being his own words'.[82]

For the most part, the person reciting the psalms utters them

> as his own words, and each sings them as if they were written concerning him, and he accepts them and recites them not as if another were speaking, nor as if speaking about someone else. But he handles them as if he is speaking about himself. And the things spoken are such that he lifts them up to God as himself acting and speaking them from himself.[83]

For Athanasius, the ability of the person praying to appropriate the psalms as his or her own words is 'astonishing' and 'remarkable'. It is at least in part this ability that seems to inspire Athanasius's repeated connection of the psalms with both the workings of grace and the activity of the Spirit.[84] Once again, it is their sacramental nature that makes the psalms special even among the other books of Scripture.

It is significant that Athanasius closely links this effective power of the psalms to how they work as distinct genres.[85] Specifically, the psalms enable a person to do all of those functions that distinguish the main psalm genres. In such a way, the psalms enable one to repent, to suffer with hope, to call out when suffering, to give thanks, to bless, praise, and confess one's faith in God.

Athanasius often describes these genres in terms of the situations that call them forth. Such situations *mandate* the use of certain types of psalms, and Athanasius sometimes groups the psalms in terms of the situations in which they must be said. Thus, for example, 'we are taught

---

82. Athanasius, 'Letter', ch. 11.
83. Athanasius, 'Letter', ch. 11.
84. See, for example, Athanasius, 'Letter', chs. 10, 12.
85. Athanasius, 'Letter', ch. 10.

how one must call out while fleeing, and what words must be offered to God while being persecuted and after being delivered from persecution'.[86] It is in the use of the right psalms in the right situation that one is 'molded' in the right way.

Those who have followed the argument of the present book to this point will, of course, recognize this intersection of setting and function as the crucial element in genre definition. For Athanasius's community, psalms may be grouped together according to the way they function in certain settings. What Athanasius adds to the previous argument is further insight into the way such psalms function in their settings. For Athanasius, these psalms are not only appropriate expressions of the feelings one might have in such settings. They are also effective means of becoming the sort of person one should be in such settings.

The psalms have the ability to shape the person who prays them. One does not necessarily pray the psalms because one is a particular type of person. One becomes a particular type of person by praying the psalms. The psalms 'mold' the person praying by bringing about a state of being. For Athanasius, this sacramental nature of the psalms lies at the heart of their uniqueness. It is also an important aspect of their genre definition.

It is significant that despite his serious concern for genre issues Athanasius specifically rules out a preference for any particular genre. Indeed, he is adamant that the readers of the book of psalms must 'read it in its entirety'.[87] The first reason for this is, as one might expect, the fact that Athanasius sees each psalm as divinely inspired. There is, however, another reason that bears directly on the point at issue in this chapter, namely, the fact that the different psalm genres are seen to correspond to all the possible settings of human existence.[88] Because of this, the psalms are like the 'fruits of a garden on which [the person praying] may cast his gaze when the need arises'.

86. Athanasius, 'Letter', ch. 10.
87. Athanasius, 'Letter', ch. 30.
88. 'For whether there was necessity of repentance or confession, or tribulation and trial befell us, or someone was persecuted, or, being plotted against, he was protected, or if, moreover, someone has become deeply sorrowful and disturbed and he suffers something of the sort that is described in the things just mentioned, and he either attends to himself as one who is advancing, being set free from his foe, or he wants to sing praises and give thanks to the Lord—for any such eventuality he has instruction in the divine Psalms'. Athanasius, 'Letter', ch. 30.

One might well contrast this with the marked preference for certain genres that one finds in Brueggemann, especially in his later work. Athanasius is certainly lacking in any sort of suspicion toward a particular genre, such as that which Brueggemann has for the psalms of descriptive praise. One reason for this, of course, is his relative lack of concern about such psalms' original setting, a setting that causes Brueggemann considerable difficulties in the case of these psalms of descriptive praise.

Athanasius's ability to embrace all the psalms is not, however, simply due to his lack of historical interest and critical sophistication. A more important reason for his inclusiveness is to be found in his conviction that the psalms have a sacramental function. Because of this assurance, such psalms as those of descriptive praise are not restricted to a particular setting among the rich and powerful who have reason for such praise in the externals of their lives. Instead, such psalms allow for praise in any circumstances.

Brueggemann, of course, saw the possibility that even the psalms of orientation could be used by those in need as a kind of 'eschatological nevertheless' by which one affirms one's faith in difficult circumstances.[89] Athanasius, however, goes further than this by raising the possibility that the psalms may be used not only to express such a faith but actually to make it a reality. The psalms of praise—both descriptive and declarative—are not only the means by which one expresses an already existent inclination towards praise. They are also the means by which one becomes the kind of individual who praises. That is to say, the psalms are the means of cultivating a particular attitude toward God.[90]

It is important for how one views the function of the psalms that Athanasius sees them as both a means of 'teaching' and a 'therapy' for the emotions.[91] Far from being simply a mirror of emotions that are already present, the psalms 'possess somehow the perfect image for the soul's course of life'.[92] Indeed, for Athanasius the psalms are part of a

89. Brueggemann, *Message of the Psalms*, p. 28.

90. It is for this reason that Athanasius both insists on reading all the psalms and prohibits any addition to or embellishment of them. Their expressions are both 'superior to those we construct' and 'more powerful as well'. 'Letter', ch. 31.

91. Athanasius, 'Letter', ch. 13. See also ch. 10 where Athanasius talks about their ability to teach one how to 'heal' the passions.

92. Athanasius, 'Letter', ch 14.

larger *imitatio Christi* on the part of the Christian. It was for this purpose that Christ made his image 'resound in the Psalms before his sojourn in our midst'.[93]

In other words, the psalms are not only a means of expressing our present state of being. They are also both a model of a better existence and the means of arriving at that existence. In this movement to a closer imitation of Christ, the psalms both teach us about the goal and enable us to move towards it. In the former activity, Athanasius sees the psalms as similar to the rest of Scripture. In the latter, they take on their unique sacramental function.

It is especially in the way that the psalms work to bring about the future that they may be seen to have a transformative function in Athanasius's thought. This transformative function is obviously not the same as the more social or communal dynamics of world creation and eschatology found in Mowinckel, although Athanasius does not rule out the possibility that the psalms may have such an effect on either the world at large or the church in particular. He is, however, more interested in the way that these prayers effect the transformation of the individuals who pray them.

Athanasius's eschatology is individualized, but it is eschatology nonetheless. Moreover, it is precisely this emphasis on the psalms' transformative value that enables Athanasius to see the value of the entirety of the psalter. Since the psalms are as much the means of effecting a different state of being as they are the expression of a present state, they are all available to the believer, whatever that believer's present state may be. Those psalms that cannot be prayed in an expressive sense may be prayed as the means of arriving at a desired state in the future.

In contrast, it is Brueggemann's reluctance to see transformative value in certain psalms that leads him to view those psalms with suspicion. One must, of course, admit that psalms may be misused, even as the devil may quote Scripture. It may well be that the psalms of descriptive praise have been used to maintain the status quo in certain situations, perhaps even in their original setting in ancient Israel. This does not mean, however, that this is their necessary or proper usage.

For Athanasius, all the psalms are able to function as agents of transformation for those that pray them. Indeed, it is precisely an

93. Athanasius, 'Letter', ch. 13.

awareness of their eschatological potential that serves as a fundamental safeguard against their misuse, even as it allows them all to be used. To limit some of the psalms to an expressive function is to invite either their neglect or their misuse.

Although Athanasius's description of the psalms as active sacramental forces is often echoed throughout the later history of their interpretation, it is one which is, without question, somewhat unusual in the modern period.[94] The distance of modern scholarship from understanding the psalms in such a way is shown by how little the radical nature of Mowinckel's sacramental view of the cult and its psalms has been adopted or even appreciated in such scholarship. In this respect, Brueggemann's attempt to reclaim Mowinckel's active view of the cult is a major advance, even if it does not quite go as far as it might have done. Nevertheless, it is worth noting that even in the modern period there are ways of looking at texts that fit quite nicely with what one finds in Athanasius and Mowinckel.

The Power of Genre: Insights from Modern Literary Theory

The preceding discussion of Athanasius has highlighted the crucial relationship between the genre definition of particular psalms and the prior question of the nature of genre itself. It is clear that Athanasius sees the basic way that the psalms work in a different way than most modern biblical scholars. As a result, he also defines and evaluates the genres of individual psalms in a different way as well.

Because Athanasius accords the psalms both expressive and transformative power, he sees the relationship between the settings and functions of individual psalms differently than do those who accord the psalms expressive power alone. A particular psalm might well function in an expressive way in some settings and a transformative way in others, depending on the needs and desires of the person praying. Because of this, it is impossible to 'deduce' a psalm's genre solely from the text of the psalm, as one might do if one sees the psalms as having only an expressive function. Each psalm is open to a number of genre

94. For a rare but important exception, see J.L. Mays, 'Means of Grace: The Benefits of Psalmic Prayer', in *idem*, *The Lord Reigns*, pp. 40-45. See also his account of the role the psalms played in Augustine's 'transformation' on p. 3 of that work.

possibilities depending on the situation and manner of its use.[95]

To what extent are Athanasius's views on genre able to inform the modern perspective on the psalms? One cannot, of course, simply accept a pre-critical perspective as valid for a critical or post-critical age. One must take into consideration changes in both historical and linguistic consciousness. More specifically, one needs to ask how well this perspective fits with modern conceptions of the way that language works.

Those familiar with recent developments in this area may well be struck by a similarity between what Athanasius is saying here and some recent tendencies in literary theory. One might think in particular of the speech act theory of Austin and Searle, as well as of certain aspects of the later Wittgenstein and the work of Paul Ricoeur. What such authors have in common with Athanasius is an emphasis on the ability of language to *do* things and even to change reality. A brief review of how these modern theories dovetail with certain aspects of Athanasius's treatment of the psalms might well provide some further insights about the source of the power of genre.

The Psalms and Speech Act Theory

The basic insight of speech act theory is that words may not only be used to make statements but also to perform actions.[96] These 'speech acts' may be of various sorts, from delivering a legal verdict to committing oneself to a particular course of behavior. In all cases, however, the performance of the action is dependent on the correct utterance of certain words that a particular society has accepted as effecting a particular result.

Of all the contemporary ways of looking at texts, speech act theory offers perhaps the most connections with Athanasius's view of the distinctive way the psalms work. Along these lines, one may recall Athanasius's remarks concerning the uniqueness of the psalms over against the rest of biblical literature. While Athanasius sees all Scripture

---

95. Thus, for example, Athanasius sees Psalm 75 (MT) as functioning in two different ways depending on whether the person praying 'wishes' to express thanksgiving for deliverance from affliction or 'needs' to confess his or her sins. 'Letter', chs. 15, 21.

96. The foundational works in speech act theory are J.L. Austin, *How To Do Things With Words* (Oxford: Clarendon Press, 1962) and J.R. Searle, *Speech Acts: An Essay in the Philosophy of Language* (Cambridge: Cambridge University Press, 1969). Also of importance is F. Recanati, *Meaning and Force: The Pragmatics of Performative Utterances* (Cambridge: Cambridge University Press, 1987).

as having an effect on the reader, the psalms bring about that effect in a different way. In terms of speech act theory, one may say that even if (as has been suggested) much of Scripture has illocutionary force, the psalms have a different type of illocutionary force than that which the rest of the Bible has.[97]

On the most basic level, the illocutionary force that most psalms would appear to have is that which Austin calls behabitive and Searle calls expressive. Such actions as praising, thanking, appealing, complaining and confessing all seem to belong to these categories in that such actions function by means of expressing what is felt by the person performing them.[98]

It is important to note that by expressing such feelings, one is doing something more than simply making a descriptive statement about one's feelings. One is performing a different kind of speech act. Thus, for example, it is a different thing to assert 'I feel gratitude' than it is to actually thank another person.[99] Clearly, for Athanasius, the psalms are a means of performing precisely the latter kind of act with respect to God.

In assessing the expressive usage of the psalms, it is also important to take note of what Searle calls the 'direction of fit' between their language and the world.[100] Unlike other kinds of speech acts, an expressive utterance does not attempt either to fit the words of the utterance to the reality of the world or to shape the world to fit with the words of the utterance. For Searle, at least, expressive speech acts assume a fit between the word and the world.[101]

---

97. For a discussion of the illocutionary force of scripture, see A.C. Thistleton, *New Horizons in Hermeneutics: The Theory and Practice of Transforming Biblical Reading* (Glasgow: HarperCollins, 1992), pp. 298-307. For attempts to relate the psalms to speech act theory, see Levine, *Sing unto God*, especially pp. 79-129, and D.K. Berry, *The Psalms and their Readers: Interpretive Strategies for Psalm 18* (JSOTSup, 153; Sheffield, JSOT Press, 1993), especially chapter 5.

98. See Thistleton, *Horizons*, p. 299. According to Thistleton, 'liturgy typically involves what Searle terms expressive illocutions, and Austin, behabitive performatives'.

99. Austin, *Words*, pp. 78-86. It is also possible for speech to combine these two functions.

100. J.R. Searle, *Expression and Meaning: Studies in the Theory of Speech Acts* (Cambridge, MA: Cambridge University Press, 1979), p. 3.

101. This assumes that the person uttering the speech is sincere. It is, of course, possible to be insincere.

While it is clear that most of the psalms can be seen as expressive speech acts, it is just as clear that neither Brueggemann nor Athanasius would view them as always having only such a neutral direction of fit. It is actually only on the simplest level that the psalms work to express a state of which the person praying is aware and intentionally wishes to express. As Brueggemann has made clear, they also work to help the person praying come to a better understanding of that state.

On this level of usage, the psalms have certain similarities to what Austin calls verdictives and what Searle calls assertives, those types of utterances by which a speaker appraises or assesses the state of things in a certain way. The difference lies in the fact that when a psalm functions in this manner it allows the person praying to come to an appraisal of his or her *own* feelings in a particular way. When this happens, the direction is one of 'word to the world'. That is to say, the act is an attempt to describe in words what already exists in the world—in this case, the feelings of the person praying.

Such an account of the fit between word and world does justice to Brueggemann's more active expressive model. It does not, however, fully do justice to the depth of Athanasius's view of the psalms. The difference is that Athanasius sees the psalms as capable of moving in the other direction as well. That is to say, they move to shape the world in the direction of the words. The words spoken have an effect on the world, and, in particular, on the person praying in that they commit the person praying to a particular way of living. As such, they no longer simply operate as expressives or assertives but also as what Austin and Searle call commissives.

In his extended discussion of modern hermeneutics, Anthony Thiselton has discussed a number of ways that speech act theory pertains to biblical texts, especially to those texts that extend a promise to the reader. In light of the earlier discussion in this chapter, it is significant that Thiselton sees such texts as both 'transformative' and 'eschatological'.[102] That is to say, these words change the world in a certain way.

102. Thiselton, *Horizons*, p. 301. Levine has also viewed the psalms in conjunction with speech act theory (as well as with the work of Bakhtin and Buber/Rosenzweig). In this connection, he specifically notes both the 'transformative' and 'eschatological' or 'messianic' aspects of the psalms in that something happens or is brought about which would not otherwise come into being. See especially the chapter, 'An Audience with the King: The Perspective of Dialogue', in *Sing unto God*.

Thiselton has a much briefer discussion of the psalms. Nevertheless, what he does say on this topic underscores some of the possibilities discussed above. According to Thiselton, a text like 'O God in thee I trust' can move in either a word to world or world to word direction.

> If the words express only the Psalmist's trust, they reflect a *word-to-world* direction of fit; if they commit the reader to an act of trust, they embody a *world-to-word* direction of fit. The latter is not force-neutral. It functions *as a self-involving illocutionary act, which carries practical consequences for the life and behavior or the reader.*[103]

One may continue to quote Thiselton on this point:

> The difference between a force-neutral reading and a self-involving illocutionary reading of 'O God, in thee I trust' *does not*…consist in some supposed second shadow-action or mental process or vocal or emotional intensity; it lies in the capacity of the same linguistic act to *count* as a commissive and as an expressive act which also carries self-involving consequences in practical life.[104]

Thiselton's distinction between these two usages goes a long way towards what one finds in Athanasius. It does not, however, go all the way. The difference lies in Athanasius's more radical claims for the ability of the word itself to bring about a change in both the world and the person praying. For Athanasius, the psalms are not merely either expressive or assertive/verdictive. They are not even merely commissive in that they commit the person praying to a particular mode of life. They are transformative and sacramental in that they are the means by which that person is changed into something he or she was not formerly.[105]

In this last case, it is not so much that the person praying effects something by means of the psalms. Rather, it is that the praying of the psalms changes the person praying in ways that would not happen without the agency of the psalms. In more theological language, the psalms are the means by which *God* affects the person praying. They are a medium of grace, a transformative and sacramental agent.

In other words, the psalms are similar to Thiselton's scriptural texts

---

103. Thiselton, *Horizons*, p. 599, italics his.

104. Thiselton, *Horizons*, p. 599, italics his.

105. In this respect, Levine comes closer to the full transformative sense when he talks about the 'identification of the worshiper's "I" and the representative, archetypal "I" in the written text (*Sing unto God*, p. 104).

of promise in that both are places in which God is actively addressing the reader. The difference between the psalms and the rest of Scripture, as Athanasius has so perceptively seen, lies in the fact that the psalms are the *means* by which the promise offered throughout Scripture is *accepted* and *actualized* in the person.

It is important to emphasize that this means of acceptance and actualization is not simply a human response to the divine promise offered elsewhere in Scripture. Rather, the fact that it is God who actually provides this response is itself one of the most intimate examples of God's grace. This is at least in part what is implied by the fact that the psalms are part of God's word in Scripture, even as they are so obviously human words to God. They are not only the way that we respond to God but also the way that God works from within.[106]

The Psalms and the Work of Ludwig Wittgenstein

This is obviously not the place to attempt an overview of Ludwig Wittgenstein's many contributions to the study of language. For the purposes of uncovering connections between modern theory and Athanasius, however, one of the most significant aspects of Wittgenstein's work is his insistence on the link between the meaning of language and its use in particular situations. In this he is at one with the practitioners of speech act theory just considered.

Particularly useful for present purposes is the later Wittgenstein's analogy between how language works and the playing of a game. According to Wittgenstein, one only comes to know what language means by examining the rules by which it is used in a given situation. 'One learns the game by watching how others play.'[107] Only then is one able to use language in a similar way, to play the game oneself, and thus to participate in the mode of life that gives that language its meaning.

Wittgenstein's empirical approach to language and meaning is obviously quite congenial to much of what the present work has argued about the relationship between setting, function and genre. Even more to the present point, however, is Wittgenstein's insistence that language

106. One may recall here Harold Fisch's description of the psalms as 'covenantal discourse' and the 'locus of an encounter between God and poet and between poet and people' (*Poetry with a Purpose: Biblical Poetics and Interpretation* (Bloomington: Indiana University Press, 1988), p. 118.

107. L. Wittgenstein, *Philosophical Investigations* (Oxford: Basil Blackwell, 1967), s. 54.

is a social phenomenon that both is dependent on and makes possible a particular mode of life. It is through its setting in the latter that language gets its meaning, while it is through language that one comes to participate in that mode.

It is this two-sided relationship between language and life that forms a natural link between Wittgenstein and Athanasius. For Athanasius, the regular use of the psalms is one of the principal means by which one participates in a Christian life. Conversely, it is the latter life that gives the psalms their meaning. Even the setting of Athanasius's comments in a letter to someone interested in developing further in the Christian life fits well with Wittgenstein's insights about the way that one becomes proficient in a particular mode of life by watching others.

The Psalms and the Work of Paul Ricoeur

Finally, one may compare Athanasius's insights to certain aspects of the work of Paul Ricoeur. Ricoeur has come up often throughout the present book, usually in connection with Brueggemann's use of his work. One may, however, go further, especially if one focuses on Ricoeur's argument that the Bible has the power to project a new world and that this projection is the means by which the reader of the Bible is afforded a new and better self.[108]

According to Ricoeur, the Bible makes a 'nonviolent appeal' to its readers to enter a new world and so become a new being. In this appeal, the different biblical genres have different roles to play.[109] Particularly significant for the present study is Ricoeur's discussion of 'hymnic discourse' such as the psalms.

For Ricoeur, these texts may be said to be revealed 'in the sense that the sentiments expressed there are formed by and conform to their object'. As such,

> thanksgiving, supplication, and celebration are all engendered by what these movements of the heart allow to exist and, in that manner, to become manifest... The word forms our feeling in the process of expressing it. And revelation is this very formation of our feelings that transcends their everyday, ordinary modalities.[110]

108. P. Ricoeur, 'Toward a Hermeneutic of the Idea of Revelation', in his *Essays on Biblical Interpretation* (Philadelphia: Fortress Press, 1980), pp. 104, 108.

109. Ricoeur's 'forms of discourse' are fairly broad, including prophetic, narrative, prescriptive, wisdom and 'hymnic' discourse. 'Hermeneutic', pp. 73-95.

110. Ricoeur, 'Hermeneutic', p. 90.

Evident here are the same sort of functions found in Athanasius and discussed above. Particularly significant is Ricoeur's understanding of these texts' ability to 'form our feelings' in such a way as to 'transcend their everyday, ordinary modalities'. In other words, the psalms are able to effect a transformation to a another level of existence in those who use them.

It may be that in this passage Ricoeur implies that the expressive and transformative functions are more inseparable than they actually are in every instance. As noted above, not every use of the psalms is both expressive and transcendent (or transformative). Nevertheless, Ricoeur is at one with Athanasius in his strong affirmation of the ability of the psalms to effect a change in the person praying.

Considering Athanasius in the context of these modern authors provides a number of clues for an understanding of the way that genre has power. It is significant that for all of these figures, it is the relationship with real life that allows texts to have a particular effect. That life provides a context within which these texts take on certain functions.

Where Athanasius differs from such theorists as Searle and Wittgenstein is in his different understanding of the life with which such special texts as the psalms interact. Because Athanasius sees God as a primary agent in this life world, the psalms can take on a more thoroughly transformative role than that of which any non-scriptural texts are capable. It is not accidental that it is Ricoeur, with his interest in 'revelation', who comes closest to Athanasius in his arguing for the transformative power of the text.[111]

Conclusions: The Power of Genre and the Genres of the Psalms

The goal of the present chapter has been to clarify the dynamics underlying the ability of genre definition to affect the way that the psalms are interpreted and used. To this end, this chapter has looked at the recent psalms scholarship of Walter Brueggemann, St Athanasius's traditional

---

111. The closest approach of purely secular theory to Athanasius may be found in those theorists who see language itself as having an ontological status. For Athanasius, however, it is God, not language, which is the ontological reality that is active in these texts. As a result, Athanasius can see the psalms as working in a sacramental way which resembles, but ultimately goes beyond, the way most modern theorists would view these or any other texts.

reflections on those texts, and some recent developments in literary theory. What has been gained from this wide ranging survey?

First of all, this chapter has outlined three different ways that the genres of the psalms may be seen to function. The most common of these in modern usage is the expressive function by which the different types of psalms are seen either to express an already existing state of being or to bring that state to better expression. A second function, the creative, was seen to be the means by which the different psalm genres create a world, a social reality. In the third function, the transformative or sacramental, the different psalm genres are the means by which one comes to inhabit that world, a process that sometimes involves the psalms' effecting a change in the person who uses them.

In contrast to someone such as Brueggemann who tends to distribute these various functions among the different psalm genres, this chapter has argued that all of the latter are capable of being used in various ways depending on the setting of the one using them. Indeed, this different usage is a fundamental aspect of what constitutes such genres as genres. As this work has so often pointed out, it is use and function that ultimately constitute genre categories. All that this chapter has done is take that insight to a deeper level.

This is not to say that instead of psalms of praise, lament and thanksgiving one should now speak of psalms that are expressive, creative and transformative. It does, however, mean that whether a psalm is being used in one of these latter ways has a decisive impact on how it functions as one of the former psalm categories. To take the example used throughout this chapter, the psalms of descriptive praise function very differently, depending on whether they are being used in an expressive, creative or transformative way. Simply to define them as psalms of descriptive praise does not determine how that praise is being actualized.

All of this leads yet again to the question with which this chapter opened, that of what gives genre its power. Much of what has been discussed in this chapter points in the same direction as the earlier chapters of this book. Genre questions seem to come into play at the point where text meets life. Indeed, this convergence points to genre as the place where text and life meet. Moreover, it appears to be precisely the ability of genre to mediate between text and life that gives genre its power.

To understand this mediating role of genre, it is useful to consider once again Ricoeur's argument that texts project a world.[112] By providing such a world to inhabit, a text also provides its reader with a possible self which that reader may become. Along these lines, Ricoeur speaks of a hermeneutics of testimony in which two exegeses converge, the exegesis of self and the exegesis of external signs.[113] One should, of course, note the way that in this process a future possibility breaks in upon the reader's present reality. The similarity to the eschatological moves of Mowinckel and Athanasius is clear.

Ricoeur's view of the way that texts work has sometimes been criticized for its lack of attention to the practical aspects of interpretation. Despite his obvious concern to lay the philosophical foundations for textual meaning, Ricoeur seems to provide little concrete assistance for deciding what a particular text actually means. Thus, even if one grants that a text may project a world, one might ask how one knows if one has adequately understood the nature of the world which that text is projecting.

It is genre that gives at least a partial answer to this question. Ricoeur has clearly seen the theological importance of genre in so far as he is aware that the meaning of the biblical revelation is not to be separated from the form in which it is given. As he notes,

> we must convince ourselves that the literary genres of the Bible do not constitute a rhetorical facade which it would be possible to pull down in order to reveal some thought content that is indifferent to its literary vehicle.[114]

Instead, 'the confession of faith expressed in biblical documents is directly modulated by the forms of discourse wherein it is expressed'.[115]

In order to appreciate this essential role of forms, Ricoeur argues that we need a 'generative poetics that would be for large works of literature what generative grammar is to the production of sentences following the characteristic work of a given language'.[116] This idea of a

---

112. One may also recall Mays's comment that the psalms evoke a setting (*The Lord Reigns*, p. 30), as well as his reference to the psalms' 'language world' (pp. 3-11).

113. Ricoeur, 'Hermeneutic', p. 112.

114. Ricoeur, 'Hermeneutic', p. 91.

115. Ricoeur, 'Hermeneutic', p. 91.

116. Ricoeur, 'Hermeneutic', p. 91.

'generative poetics' is very suggestive, even though Ricoeur does not develop it in his essay.[117]

In this respect, one may profitably follow up on Ricoeur's analogy with the production of sentences in a language. One becomes fluent in a language when one is not only able to understand what is being said in that language but is also able to produce meaningful utterances in that language on one's own. Similarly, one becomes fluent in a genre when one not only can recognize the ways previous communities have grouped and used texts, but when one can also use these texts in similar ways. Even more, one becomes fluent in a genre when one can recognize the potential of other texts to be read in conjunction with that original genre grouping.

This does not mean that one will necessarily have the same genre groupings as these previous communities, just as other speakers of a language will not say the same things. It does mean, however, that how one uses such texts should be able to be understood by other users of these texts, just as two speakers of the same language are able to understand each other to a certain extent. Such mutual understanding is possible because speakers of the same language follow the same rules of language.

Similarly, a generative poetics of biblical genres is one that is informed by certain rules. Such rules are provided by both the historical and the contemporary community, and they are usually referred to by concepts such as tradition, the rule of faith and the *sensus fidelium*. The latter provide the rules according to which genre is able to relate a text to a particular mode of life.

This is, of course, the other side of the coin to the idea that was so important in the earlier chapters of this work, namely, that genre is defined by function. To see a text as belonging to a certain genre is to describe how that text fits into a particular mode of life. Indeed, to define a genre is to entertain a particular mode of life as possible for one's own life.

The world implied by a particular text is a world either already inhabited or potentially inhabitable. In the first instance, one approaches the world of a particular text by means of a genre competence that has

117. For attempts to develop this aspect of Ricoeur's thought, see Tracy, *Analogical Imagination*, pp. 128-29; M. Gerhart, 'Generic Studies: Their Renewed Importance in Religious and Literary Criticism', *JAAR* (1977), pp. 309-327; 'Genre as Praxis: An Inquiry', *PreText* 4 (1983), pp. 273-94, and *Genre Choices*.

its roots in the real life of a community. The way a community lives has a critical impact on the way a community groups its texts. Conversely, the way a community groups its texts helps to perpetuate a particular mode of community life. In such a way, it was the religious experience of western Christianity that was responsible for the textual grouping of the seven penitential psalms, even as this particular grouping helped to make possible a particular religious experience for that community.

This is not, however, to say that one inevitably constructs one's genres according to what one already is, as some modern literary theorists would argue. One may, after all, move from one community to another, and it is often one's textual experiences that either prompt or facilitate such a move. As Jauss has shown, one's experience with a certain text may result in a radical re-evaluation of genre categories. So may one's experience with a certain community. Both the text and the community have power to reshape one's world, and one corollary of that power is the ability to group texts in a particular way.

Genres have power because they both reflect and make possible different modes of existence in the world. To define a text as belonging to a particular genre implies a certain world view. This is especially the case with regards to 'classic' texts that engage life in a way that has been judged to be particularly serious or productive.[118] Indeed, it is most especially the case with texts that are determinative of a community, such as the Bible. To enter that world is either to join or to found a community of fellow interpreters.

Biblical genres have power because they arise out of and help to actualize the life potential of those communities for whom the biblical text is foundational. Among these biblical genres, those found in the psalms have long been thought to be uniquely effective in bringing about a particular mode of life. As has been seen by authors as diverse as Athanasius and Mowinckel, it is the transformative power of these texts which sets them apart from the rest of Scripture.

---

118. On the special qualities of 'classic texts', see Tracy, *Analogical Imagination*.

Chapter 5

KING DAVID'S GENRES: THE RELATIONSHIP BETWEEN
AUTHORSHIP AND GENRE IN THE PSALMS

This book has argued strongly for a definition of genre that centers on function as one of the primary determinants of how texts are grouped. In support of this view, the last chapter has pointed to the crucial importance of a genre's relationship to a particular mode of life and social community. If genres are defined according to their functions, it is their relationship to their social settings that make such functions possible.

One important issue has often surfaced in the course of this discussion, an issue that has been addressed throughout but that is nonetheless in need of some further discussion. This issue is the question of how one assesses the validity of a particular genre definition. Does defining genre by function mean that a group of texts may be put to any use that its readers feel is appropriate? If so, does this mean that the text is completely at the mercy of the reader and, as such, is incapable of the independent address that one certainly expects from such texts as the Bible?

It will be recalled that a number of safeguards for the genre definition of biblical texts have been offered in the preceding chapters, among them community usage, tradition and canonical context. Missing from this list of suggested safeguards is one that until recently would have been foremost in biblical interpretation, that of the intention of the author. This omission is not accidental, as one may see from the fact that the preceding chapters have often been at pains to point out how even such forward looking authors as Brueggemann have been limited by their commitment to the genre definition of a biblical text's original setting.

The role of the author is a controversial subject in biblical studies at the present time, just as it is in the wider humanities. This chapter will take a closer look at this controversial subject, with special attention to its relationship to genre questions and to the psalms.

Author and Genre in Contemporary Literary and Biblical Studies

There is no doubt that for many modern interpreters the intention of the author remains the primary goal of literary investigation. While some of these interpreters are motivated by historical interest in the author and his or her times, others are undoubtedly attracted to the author's intentions because they feel that such intentions provide a fixed point of meaning for a text. As such, these interpreters are hoping to avoid the dangers of what they see as subjective and relativistic interpretation.

Partly because of its inescapable historical interests, biblical studies has, if anything, been even more firmly committed to the author's intentions than the rest of the humanities. Only in the very recent past has there been any real movement away from such intentions as the goal of biblical interpretation. Even now, much of the field remains firmly committed to such an approach as the only effective hedge against the 'eisegesis' of the biblical text.

In such a context, genre plays an extremely important role as a link between the author and the reader. Because genres transcend the individual text and are known to both author and reader alike, the author's choice of a particular genre provides a vital clue as to how that author wishes the reader to understand his or her work. The prominent literary critic, E.D. Hirsch, Jr, has provided a strong defense of both author's intentions and the role of genre in ascertaining those intentions. Not coincidentally, Hirsch is also a strong advocate of determinacy in textual meaning.[1]

1. This concern is evident from the title of Hirsch's major work, *Validity in Interpretation*. For Hirsch, the correct identification of the genre chosen by an author is a crucial element in understanding that author's purpose in a particular text. The difference between Hirsch and the present work is that the former is interested in a text's 'purpose', while the latter is interested in its 'function'. It is, however, striking that even such a strong advocate of authorial intentionality as Hirsch recognizes that certain texts, such as the Bible and the Constitution, 'do seem to require that meaning go beyond anything that a human and historical author could possibly have willed' (pp. 121-22). In such a case, he sees the need for an authoritative interpreter, such as the *consensus ecclesiae* or a court of law (p. 123). He does, however, also argue that subsequent interpretation should be true to the 'type' chosen by the author. If it does not, it is actually an interpretation of a different text.

Other modern critics are, of course, less enamored of the author's status in the interpretation of texts.[2] For such critics the author's choice of genre is not definitive since the reader does not necessarily read a text in terms of its original genre. Certainly, much of what has been discussed previously in this book would seem to move in this direction in that it has shown the adaptability of a text's genre to different readers over the course of that text's history.

Given the prominent place of the author in the until recently dominant historical-critical approach to the Bible, it is necessary to come to terms with the role of the author in a more direct fashion. Nevertheless, it should be obvious from what has been said so far in this work that the relationship of author and genre in biblical studies is by no means as clear as someone like Hirsch would see it.

Indeed, when one looks at the psalms in particular, one sees a certain tension between the quest for authorial meaning and an appreciation of a psalm's genre. Thus, for example, it was precisely the nineteenth century's rigid insistence on tying interpretation to a knowledge of the historical particulars of composition (time, place, historical situation) which was challenged by Gunkel and his genre-oriented form-critical method. While Gunkel by no means neglected such historical specifics when available, he emphasized forms as things which transcended such particulars in so far as they belonged less to individual authors than to the communal tradition.

Obviously, Gunkel would not deny the fact that an author's choice of a particular genre is a significant datum to be considered in our understanding of any given text. Nevertheless, to the extent that we are not dealing with recognizable historical authors, the emphasis clearly falls on the text or the communal setting instead. In other words, as noted in the previous chapters of this work, Gunkel's focus on form is a generalizing move away from individual authors as such.

It is, however, significant that one of the main reasons the relationship between author and genre is so problematic in biblical studies is because of the author's shadowy and speculative nature. Especially in

In the case of the Bible, Hirsch raises the possibility that interpretation that goes beyond the type chosen by the human author can only be defended as an interpretation of the text of the divine Author (p. 126).

2.   One may include a wide array of critical schools, ranging from the New Critics to various types of post-structuralists, among those who see the author as 'dead' with respect to the current act of interpretation.

the case of the psalms, it was precisely this shadowy nature that made the author so dispensable for Gunkel in the first place. As such, Gunkel's liberating move essentially consisted of bracketing the author in favor of wider communal traditions and setting.

Given this critical bracketing of the author, it is all the more note-worthy that the book of Psalms is one of those biblical books where authorship is a persistent concern of the book itself. This is pre-eminently to be seen in the frequent attributions to be found in the titles of the psalms, as well as in the summary statement of Ps. 72.20, which attributes the preceding psalms to David. The early historical critics, of course, saw this Davidic authorship as a pious fiction, a judgment that opened the door to their own speculative search for the 'real' authors of the psalms.

As has recently become clear, the claim of Davidic authorship raises significant interpretive issues that are not identical with the question of the historical accuracy of that claim.[3] What have not yet been sufficiently appreciated are the implications of this for questions of genre. Once again, a look at both the history of interpretation and recent scholarly trends helps to clarify these genre issues.

King David as the Author of the Psalms: The Claim and its Dilemmas

The roots of the traditional view of David as the author of the psalms are to be found in both the Psalter itself and the books of Samuel and Chronicles. In the Psalter one finds the common superscription *l^{e}dāwid* which, while not necessarily indicating authorship, was easily and early taken to imply such authorship.[4] The same is true of the concluding formula in 72.20, even though this formula presents some obvious difficulties for the Davidic authorship of all the psalms.

Other indications of David's authorship of the psalms are to be found in the 13 psalm titles that allude to specific incidents in David's life.

---

3. Especially important here is the work of Childs ('Psalm Titles'; *Introduction to the Old Testament*, pp. 504-525); Ackroyd (*Doors of Perception*); and Mays ('David'; *Psalms*; *The Lord Reigns*).

4. This superscription occurs 73 times in the MT, and, as noted below, more in the LXX and the other versions. On the range of this expression's possible meanings, see J. Kugel, 'David the Prophet', in *idem* (ed.), *Poetry and Prophecy: The Beginnings of a Literary Tradition* (Ithaca, NY: Cornell University Press, 1990), pp. 45-55 (49).

Perhaps the best known example is the title of Psalm 51, which relates that penitential psalm to the great sin of David with Bathsheba. Other examples include Psalms 3, 7, 18, 34, 52, 54, 56, 57, 59, 60, 63 and 142.[5]

Supporting Davidic authorship are the association of David with the lyre in 1 Samuel 16 and his purported composition of poetic pieces throughout 1 and 2 Samuel. Along these lines, one thinks in particular of his dirge for Saul and Jonathan in 2 Samuel 1, which was both written down in a book and ordered to be taught to Israel.[6] Such traditions prompted other pieces to be attributed to David. Among these are 2 Samuel 22 and 23, the former of which has a parallel in Psalm 18. Indicative of David's musical and poetic status was his designation as *n^e'îm z^emirôt yiśrā'ēl* in 2 Sam. 23.1.[7] As Amos 6.5 shows, David's connection with song was proverbial from an early period.

Further traditions that indicate a connection between David and Israel's songs are to be found in Chronicles. According to that work, David was responsible for the founding and organization of the singing cult.[8] He also apparently was seen to have been responsible for some of the works performed in that cult.[9]

With all of this biblical support for a connection between David and the psalms, it is not surprising that post-biblical interpretation tended to see him as the author of the psalms from an early period. The multiplication of psalms attributed to David in the LXX and the other versions is a clear indication of this trend.[10] One also sees signs of an acceptance of

5. See Childs, 'Psalm Titles'; Mays, 'David'; and E. Slomovic, 'Toward an Understanding of the Formation of Historical Titles in the Book of Psalms', *ZAW* 91 (1979), pp. 350-80. As in the case of the *l^edāwid*, the later versions have added to the number of superscriptions which allude to incidents in David's life.

6. See Mays, 'David', p. 148.

7. The connection of this phrase with songs is clear. It may also have prophetic implications as well. See Kugel, 'David the Prophet', p. 48, as well as J.D. Levenson, 'A Technical Meaning for *N'M* in the Hebrew Bible', *VT* 25 (1985), pp. 61-67.

8. On this, see 1 Chron. 15.16, 16.4, 23.5-6; 2 Chron. 7.6.

9. So 2 Chron. 29.30 and possibly 2 Chron. 7.6. See Mays, 'David', p. 150.

10. The fact that the Greek translation of *l^edāwid* sometimes changes from the dative to the genitive also appears to be an attempt to solidify the claim of Davidic authorship. On this, see A. Pietersma, 'David in the Greek Psalms', *VT* 30 (1980), pp. 213-26.

Davidic authorship in Ben Sira and at Qumran, as well as in Josephus and the New Testament.[11]

It is, however, important to note that the biblical evidence for Davidic authorship of the psalms (or, at least, for his authorship of all the psalms) is not unambiguous. Thus, for example, there are a number of psalm titles that suggest non-Davidic authorship. Other illustrious figures of Israel's history, such as Moses and Solomon, are connected with individual psalms, while various singers and singing groups are associated with other psalms.[12] If one sees the *l^{e}dāwid* as indicating Davidic authorship, the similar attribution of other psalms to different figures would certainly seem to count against their connection with David. One might also mention that a number of psalms are apparently anonymous, their titles offering no clue as to their possible authorship.

Another feature that would seem to count against Davidic authorship of at least some of the psalms is the presence of historical elements that are difficult to reconcile with David as their author. Thus, for example, Psalm 137 clearly implies a setting in the Babylonian exile, seemingly demanding a different author. Even Psalm 51, whose full biographical superscription relating to the David and Bathsheba episode fits well with the overall penitential nature of the psalm, has problems along these lines. As has often been noted, the final verses of this psalm call for a restoration of the walls of Jerusalem, something which would be incompatible with a setting in David's time.

Such conflicting evidence played a major role in the critical rejection of Davidic authorship for many of the psalms, a rejection that opened the way for both the search for alternate authorship and the more general form-critical approach. Nevertheless, earlier commentators also saw the difficulties involved in a claim of Davidic authorship, even as they, for the most part, proceeded to reaffirm that claim.

11. See Ben Sira 47.8-11, the biographical sketch in 11QPs^a, Josephus's *Ant.* 7.12.3; *Apion*, 1.8; Mt. 22.43; Mk 12.36-37; Acts 1.16, 4.25; and Rom. 4.6. According to Kugel, this trend to ascribe the Psalms to David went hand in hand with a tendency to see this text as revealed Scripture. See his 'Topics in the History of the Spirituality of the Psalms', in Arthur Green (ed.), *Jewish Spirituality from the Bible through the Middle Ages* (New York: Crossroad, 1986), pp. 113-44 (135). Such a tendency also apparently strengthened the claim of David to be a prophet. So Kugel, 'David the Prophet', pp. 54-55.

12. Thus, Ps. 72 is associated with Solomon and Ps. 90 with Moses, while Pss. 50, 73–83 are associated with Asaph and Pss. 42–49, 84, 85, 87, 88 are associated with the sons of Korah.

What is especially noteworthy from the point of view of the present study is that these earlier authors often defended Davidic authorship by defining the genre of the psalms in a certain way. As has been seen throughout this work, such genre definitions are interesting in their own right, but they are also significant in terms of their implications for any modern approach to the question of genre in these texts. As such, it is well worth looking at what even a limited survey of these views tells us about our own critical stance with respect to authorship and genre in the psalms.

David and the Psalms in Rabbinic Tradition

Nowhere can one find a longer or more determined wrestling with the question of the Davidic authorship of the psalms than in the rabbinic tradition. On the whole, this tradition continues the early Jewish tendency towards attributing the psalms to Davidic authorship. Thus, *Midrash Tehillim* contains the statement that 'as Moses gave five books of laws to Israel, so David gave five Books of Psalms to Israel'.[13] Similar sentiments are to be found in the Babylonian Talmud,[14] prompting the judgment of E. Slomovic that the 'prevailing opinion' was that of *Midrash Tehillim*.[15]

Davidic authorship is also accepted by many of the later commentators, though not perhaps in quite as unanimous or as thoroughgoing a manner. Thus, Saadiah Gaon sees David as the author of all the psalms, a view that he claims is the consensus view of the entire nation of

---

13. *Mid. Teh.*, on Ps. 1.1, trans. Braude.

14. Along these lines, one may note the statement of R. Meir in *b. Pes.* 117a that David uttered all the praises in the book of Psalms. It is interesting that he supports this assertion by his rereading of the *kallu* in 72.20 as *kol ellu*, thus turning a verse which could well be seen as evidence against all-encompassing Davidic authorship into an argument for such authorship.

One also may note the statement of R. Judah the son of R. Simeon b. Pazzi in *b. Ber.* 9b that David composed 103 psalms before saying Hallelujah, waiting until he saw the downfall of the wicked in 104.35. While this does not address the question of Davidic authorship after this point in the psalter, it clearly asserts such authorship for some of the more problematic psalms, such as Ps. 90.

On the well known but somewhat more complicated statement of *B. Bat.* 14b-15a that David wrote the book of Psalms 'upon the hands of' ten 'elders', see further below.

15. Slomovic, 'Historical Titles', p. 353 n. 11.

Israel.[16] Davidic authorship of most (though not all) of the psalms is also accepted by such commentators as Ibn Ezra and David Qimḥi.[17]

Such traditions that accept Davidic authorship are, however, complemented by others that show an awareness of the difficulties involved in making such a comprehensive claim. In such a way, another passage in the Babylonian Talmud states that David wrote the psalms 'upon the hands of' (*'l ydy*) ten 'elders': Adam, Melchizedek, Abraham, Moses, Heman, Jeduthun, Asaph and the three sons of Korah.[18] Such a tradition clearly is an attempt to reconcile a strong trend towards Davidic authorship with the conflicting evidence of the different psalms titles.

Shir HaShirim Rabbah is similar in its arguing that 10 righteous men sought to compose the book of Psalms.[19] While all were acknowledged to be pleasing and devoted, praiseworthy and fit to sing a hymn before God, David was the one whom God chose to compose Psalms through all of them. The reason for this choice was the sweetness of David's voice (cf. 2 Sam. 23.1). Indeed, it is David who 'makes the songs of all Israel sweet'. One finds a similar tradition in *Midr. Teh.* 1.6.[20]

Worthy of note here is the attempt to connect David with all the psalms while in some way respecting the contrary evidence of the different psalm titles. In a certain sense, one may see this as an ambivalence over whether David is an author or an editor. The question is whether he actually has a hand in the composition of all the psalms or whether he simply includes in his book psalms composed by others alongside those he himself has composed.

The issue is perhaps most crucial in that case where a psalm is apparently attributed to Moses, since Moses both precedes David in time and is his rival for equal or greater prestige. Thus, for example, the title of

---

16. See U. Simon, *Four Approaches to the Book of Psalms: From Saadiah Gaon to Ibn Ezra* (Albany: State University of New York Press, 1991), p. 13. The claim is based on the liturgical reference to the 'songs of David' in the *Siddur*.

17. On Ibn Ezra, see Simon, *Four Approaches*, pp. 176-82. The early article of A. Neubauer, 'The Authorship and the Titles of the Psalms According to Early Jewish Authorities', in *Studia Biblica et Ecclesiastica*, II (5 vols.; Oxford: Clarendon Press, 1890), pp. 1-57, is also of interest in detailing the tendency to ascribe the Psalms to Davidic authorship.

18. *B. Bat.* 14b. According to this tradition, Ethan is understood as identical with Abraham.

19. *Shir. R.* 4.3.

20. One might also note that *Midr. Teh.* seems to have few problems in attributing Ps. 90 to Moses.

Psalm 90 indicates Mosaic authorship for that psalm, and some have even attributed the following 10 unattributed psalms to Moses as well.[21] Others, however, not wishing to deny David the authorship of this psalm, have interpreted the *lᵉmōšeh* as 'for the sons of Moses'. By this they mean that David composed this psalm for performance by those levitical singers who may be seen to be the sons of Moses.[22]

A similar issue is to be found in the Talmudic discussion of the Hallel psalms which were recited at Passover (Pss. 113–18).[23] This passage contains the straightforward assertion by Rabbi Meir that all the psalms are the work of David. In contrast to Rabbi Meir, Rabbi Jose cites the view of his son, Rabbi Eleazer, that the Hallel psalms were first uttered by Moses and Israel at the time of the Exodus. Rabbi Jose also notes that Rabbi Eleazer's colleagues disagreed with him, arguing in favor of Davidic authorship, but he continues to argue that in this case Rabbi Eleazer is in the right. The reason for this assertion is that it is impossible that Israel slaughtered their Passover offering and took their palm branches without uttering song until the time of David.[24]

This wider provenance of the psalms is also to be found in the commentary of David Qimḥi. Qimḥi is somewhat restrained in his estimation of Davidic authorship, attributing to David only the *lᵉdāwid* psalms and those which are anonymous. He even entertains the possibility that in certain cases *lᵉdāwid* may mean 'concerning David' rather than implying actual authorship. Nevertheless, Qimḥi sees the psalms as reflecting either events which happened to David directly or to Israel as a whole. Indeed, these latter events include those which happened after David's time, such as the Babylonian captivity and the restoration of the house of David to its former position. This was possible because David composed the psalms with the help of the Holy Spirit.[25] Once again, David is seen as giving the psalms to the singers to recite.

21. So Rashi and others. These psalms are sometimes seen as having been composed by Moses for the 11 tribes of Israel named in the Mosaic blessing in Deut. 33.

22. So Saadiah Gaon. Qimḥi tries to combine the two views by raising the possibility of Mosaic authorship and Davidic editing and inclusion in the book of Psalms.

23. *b. Pes.* 117a.

24. The passage also argues that it would have been impossible to compose these psalms while Micah's idolatrous image was in existence at Beki. Thus, it must have been composed before this by Moses at the Red Sea.

25. Though this is apparently to be distinguished from prophecy proper.

What the rabbinic evidence seems to indicate is a general impetus to connect the book of Psalms to David in some way. A number of commentators are willing to see a role for other individuals (especially Moses) in the creation of certain psalms. Even in the latter cases, however, David seems to function as the inspired medium by which the psalms were made available to the rest of Israel. Indeed, it is David's privileged place of standing before God in prayer and song which make the psalms especially effective prayers for the ongoing life of the people.

David and the Psalms in Christian Tradition

The rabbinic tendency to connect the psalms to David in some way is echoed in the Christian tradition. Various New Testament authors cite David as the author of certain psalms,[26] and this tradition was, on the whole, followed by the early church. As in the rabbinic tradition, Christian sources are to some extent ambivalent as to whether David is the author of all the psalms. Augustine argues for the maximalist view, claiming for David a unique authorship of the psalms.[27] As is often the case in scriptural matters, Jerome takes the opposite stance.[28]

Both points of view continued into the medieval church, although the more inclusive position of Augustine tended to prevail in a way similar to that in which his views on other scriptural matters prevailed.[29] The Reformation, on the other hand, was more reserved in its views on Davidic authorship. Thus, for example, both Luther and Calvin see Moses as the author of Psalm 90, and Calvin sees Psalm 137 as a product of the Babylonian exile. Such readings are, of course, quite in keeping with these reformers' greater appreciation for the literal sense of the text and their lesser appreciation for the authority of church tradition.

26. See, for example, Mt. 22.43; Acts 1.16; and Rom. 4.6. Whether coincidentally or not, all of the psalms cited in these passages have the superscription *le̊dāwid*.

27. So *City of God*, 17.14; *En. Ps.* 9.35.

28 Letter 146 to Cyprian, s. 4. Also note Jerome's apparent acceptance of the rabbinic tradition of Mosaic authorship for Ps. 90 and the psalms which follow (*Contra Rufinum* 1.13).

29. Thus, in the later middle ages, the more literal Lyra preferred the position of Jerome, while Paul of Burgos argued for a more comprehensive Davidic authorship.

One complicating factor in this Christian view of Davidic authorship will be discussed at length below, but it should be at least noted here. Even when the early church speaks of David as the human author of a particular psalm, it very often means by this that Jesus spoke that psalm through him. The interpreters of the Reformation, on the other hand, are perhaps less likely to see David as responsible for all the psalms but more likely to interpret a psalm in accord with the actual circumstances of his life. In such a way, David may be seen as having had a wider but less concrete presence prior to the Reformation and a less encompassing but more substantial presence after that event.

The Modern Retrieval of Davidic Authorship: Implications for Genre

From the above survey, it is clear that there is a strong pre-critical tendency to attribute most, if not all, of the psalms to David. This is the case despite elements in both the psalm titles and the bodies of the psalms themselves which pose difficulties for such Davidic authorship. It is, of course, precisely this conflicting evidence that has led to a widespread reluctance on the part of modern interpreters to attribute any particular psalm to Davidic authorship.

Few modern critical scholars would want to affirm the Davidic authorship of any particular psalm on the historical level.[30] As noted above, however, there is at present a growing appreciation of the hermeneutical significance of Davidic authorship. One important voice in this direction is that of Brevard Childs who has argued that the Davidic tradition of authorship is an important feature of the canonical interpretation of the Psalms.

For Childs, the significance of Davidic authorship is best seen in those superscriptions that relate the psalms to specific incidents in the life of David.[31] Such superscriptions are the means by which 'psalms

---

30. For a rare modern attempt to place some of the psalms in David's life, see M. Goulder, *The Prayers of David Psalms 51-72: Studies in the Psalter. II* (JSOTSup, 102: Sheffield, Sheffield Academic Press, 1990). According to Goulder, these psalms were actually written for David by a priest. They now appear in chronological order in the text and they correspond to significant events in David's life stretching from the Bathsheba incident to the accession of Solomon. One should note that in this proposal Goulder accepts the historical idea behind the biographical superscriptions of these psalms, though he rejects the actual historical details of many of them.

31. Childs, *Introduction to the Old Testament*, pp. 520-22.

which once functioned within a cultic context were historicized by placing them within the history of David'. As a result, the psalms now function to provide access to the 'inner life' of David, a man 'who displays all the strengths and weaknesses of all human beings' and who 'experiences the full range of human emotions'.[32]

According to Childs, this link to David helps to make the psalms 'immediately accessible to the faithful'.[33] Rather than grounding the psalms in the past, the Davidic superscriptions help to 'contemporize and individualize' them for every generation. Through David, they 'testify to all the common troubles and joys of ordinary human life in which all persons participate'.

Peter Ackroyd has moved in a similar interpretive direction in a suggestive book published in 1978. In this work, Ackroyd calls attention to the new dimensions of meaning that occur when a psalm is read in conjunction with a narrative context.[34] Indeed, Ackroyd notes that such an association of psalms and narrative has long been a part of the tradition, as may be seen from those manuscripts of Samuel that apparently leave spaces at appropriate places so that relevant psalms might be recalled.[35]

Like Childs, Ackroyd has seen the significance of the Davidic psalm titles for the interpretation of certain psalms. Thus, he notes that by connecting Psalm 3 to the story of David and Absalom, that psalm's superscription invites the reader 'to see in the story of David an example of experience from which he can learn to assess his own fears and anxiety'.[36] It is by this reading of the psalm alongside the story of David and Absalom that the psalm 'becomes a vehicle for the religious needs and aspirations of the worshiping community and individual'.[37]

A third scholar to stress the hermeneutical significance of David is

---

32. Childs, *Introduction to the Old Testament*, p. 521. See also his 'Psalm Titles', p. 149.

33. Childs, *Introduction to the Old Testament*, p. 521.

34. See Ackroyd, *Doors*, p. 32.

35. Ackroyd, *Doors*, p. 35. On this, cf. also M. Fishbane, *Biblical Interpretation in Ancient Israel* (Oxford: Clarendon Press, 1985), pp. 405-406. Fishbane sees such purposeful placing of lacunae as indicative of at least a nascent unifying scriptural vision.

36. Ackroyd, *Doors*, p. 34. Note the emphasis on learning in light of what was discussed in the previous chapter.

37. Ackroyd, *Doors*, p. 35.

James Luther Mays.[38] Like the two previous scholars, Mays notes the long Christian tradition of using David's life to give the psalms 'human and dramatic context'.[39] For such traditional interpretation, the 'connection with David has been a central hermeneutical principle'.[40] According to Mays, both the psalms with narrative superscriptions and the more numerous *l^edāwid* psalms 'hold their users in continuity with David and in relation to David's God'.[41]

More specifically, Mays sees the book of Psalms as presenting David in three distinct though related ways. First of all, David is 'one of the lowly', the 'model of the piety of those who depend on the LORD in the midst of the exigencies of life'.[42] Secondly, David is the anointed of the LORD, in both its historical and messianic senses. As such, David is not simply one of the lowly but also a sign of hope for the lowly.[43] Finally, David is 'the source and patron of praise and prayer for the worship of the LORD'.[44]

For such scholars, the figure of David functions as what Alan Cooper has called a 'productive interpretive strategy'.[45] This does not mean that

38. See especially his 'David', and *Psalms*, as well as *The Lord Reigns*, pp. 123-27, and 'Psalm Study'.

39. Mays, 'David', pp. 144-45. See also *The Lord Reigns*, pp. 49-50, where he notes that 'in time the story of David became the context, first for the individual prayers, and then for many of the psalms'. In this tradition, David was not 'a strictly historical figure'. Rather, David was 'a paradigm and prototype in a canonical context' ('Psalm Study', p. 148).

40. Mays, *The Lord Reigns*, p. 123. Significantly, Mays sees the rediscovery of this approach as connected to a renewed emphasis on reading the Psalms as a book. For Mays, 'the connection made between David and the Psalms is a dominant feature of the book'.

41. Mays, 'David', p. 153.

42. Mays, *The Lord Reigns*, p. 123. Like Ackroyd, Mays sees Ps. 3 as crucial for this picture of David in that 'it sets the tone for all the rest'.

43. Mays, *The Lord Reigns*, p. 124. Mays also argues that those psalms that specifically mention David as God's chosen king work to cast a 'messianic construal' over the entire collection ('David', p. 153). This in turn points to the idea of the kingdom of God as the 'organizing, unifying subject of the psalter' ('David', p. 155; *Psalms*, p. 18).

44. Mays, *The Lord Reigns*, p. 125. Such a role is implied by 'elements of the superscriptions, the juxtaposition of David psalms with those of the Asaphites and Korahites, and the conclusion of the Psalter'.

45. A. Cooper, 'The Life and Times of King David According to the Book of Psalms', in R.E. Friedman (ed.), *The Poet and the Historian: Essays in Literary and*

it is the only such interpretive strategy of which the psalms are capable, a point which is well made by Roland Murphy.[46] It does, however, have the advantage of taking seriously both the witness of the interpretive tradition and the canonical shape of the book of Psalms itself.

Davidic Authorship and Genre: The Question of Typicality
The retrieval of the hermeneutical importance of David for the psalms that one sees in such scholars as Childs, Ackroyd and Mays has a number of implications for our understanding of genre. Clearly none of these scholars would wish to return to a pre-Gunkel view of the psalms which was not sensitive to questions of literary form and social setting. At the same time, they have suggested a different approach that is in major ways not directly dependent on Gunkel's analysis.

It would be a mistake to see the renewed emphasis on David as inimical to a genre-based approach to the psalms. Indeed, the new appreciation of David as a figure of hermeneutical significance raises genre issues of great importance. The place where such issues of authorship and genre intersect is the question of typicality.

Both Childs and Ackroyd emphasize the interpretive significance of David's role as a typical figure. Thus, for Childs, it is because David is a typical human being like ourselves that we are able to relate to the psalms through him. Important in this is the fact that David experiences 'the full range of emotions'. Because of this, the psalms 'testify to all the common troubles and joys of ordinary human life in which all persons participate'.[47]

According to Ackroyd, the figure of David is particularly appropriate for the role of representative human being because the Davidic tradition was 'extensive and varied'.[48] David is a 'real personality', who is 'both heroic and tragic'. As such, his experience can be seen as 'typical, as

---

Historical Biblical Criticism (HSS, 26; Chico, CA: Scholars Press, 1983), p. 125.

46. For Murphy's reservations about Childs's Davidic interpretation of the psalms, see his *Psalms*, pp. 22-26. As noted in the text, Murphy does not object to this approach per se. Indeed, he sees it as stemming from an 'honorable and respectable tradition' and makes use of it himself. He does, however, worry that such an approach will excessively limit the modern interpretation of the psalms, a point which is well taken. Both Childs and Mays make similar points, as will be seen in the next chapter of this work which deals explicitly with the question of whether the psalms admit to only one mode of interpretation.

47. Childs, *Introduction to the Old Testament*, p. 521.

48. Ackroyd, *Doors*, p. 76.

providing patterns for the understanding of the reader's own experience, and as enabling him to see his own needs and uncertainties in a
wider context'.[49]

Mays seems to put less emphasis on David as a typical human figure
and more on his specific roles as one of the lowly, a messianic figure
and a patron of divine worship. In the first of these roles, David is
'identified' with the lowly, even as he is 'the model of the piety of those
who depend on the LORD in the midst of the exigencies of life'.[50] As
such, he seems to function for Mays as an 'ideal type', to which the
believer should conform.[51]

One finds a somewhat similar approach in the work of Gerald
Sheppard.[52] Sheppard emphasizes the 'particularity' of David's life and
argues against seeing him as an 'unhistorical, ideal, or typological
figure, an "everyman"'. According to Sheppard, 'David's life strikes in
all of us some familiar notes, not because it is so typical but because it
is so thoroughly human, not because it provides a universal pattern of
human distress but because of its psychological depth'.[53] Sheppard further argues that 'we are invited by the biblical portrayal more to identify with some of David's ordinary actions and feelings than to compare
our experiences with his'. In David, 'we confront the reality and frailty
of human life'.

While there are important differences between them, all of these
scholars see some sort of a connection between David and the rest of
humanity as important for how one approaches the psalms. At the same
time, there also seems to be an awareness of David's own specific history and personality, especially in the case of Mays and Sheppard.
What needs to be looked at further is the way these two aspects of the
reader's understanding of David affect the appropriation of the psalms.

More specifically, one might ask how the issue of David's status as a
typical figure relates to the way the psalms function in genre terms. In
answering this question, it will help to remember that it is precisely the
sharing of common human experiences that Brueggemann saw as the
link between the ancient Israel that created the psalms and the modern

49. Ackroyd, *Doors*, p. 76.

50. Mays, *The Lord Reigns*, p. 123.

51. As will be noted below, Mays is more inclined to use typicality language
similar to Childs and Ackroyd when he relates the psalms to the suffering of Jesus.

52. G. Sheppard, 'Theology and the Book of Psalms', *Int* 46 (1992), pp. 143-55.

53. Sheppard, 'Theology', p. 148.

reader. Because of such common experiences, Brueggemann was able to assume that the psalms continue to have the same 'typology of function' that they did in ancient Israel.[54] To some extent, Brueggemann saw this similar functioning as dictated by the text of the psalms themselves, though, as noted above, the extent of this functioning actually varied with the different types of psalms. Nevertheless, what makes it possible for the psalms to continue to function for Brueggemann is what he sees as their direct link to universal human experience.

As noted in the previous chapters of the present work, the history of the psalms' reception raises some questions about whether the psalm texts can be correlated to universal experience quite as directly and as neatly as Brueggemann has contended. Denying such an immediate appeal to universal experience does not, however, rule out all claims to 'typicality'. In fact, it is precisely the psalms' connection to the specific yet representative figure of David that provides the 'typicality' necessary to talk about genre links between past and present.

The psalm titles show exactly how this works, especially in those cases where they situate certain psalms in the life of David. As Childs has argued, such titles work to provide us with greater access to David's inner life.[55] Such access, however, not only satisfies our curiosity about a biblical hero, it also provides us with examples of the appropriate use of the psalms.

The superscription gives us a readily accessible setting for the psalm. Because we have been in similar situations, we are able to identify with David in his need, his shame and his joy. As is always the case, our knowledge of a psalm's setting helps to illuminate the way a psalm functions. In such a way, setting the psalms in David's narrative works to provide the reader with an example of how one should respond in similar circumstances.[56]

By situating a psalm in David's life, a superscription gives that psalm a specific context of interpretation. This context is similar, but not

54. Brueggemann, 'Life of Faith', p. 5.
55. Childs, *Introduction to the Old Testament*, p. 521; also 'Psalm Titles'.
56. Thus, according to Mays, the psalm titles are 'hermeneutical ways of relating the psalms to the lives of those who lived in the face of threats from enemies within and without and from their own sin, and who sought to conduct their lives according to the way of David'. In such a way, David 'becomes model and guide for those who study the psalms and sing them in worship' ('David', p. 152).

identical, to familiar contexts from our own lives. Both the similarities and the differences have interpretive significance. In other words, the superscription functions as both an interpretive bridge to the psalm and a means of gaining perspective on the psalm.

To recognize a difference between ourselves and David does not distance us from the psalm any more than recognizing a difference between our own ambition and that of Macbeth distances us from Shakespeare's play. To use a word found in a number of the above authors, we are able to 'identify' with David, even as we realize that we are not identical with him.[57] The magnified example of David helps us to realize our own shortcomings and our own neediness.

It is, however, important to see that while our human situation may well mirror David's, it is not necessarily the case that our response will be the same as his. Indeed, it is only through the psalm that we are able to make David's response our own. The psalm does this first of all by providing a 'model' of what the proper response should be. Even more significantly, however, the psalm is what 'enables' us to respond as David did. In the words of the last chapter, the psalm functions as a means of transformation.

One may again quote Athanasius in this regard: 'You too, practicing these things and reciting the Psalms intelligently in this way, are able to comprehend the meaning in each, being guided by the Spirit. And the kind of life the holy, God-fearing men possessed who spoke these things—this life you also shall imitate'.[58] For Athanasius, the lives of those who say the psalms provide a model to be imitated, while the psalms themselves are the means by which the Spirit works to transform them into such people.

In such a way, the connection with the narrative helps to further the transformative use of the psalms. According to Brueggemann, the use of a particular genre is often directly dependent upon one's existing experience or situation. If, however, the reader has become involved with the story of David, he or she will be able to appropriate the psalms even if his or her life situation is not entirely identical with the

---

57. In stressing such an identification with David and the situating of the psalms in his life story, these authors are very much in keeping with the tradition of Augustine and the medieval period. On this, see Kuczynski, *Prophetic Song*, p. 55 and *passim*.

58. Athanasius, 'Letter', ch. 33.

sentiments of those psalms.[59] The narrative of David provides an avenue of access to the psalms by helping to engender the appropriate state in which they can be best be used. In turn, the psalms enable us to become more like David himself.

It may well be that the setting of the psalms in the specific context of David is a somewhat more flexible approach than Brueggemann's direct appeal to universal human experience. Thus, instead of seeing the psalms as fitting our situations or even giving them form, as Brueggemann has done, Ackroyd sees them as 'giving us a wider context for where we stand'.[60] Ackroyd continues:

> The uniqueness of our own moment of experience is not to be denied. But it is possible to see it now related to typical experiences, to declarations of need and confessions of faith which lift it out of its uniqueness into a larger sphere, where we may both learn from the rich traditions of the psalms and ourselves contribute to their continuing understanding. It is here that we may understand why the psalms came to be known as the 'psalms of David'. Associated with the life of that one particular personage of Israel's past, they came to express the needs and hopes of every worshiper. Seen as showing David's response to changing fortunes and experiences, they came to express the nourishing of religious life in every age.

Both Brueggemann and Ackroyd see the bridge between the psalms and the modern reader as somehow connected with the 'typical'. The difference between them is to be found in how each conceives of the typical. For Brueggemann, the psalms—or at least the laments—can be used by both ancient and modern worshipers because they clearly belong to the universal situation of human suffering. In other words, the texts themselves indicate their setting, and this setting is one shared by ancient and modern alike.[61]

It was, of course, the argument of the third chapter of the present work that even the laments were not so determinative of their setting as Brueggemann claimed. If, however, that chapter's argument were to be accepted, could any claim be made for typicality? It is precisely at this point that the figure of David comes in.

---

59. One may recall Ackroyd's observation about the spaces left in the books of Samuel for the insertion of the appropriate psalms.

60. Ackroyd, *Doors*, p. 73.

61. Once again, this is especially true of the laments. For Brueggemann, the function of the other types of psalms may vary according to the setting.

For Ackroyd, it is not the psalms themselves that indicate a typical situation. It is instead the figure of David that is typical in that he is a human being like the rest of us, with all our strengths and weaknesses. Through the superscriptions, a connection is made with the situations in which the psalms are appropriate. We are given access to the psalms through our involvement in the story. In other words, it is not simply the psalm text that determines its own setting. Rather, a setting is provided through the 'typical' figure of David.

This seems a bit less direct than Brueggemann's approach, but much is gained in this long way around. Thus, Ackroyd is able to see an ongoing tradition stretching from David to the present, a tradition of 'unique experiences' which continually provide new meaning to the psalm. All of this tradition is summed up in David, though each worshiper makes a contribution.

In the process of ongoing interpretation and reinterpretation, Ackroyd sees the psalms as having come to perform a 'function' different from that which they may have originally performed.[62] Nevertheless, the fact that we stand in a line of a long tradition of interpretation means that 'we cannot detach our own reading from that of our predecessors'.[63]

One may well think of the perspective of medieval exegesis here. David is the type, while later worshipers are the anti-types.[64] The latter provide a new perspective on the former, even as the former in some way anticipates the latter.[65] Each interpreter continues to embody the tradition anew out of his or her unique situation.

Ackroyd's approach is notable for the way he uses canon and tradition as interpretive categories. It is the canonical placing of the psalms alongside the figure of David that provides the essential hermeneutical clue. However, it is the use of the psalms over the centuries that has furnished the context for our own contemporary reading of the psalms. Indeed, Ackroyd even talks about the 'transformation of psalmody' which is 'essential to its continuing use'.[66] It is the more flexible nature

62. Ackroyd, *Doors*, p. 50.

63. Ackroyd, *Doors*, p. 43.

64. According to Mays, David's story is the 'pattern and type of what is to be' ('David', p. 148).

65. The fact that for Christian readers the crucial anti-type is Jesus constitutes an interpretive move of some importance which will be looked at shortly.

66. Ackroyd, *Doors*, p. 50. Through this transformation, these poetic texts have 'enabled later readers, both Jews and Christians, to gain deeper insight both into the

of his David-centered typicality that allows both this transformation and this continued use.

Davidic Authorship and Genre: Some Examples

What follows are two examples of how taking the biographical super-scriptions seriously affects the way that the psalms are appropriated in genre terms. The first example is that of Psalm 51, whose extended superscription places that psalm in the context of David's great sin with Bathsheba and Uriah. The second example includes a number of the other biographical superscriptions, those in which David is seen to be in times of need.

One will recall that Psalm 51 is one of the seven penitential psalms. It is, in fact, the only one of the seven that is fully endorsed as a penitential psalm by both the tradition and modern form-critical analysis. As such, there is an obvious fit between the content of the psalm and the setting indicated by the superscription. If one takes the superscription seriously, one is given an insight into the character of David at a crucial moment in his life. One is also given a model of the ideal way in which one can repent one's sins.

Obviously, this usage is not 'typical' in that not everyone has committed a transgression of the same magnitude as David, nor is everyone visited by a prophet when guilty of some major sin. Nevertheless, few readers would have trouble relating to David in both his transgression and his unmasking. David is, in a sense, all of us writ large.

A look at Luther's commentary on this psalm shows how both the similarities and the differences between David and the reader are significant. For Luther, it is the very seriousness of David's crime that makes his petitioning of God's mercy so significant for us. After all, Luther reasons, if David, who was granted so much and had fallen so far, could still seize hold of God's mercy, what excuse could there be for the rest of us to think that our sins prevent us from approaching God?[67] For Luther, David is an extreme example of both the sin that necessitates the praying of this psalm and the faith that makes it possible. By praying this psalm and imitating David in his repentance, one takes on the proper stance before God.[68]

religious traditions in which they stand and into the particular moments of their own experience and their own contemporary situation'.

67. Luther, *Selected Psalms*, I, pp. 318-19 and *passim*.

68. On the imitation of David and the other 'Old Testament faithful' as an

The second example to be noted here has to do with the way that the various contexts specified by the superscriptions effectively work to group the psalms according to setting. Thus, a number of the biographical superscriptions describe situations of flight and anxiety.[69] As might be expected, given this context, all of these psalms have at least some connection with the genre of the individual lament.[70] Within this genre definition, however, there is considerable variation of emphasis.

While most of these psalms are fairly standard lament psalms, one at least (Ps. 3) moves a long way towards being more of a psalm of trust.[71] Another (Ps. 52) is more a rebuke of the enemy and an assertion of the psalmist's own confidence.[72] A third (Ps. 63) links statements of thanks and trust to a desire for and an experience of God's presence.

In such a way, these psalms portray David as having a range of reactions to his times of need. In this, he may be seen as a model for those who find themselves in similar situations, even if the latter are not quite so desperate as those of David. Like David, one can both lament one's sufferings and assert one's confidence in God's deliverance. David's example shows that more than one response is appropriate in such settings.

One may note in passing the difference between the context implied for some of these psalms by the superscriptions and that proposed by Brueggemann in *Message*. For Brueggemann, the psalms of trust follow upon and generalize the experience described in the thanksgiving psalms.[73] As such, he specifically sees Psalm 63 as a psalm of new orientation which celebrates God's past saving action.[74] If, however, one considers the context implied by its superscription, one finds that this psalm has clearly been considered to be quite appropriate to times

important characteristic of Luther's hermeneutical approach, see Preus, *From Shadow to Promise*, p. 197. For the view that the imitation of David is a standard medieval hermeneutical stance, see Kuczynski, *Prophetic Song*.

69. Cf. Pss. 3, 52, 54, 56, 57, 59, possibly 63, and 142.

70. So Gunkel, *Einleitung in die Psalmen*, p. 172, which is followed by most subsequent commentators.

71. Thus, according to Gunkel, 'im ganzen tritt das Vertrauen hervor, Klage und besonders Bitte zurück' (*Psalmen*, p. 13).

72. Gunkel finds the genre of this psalm difficult, though he does see at least a connection with the individual lament. Cf. *Psalmen*, p. 228, and *Einleitung in die Psalmen*, p. 172.

73. Brueggemann, *Message of the Psalms*, p. 152.

74. Brueggemann, *Message of the Psalms*, p. 200 n. 50.

of 'disorientation'. As such, it presents the person in such times with another canonically sanctioned genre option besides that of the lament.[75]

Of course, not every psalm has a biographical superscription such as those considered here. Even if one accepts the hermeneutical construct of Davidic authorship as significant for the rest of the psalms, one must ask how one makes the connection between those psalms and David's life. The answer is undoubtedly that one makes this connection by means of analogy to those psalms that do have such biographical super-scriptions.[76] In such a way, the latter psalms serve as a hermeneutical prism through which all the psalms may be both related to David and appropriated by his successors.

One may profitably use the language of the previous chapter to sum up the genre implications of these psalms' link with David. The narrative of David presents a complex human life that is in many ways similar to our own. In their different genre possibilities, the psalms present David's inner responses to that life, responses which together are paradigmatic for a particular 'mode of life'. The psalms invite us to that life and, even more, help to make that life possible for us. By praying the psalms, we are able to appropriate that mode of life and to be transformed along the lines of God's servant, David.

David as Prophet: Implications for Genre

So far this chapter has examined the genre implications of following the lead of those psalm superscriptions that present David as a hermeneutical key for the psalms. If one does this, however, one is also forced to consider those elements of the psalms that were seen above to be difficult to reconcile with such Davidic authorship. In particular, one needs to consider those elements of the psalms that are historically anachronistic for David.

75. This grouping of the lament and psalm of trust is more in line with the thinking of someone like P. Miller who includes both psalms in a chapter entitled 'Prayers for Help'. Seeing them as appropriate to the same situation does not, however, keep him from noting the 'inherent tension' between these two types of prayer or from also including the psalms of trust in his chapter on thanksgiving. See his *They Cried to the Lord: The Form and Theology of Biblical Prayer* (Minneapolis: Fortress Press, 1994).

76. Cf. Mays, 'David', p. 152. The tradition is sometimes even more explicit in tying these psalms together. Thus, for example, Qimḥi places Ps. 4 in the same setting as that specified in the superscription of Ps. 3.

One may in this respect consider Psalm 137, a psalm that is clearly difficult to fit with a Davidic provenance.[77] If all the psalms are attributed to David, what is one to make of the obvious non-Davidic setting of this particular psalm? One could, of course, follow the lead of those authors who would deny this psalm to David because it is lacking a Davidic superscription. Even this, however, does not solve all the anachronisms one finds in the Psalter.

This is clear from Psalm 51, a psalm that was seen in the previous section to have one of the closest links between superscription and psalm content. Despite this close link, Psalm 51 ends with a plea for God to rebuild the walls of Jerusalem as a precondition for the resumption of acceptable sacrifice. The problem is, of course, that the walls of Jerusalem were not in need of such repair in the time of David. Indeed, these verses are most appropriate in the same exilic setting which was so problematic for the David authorship of Psalm 137.

How is it possible to take Davidic authorship seriously—even as a hermeneutical construct—in the face of such details? Does this obvious critical tension have any significance for the genre definition and function of the psalms? Once again, a look at how this question was treated throughout the history of interpretation may provide some insight into the issues involved.

Important here is the tendency to see David as, in some way, a prophetic figure.[78] This tendency was from the beginning quite prevalent in Christian interpretation. The New Testament, for example, clearly sees David as inspired by the Holy Spirit (Mk 12.36) and specifically calls him a prophet (Acts 2.29-30). For the early Christians, David's prophetic status was seen especially in the way the psalms predict the events of the life of Jesus. Indeed, in the early church, it was precisely those psalms that could be taken to refer to Jesus that were seen as central.[79]

This tendency to ascribe prophetic status to David was not, however, a Christian innovation.[80] The connection between David and prophecy

---

77. Given the obvious difficulties, it is striking that the LXX has added a Davidic superscription to this psalm.

78. See Kugel, 'David the Prophet' for an overview of the early stages of this tradition. Kugel specifically notes the way psalms such as Ps. 137 must have contributed on the development of the view of David as a prophet (cf. p. 50).

79. So Acts 2.25-28, 34-35. Cf. Linton, 'Interpretation of the Psalms'.

80. So Kugel, 'David the Prophet', p. 46.

was already present in the Jewish tradition before the rise of Christianity, as may be seen from Philo and the brief biographical note that is part of 11QPs[a].[81] Josephus also sees David as someone to whom God had shown the future.[82]

David's prophetic status continues to be affirmed in the later rabbinic tradition, as may be seen from Naḥmanides' reference to him as 'the illustrious prophet in kingly garb and crown'.[83] Those rare exceptions who denied the prophetic nature of the psalms also tended to deny their wholesale attribution to David because of the historical problems created thereby.[84] More common among the commentators than such denials were discussions of the exact nature of David's prophecy.[85]

According David prophetic status takes away the historical difficulty of those psalms and sections of psalms that cannot be reconciled with a setting in David's own lifetime. It does so, of course, by adding another dimension to the hermeneutical role of David, a move not without its potential problems. Thus, for Ackroyd, the prophetic use of the psalms

81. Thus, Philo refers to the author of Ps. 84 as 'a certain prophetic man'. (See Kugel, 'David the Prophet', p. 54, for a discussion of this text.) The Qumran text details David's literary output which it claims was spoken through prophecy (*bnbw'h*). As Kugel notes, this claim to prophecy apparently does not have the same predictive force that one finds in Christianity. It has instead more to do with the need to guarantee the special scriptural nature of the Psalms with which David was so intimately associated. See 'David the Prophet', pp. 46, 54-55.

82. Cf. *Ant.* 8.109-110, where Solomon claims that God showed David 'all things that were to come to pass'. One also sees a prophetic David in the 'Songs of David', an apparently first-century work. Cf. Kugel, 'David the Prophet', pp. 46-47.

83. See Kugel, 'David the Prophet', p. 47.

84. Such apparently was the position of the learned grammarian of the eleventh century, Moses Ibn Giqatilah. For an overview of his position and an analysis of how it relates to the work of Ibn Ezra, see Simon, *Four Approaches*.

85. Thus, for example, in their explanation of the different psalm titles some authorities see a difference between *l[e]dāwid mizmôr* and *mizmôr l[e]dāwid*, according to whether the Holy Spirit came upon David before or after the composing of a particular psalm (though later commentators saw no difference, probably because they wished to preserve a connection with the Holy Spirit for all the psalms). On this, see Neubauer, 'Authorship'.

Qimḥi is interesting in this respect as well. He also sees David as composing the psalms with the help of the Holy Spirit, though this was in some way to be distinguished from prophecy proper. David spoke of events after his time—such as the Babylonian and other captivities. He also pronounced consolation in view of the restoration of the house of David to its former position.

'has its limitations', in that it is 'much more concerned with finding
confirmation for what is already believed, means of expressing in familiar terms new elements of religious experience, than with letting the
psalms speak out of their poetry'.[86]

Clearly, Ackroyd is correct in calling attention to the danger that a
prophetic reading will allow the tradition to suffocate the text. It is,
after all, a significant genre shift to move from prayer to prophecy, and
one which is by no means obvious from the text of the psalms themselves. Nevertheless, there is an aspect of David's status as prophet that
relates directly to his hermeneutically important role as a representative
person. Moreover, it is this connection that seems to be of the highest
significance in the tradition.

To understand this link between David as prophet and David as representative person, one may begin by noting the discussion in *b. Pes.*
117a as to whether David uttered the psalms with reference to himself
alone or with reference to the community. In this discussion, Rabbi
Eliezer argues that David spoke all the psalms with reference to himself, whereas Rabbi Joshua argues that David spoke them with reference to the community. The sages give a middle opinion, asserting that
some psalms refer to the community while others refer to David himself. More specifically, they see the psalms that use the singular as bear-
ing upon himself, while those in the plural allude to the community.[87]

Those familiar with modern form-critical discussions will not fail to
catch an echo of the long-standing debate over the personal or communal nature of the psalms. This is a basic form-critical distinction and
one which is crucial for these texts' modern genre definition. To see
only this, however, would be to miss the real significance of this rabbinic debate. After all, one is not simply talking about psalms of the
individual and psalms of the community. One is talking about psalms
that arise out of the circumstances of David's own life and those that
refer to situations of Israel's wider history. The crucial point here is that
David composes prayers both for himself and for others.[88]

Other rabbinic texts take this crucial point one step further. According

86. Ackroyd, *Doors*, pp. 75-76.
87. This debate is apparently cited in *Midr. Teh.* 24.3. Cf. also 4.1 and 18.1,
though see further below on the last of these passages.
88. This assertion that David composed psalms for others is in some ways similar to those traditions which connect David to the individuals named in the other
psalm titles.

to *Midrash Tehillim*, it was taught (by Rabbi Yudan in the name of Rabbi Judah) that 'all that David said in his Book of Psalms applies to himself, to all Israel, and to all the ages'.[89] As Slomovic notes, this principle allows the rabbis to move beyond a Davidic reference in a given psalm text to events that either precede or follow David's times.[90]

In this rabbinic principle, one sees the special significance of David's prophetic status for the book of Psalms. Such status is not simply a safeguard of the inspiration and authority of that book. Rather, David's ability to foresee all of Israel's history allows him to be the privileged representative of Israel with regard to Israel's history.[91] As such, David is able to provide the appropriate, divinely inspired response to that history.

David's prophetic status allows him to compose texts not only for himself (and for the community of his own time) but also for the Israelite community throughout its history. Indeed, a particular psalm may refer to the events of many different periods. In such a way, David's own history is intertwined with the history of his people, and David's response is appropriate for later generations as well.

Given this principle of interpretation, the rabbis are free to situate a given psalm in Israelite history while still maintaining a link with David. Thus, according to *Midrash Tehillim*, Psalm 137 shows that God allowed David to see the destruction of both the first and the second Temples.[92] With this in mind, the psalm is not interpreted with reference to David's own life but with regard to the catastrophes of later years. Nevertheless, it is clearly felt that David has provided the appropriate response to these catastrophes.[93] Because David is a prophet, he is able to foresee Israel's future history. This is, however, the least important aspect of his prophetic activity, especially for those on the other side of the events. More important is the fact that he is also able to

---

89. *Midr. Teh.* 18.1. trans. Braude.

90. Slomovic also notes that this is the case 'even when a historical heading is already provided in the text'. See Slomovic's example of *Midr. Teh.* 18.11, which refers to Babylon, Media, Persia, Greece and Rome. Cf. Slomovic, 'Historical Titles', pp. 353-54.

91. For N. Sarna, this verse from the Midrash shows that David was seen as a 'corporate personality'. See his introduction to M. Buttenwieser, *The Psalms, Chronologically Treated with a New Translation* (New York: Ktav, 2nd edn, 1969), pp. xiv-xv.

92. V. 1 is felt to refer to the former and v. 7 to the latter.

93. One sees a similar view of David's role in Qimhi as well.

provide Israel with the correct response to that history. Thus, just as David was able to lament his own sufferings in the most appropriate way, he was also able to furnish Israel with the most appropriate way to lament the exile and other misfortunes. Similarly, the David who was able to repent his own sins was also able to provide Israel with the correct words to turn back to God after its transgressions.

David's prophetic status is important because it adds a communal dimension to his role as a representative person. Just as David's personal life anticipates the life of every individual, so he is able (through prophetic means) to anticipate the entire history of Israel as a nation. Since David as king was both a private and a public person, it is fitting he was able to provide appropriate prayer for both every individual and the entire nation.[94]

Just as the prayers that arise from David's personal life witness to and make available the special relationship that he had with God, so the communal prayers that David has provided witness to and make available such a relationship for Israel as a whole. While the hermeneutical approach is clearly different in each case, both types of psalms have expressive and transformative possibilities. Both David as an individual and Israel as a nation have a role as God's servant. Through the words of David, every generation of Israel is able to speak in a way befitting God's servant. By doing so, Israel is ever more transformed into just such a servant.

David's Genres in Christian Tradition

According to much of Jewish tradition, David functions as the hermeneutical center of the psalms, both in his role as the representative man of prayer in his own right and in his role as the authoritative composer of prayers for all succeeding generations of Israel. To some extent, David retains these roles in Christian tradition as well.

Here again, the psalm titles may be seen to have had considerable influence on the interpretive tradition. Psalm 51, for example, was often interpreted in the light of the Bathsheba episode, with David being held

---

94. As is quite evident from Ps. 51, both of these aspects of David's life may be present in the same psalm. Whether or not one wants to see the psalms as taking on a more general corporate reference (cf. Childs, *Introduction to the Old Testament*, pp. 519-20), it seems clear that the rabbinic tradition has seen David as an important means for both the individual and the communal appropriation of the psalms.

up as a model of penitence who could well be imitated by the reader.[95] In a more general way, Christian authors from the New Testament on routinely speak of David as the author of the Psalms. They also follow their Jewish counterparts in sometimes seeing David as a prophet whose words apply to their own circumstances.[96]

Despite these similarities in appropriating the psalms through the person of David, the Christian tradition has one major difference from its Jewish counterpart. Not surprisingly, this difference has to do with the fact that for the Christian interpreter a figure has arisen with even more authority and access to the Holy Spirit than David. Indeed, for the Christian, Jesus is the new David, the antitype of whom the old David is merely the foreshadowing. The relationship of this new David to the psalms is of great interest for the present discussion of authorship and genre.

The early church was, of course, particularly attracted to those psalms that could be seen as messianic prophecies. Such psalms were felt to have great apologetic value and as such to be particularly useful for spreading the gospel. It is, however, important to note that the early church saw two distinct ways in which the psalms worked as prophecy.

The first of these is where David speaks as a prophet who sees ahead to the events of Jesus' life. Thus, for example, Acts 2.33-35 sees David as prophesying in Psalm 110 concerning Jesus' ascension and enthronement. Similarly, Athanasius sees Psalm 45 as being addressed by David to his 'daughter' Mary concerning Jesus' human birth.[97]

As important as this first prophetic usage was for early Christianity, a second usage was even more important for later interpretation. In this second usage, David is a prophet in that it is through him that Jesus himself may be seen to be speaking beforehand. This mode of interpretation may already be seen in the New Testament. Thus, for example, the point of Peter's quotation of Psalm 16 in Acts 2.25-28 turns on the

---

95. See, among other examples, 1 Clem. 18.1 and Augustine's treatment of Ps. 51 in his *Enarrationes*. Also see Athanasius's reference to the narrative superscriptions of Pss. 52 and 54 in *Letter to Marcellinus*, ch. 20. For a very informative discussion of the medieval view of David as a moral prophet who taught by both word and example, see Kuczynski, *Prophetic Song*, especially Chapter 2, 'Imitating David'.

96. So, for example, 1 Clem. 19. Also, see Kuczynski, *Prophetic Song*, for a detailed discussion of this use of the psalms from antiquity through the middle ages.

97. Athanasius, 'Letter', ch. 6.

fact that David, as someone who is dead and buried, cannot be speaker of this psalm (so v. 29). For Luke, only Jesus can be the speaker of this psalm since he has not undergone corruption.[98]

Justin Martyr's similar argument with regard to Psalm 22 has the advantage of being even more explicit as to the method involved.[99] According to Justin, when David speaks in that psalm about a piercing of hands and feet and a dividing of garments, he cannot be referring to his own situation, since these things never happened to him. Instead, he is speaking 'out of the person of Christ' (*apo prosōpou tou Christou*). That is to say, it is really Jesus who is speaking prophetically through David here.

For many of these early Christian authors, determining the identity of the speaker is the most important interpretive task for a particular psalm.[100] There are a range of possible speakers, including God, Jesus (in either his humanity or his divinity), David or the faithful, especially the church. Naturally, when such interpreters focus on Jesus as the real speaker of a particular psalm, David, the prophetic medium of this speech, tends to fade into the background.

Perhaps the most interesting aspect of this particular appropriation of the psalms is the fact that it requires an act of genre definition similar to that made in the Jewish tradition when it saw David as responsible for all the psalms. One may remember that in that tradition David was seen as uttering some psalms on his own behalf while providing others for the benefit of the Israel of a later time. In a similar way, the early interpreters describe Jesus as speaking some psalms with reference to himself, while praying others on behalf of the 'saints' or the 'pious'.[101]

98. One may profitably note Linton's very perceptive analysis of the hermeneutical method involved here ('Interpretation of the Psalms'). First, the interpreter takes the words of the psalm in an exaggeratedly 'verbal' way, a move which makes it impossible to accept the 'natural' subject of the psalm. This in turn prompts a 'reintroduction of the correct subject'. Linton sees this as similar to what takes place in rabbinic interpretation.

99. Justin Martyr, *Apology* 35.6.

100. So Linton, 'Interpretation of the Psalms'.

101. Thus, Origen sees Ps. 91.11-12 as referring not to Christ himself but *de sanctis generaliter*, as it says in the Latin version of his commentary on the Gospel of Luke (*Homil. in Lucam* 31, GCS 49). In Greek, the authors often refer to speaking *ek* (or *apo*) *prosōpou tou Christou*. Again, see Linton, 'Interpretation of the Psalms', for a representative survey. His discussion of Eusebius (pp. 151-52) is particularly instructive.

Using more technical terminology, one may say that Jesus prays some psalms *personaliter* and others *generaliter*.[102]

In the case of David, it will be remembered that the distinction between David's personal psalms and those composed for Israel was made on the basis of two factors. First of all, those psalms that were of a communal nature were seen to be more appropriate for a wider setting in the life of the nation. Secondly, psalms that raised historical difficulties for a Davidic setting were also seen to be home in a wider national setting.

In the case of Jesus, the grounds for distinguishing *personaliter* from *generaliter* references are similar in some cases but different in others. Thus, some references (such as the Psalm 22 verses discussed by Justin Martyr) are obviously assigned to Jesus on the basis of their historical appropriateness or their actual citation in the New Testament. On the other hand, passages that were seen to refer to Jesus' divinity (such as Ps. 2.7) are denied to other speakers on more ontological grounds. Thus, for both historical and ontological reasons, Jesus was seen to speak certain psalms *personaliter*.

Another dividing line between the psalms that Jesus speaks *personaliter* and those that he speaks *generaliter* is that of whether a psalm either admits sinfulness or asserts innocence.[103] Because Jesus was considered to be without sin, it was obviously impossible for him to pray the former psalms on his own behalf. This does not mean that the early Christian authors did not see Jesus as praying these psalms. Rather, they saw him as praying them for the Church, which is in great need of such intercession. On the other hand, the Church, being sinful, obviously cannot pray the psalms of innocence in its own right. It is only the sinless Christ who can properly pray such psalms, and so these are properly only applicable to him personally.[104]

As in the case of the distinction between David's own personal

---

102. On these terms, cf. Linton, 'Interpretation of the Psalms'.

103. Again see the discussion in Linton, 'Interpretation of the Psalms', pp. 152-53.

104. Cassiodorus has a useful summary of the ways that the psalms relate to Christ in ch. 13 of the preface to his *Expositio*. For an English translation, see his *Explanation of the Psalms* (trans. P.G. Walsh; Ancient Christian Writers, 51; New York: Paulist Press, 1990), pp. 34-35. Cassiodorus sees the psalms as referring to Christ either according to his humanity, his divinity, or his body, the Church. The medieval view is similar. See Kuczynski, *Prophetic Song*.

prayer and those Davidic compositions meant for wider use, the distinction between Jesus' *personaliter* and *generaliter* prayer is capable of great hermeneutical nuance and sophistication. Thus, those prayers that Jesus prays *personaliter* are not excluded from the prayer life of the Church, even though the Church is formally unable to pray them in its own right. Instead, such prayers become the *means* of becoming more like Jesus. Indeed, they are seen as the instruments of God's grace, a way of union with Jesus.[105]

Similarly, those psalms that the Church properly prays in its own right, such as those that contain cries of distress or penitence, become powerful precisely because Jesus has also prayed them.[106] Indeed, they become powerful because Jesus has prayed them in a way and to a depth that the Church is incapable of praying them on its own.[107] It is the fact of Jesus' taking on human suffering that gives a psalm such as Psalm 22 its particular power. Similarly, it is because Jesus has taken on human sinfulness that the Church's praying of the penitential psalms has real efficacy. In both cases, what guarantees the effectiveness of these psalms is the fact that the Church joins Jesus in the praying of these prayers even as Jesus has joined the Church in its situation of need.[108]

As was the case with David, seeing Jesus as the one praying the psalms provides a setting for the psalms in a life story which is avail-

---

105. On this, see especially Linton's discussion of Augustine in 'Interpretation of the Psalms', p. 155. For a modern example of this type of interpretation, see D. Bonhoeffer, *Psalms: The Prayer Book of the Bible* (Minneapolis: Augsburg, 1970), pp. 50-55.

106. One finds something similar to this in the rabbinic view of David as the one who makes all the songs of Israel pleasing to God. Cf. *Shir. R.* 4.3.

107. The words of Bonhoeffer are in keeping with much of the interpretive tradition: 'How is it possible for a man and Jesus Christ to pray the Psalter together? It is the incarnate Son of God, who has borne every human weakness in his own flesh, who here pours out the heart of all humanity before God and who stands in our place and prays for us. He has known torment and pain, guilt and death more deeply than we. Therefore it is the prayer of the human nature assumed by him which comes here before God. It is really our prayer, but since he knows us better than we know ourselves and since he himself was true man for our sakes, it is also really his prayer, and it can become our prayer only because it was his prayer'. *Psalms*, pp. 20-21.

108. Cf. Westermann's essay, 'The Role of the Lament in the Theology of the Old Testament', in *Praise*, pp. 259-80.

able to Christians in literary form. As Mays notes, this is particularly
true of Jesus' passion in which the psalms play a major interpretive
role.[109] Once again, both the similarities and differences between that
life story and that of Christians provide valuable hermeneutical connections and perspectives through which Christians can appropriate the
psalms.

Thus, for example, placing Psalm 22 on the lips of Jesus on the cross
allows a connection between him and human suffering, even as it puts
individual human suffering in a wider perspective. For Mays, the use of
this psalm helps to bring out the 'typicality' of Jesus' suffering, something that Jesus shares with the rest of humanity.[110] At the same time,
however, Jesus' use of this psalm also puts certain individuals' relative
lack of suffering in perspective, namely as a natural but still less than
faithful resistance to sharing Jesus' cross and the suffering of others.

To those who are suffering, Jesus' appropriation of Psalm 22 is an
assurance that 'I am with you on your cross'. To those who attempt to
keep such suffering at a comfortable distance, Jesus' praying of this
psalm asks 'Why are you not with me on my cross?' or 'Why have you
not taken up your cross and followed me?'

Crucial here from the perspective of genre is how a change in the
way one views the speaker of the psalms results in different groupings
of those texts. Thus, for example, a psalm like Psalm 25 may be seen in
either a personal or a general way, depending on whether one sees
David or Jesus as the speaker. The Jewish tradition sees the psalm as
clearly appropriate to David personally, since it is an individual psalm
which fits well with the particulars of David's own life.[111] In the
Christian tradition, on the other hand, this psalm must be understood
generaliter, since its confession of sinfulness is not at all appropriate
for the sinless person of Jesus.[112] In each tradition, such a psalm is able
to be read alongside other personal or general psalms. The configuration
is, however, different in each case.

It is important to recognize that the Christian tradition on the appropriation of the psalms is a long and varied one. Not all Christian authors
have used a Christ-centered approach to the psalms. Especially in the

---

109. Mays, *The Lord Reigns*, p. 51.

110. Mays, *The Lord Reigns*, p. 51.

111. In such a way, Qimḥi sees the greatness of David's guilt in v. 11 as related
to the Bathsheba episode.

112. So Augustine in his *Enarrationes*.

more recent past, this approach has not been much in evidence, with someone like Bonhoeffer a significant but lonely exception. Much more common since the Reformation has been the Davidic approach to the psalms. Indeed, as was seen in the second chapter, the change from Jesus to David as the speaker of the psalms was a significant hermeneutical shift.[113]

In the modern era, of course, even the Davidic approach has given way in favor of other more critical approaches. Whether these latter approaches are more appropriate for the modern age must be left for the reader to decide. Nevertheless, to turn one's back completely on the hermeneutical insights of the past would seem to be wasteful at best. There is much treasure to be retrieved from these approaches in general and from a reclaiming of David's connections with the psalms in particular.

Conclusions

One may conclude by offering several observations on the general question that began this chapter concerning the relationship between author and genre in the case of the psalms. First of all, the actual historical authors of the psalms are unknown. Even the date and historical circumstances of their composition are only rarely able to be ascertained with any real probability. As a result, any attempt to situate the genre of the psalms historically must go the form-critical route of institutional setting. Even this, however, may be seen to be a rather speculative task. As a result, such modern authors as Westermann and Brueggemann have sought less to discover the institutional setting of the psalms than to situate them in either a larger theological relationship between God and Israel or in a wider existential human setting.

As has often been pointed out in this work, both the classic form-critical enterprise and the more recent work of Westermann and Brueggemann may be seen as generalizing moves away from individual historical authors. With respect to the question of authorship, however, the practical import of this move is to make progressively easier an identification of the reader with the supposed 'original context'. In reality, however, such a context is more an ideal construct, representing

---

113. Though the reformers still draw connections between David, Christ and the Church. Thus, in his exposition of Ps. 109, Calvin sees David as both mourning his own sufferings and representing Christ and the Church, prefiguring their sufferings.

what one sees as either distinctively Israelite or universally human.

Because the historical author has receded from consideration in the case of the biblical psalms, the focus has instead tended to center on those aspects of the psalms that are most compatible with a particular audience in a particular age. This interest in connecting the psalms to their audience has always been an important factor in their use and genre definition. What the present chapter's overview of the interpretive tradition has shown is that this move was often complemented by a reference to a specific authorial figure.

Thus, despite the difficulties in applying Hirsch's genre model to the psalms, it is nonetheless clear from the history of the psalms' reception that the concept of author is not irrelevant to their interpretation or their genre definition. Indeed, the quest for a suitable author frequently led the Jewish tradition to attribute even the anonymous 'unsuperscripted' psalms to David. The Christian tradition either made a similar Davidic attribution of the psalms or saw their real author in the person of Jesus. In both cases, there seems to have been a felt need to 'situate' the psalms with respect to a particular personality.

Modern authors have begun to rediscover the power of situating the psalms in such a way. The work of such scholars as Childs, Ackroyd and Mays clearly suggests that there are significant hermeneutical advantages to be gained from this sort of approach. Among these advantages is the ability to consider the psalms in a context that is in conversation with the rest of Scripture. This context, in turn, helps to provide guidelines for both the general interpretation and the genre definition of the psalms.

Since attention to their author was a prominent feature of much of the Jewish and Christian interpretation of the psalms, the modern retrieval of such an approach has the advantage of bringing contemporary interpreters into conversation with a rich and fruitful tradition. In addition, the connecting of the psalms with the figures of David and/or Jesus has the further advantage of bringing both the psalms and those who pray them back into dialogue with the history of salvation. It does this without tying the interpreter down to a speculative search for elusive historical authors or equally elusive historical situations.

What the present chapter has attempted to bring out are the genre implications of this retrieval of authorship as an interpretive category. Once again, the discussion has served to highlight such concepts as setting and function. By situating the psalms in the life of a particular 'author', one is given an insight into the way such psalms may continue to function in the present day. This process sometimes suggests settings and functions that are different from that implied by both standard form-critical analysis and its more recent development. However, even where it does not result in such different functions, situating the psalms in the life of an author deepens their use by providing an example of an ideal figure with whom the reader may identify.

In summary, then, the canonical text and the interpretive tradition provide a ready ideal author for the psalms even as they frustrate any search for their real author. While this ideal author does not allow for the same type of genre analysis that a real author would, taking such a figure seriously does have concrete implications for the grouping and use of the psalms. One should obviously remember Roland Murphy's warning that this approach is not the only way of appropriating these texts. Still, the present chapter has shown that situating the psalms in the context of their ideal author clearly raises important issues for their genre definition and continued use.

Chapter 6

THE PARTS AND THE WHOLE: THE GENRE DEFINITION
OF THE PSALMS AND THE CANONICAL SHAPE
OF THE PSALTER

The preceding chapters have surveyed a number of possible settings for the psalms. These settings have ranged from the historical situation of ancient Israel to the existential situation of the modern interpreter. They have encompassed both real flesh and blood Israelite singers and an ideal literary portrait of David, the sweet singer of Israel. Each of these possible settings has, in turn, been seen to have serious implications for the main concern of this book, the genre definition of the psalms.

Yet one more setting needs to be considered here, one that has begun to have an important impact on psalms research. This is the setting of the Psalter itself. A number of recent scholars have emphasized the fact that the psalms no longer exist as individual units. Instead these texts now constitute a unified collection, a 'book' of scripture among other books of scripture. In such a context, the individual psalm is important not so much in its own right but rather as an element of a larger literary whole with a specific canonical shape and attendant meaning.

Such an approach clearly constitutes a major shift in a field that has been dominated by its almost exclusive concern for the individual psalm. A number of perceptive insights have arisen from this new perspective, as will be seen below. Nevertheless, as one might well expect, such a dramatic shift is not without its implications for the main concern of this book, namely, the genre definition of the psalms.

The present chapter will examine these new considerations of the canonical shape of the Psalter with an eye towards understanding their significance for the genre analysis of the psalms. As part of this examination, the chapter will consider the way in which the practitioners of this new approach understand and use genre categories in their work on the psalms. It will also suggest certain ways in which some of these recent studies need to be augmented by a more developed awareness of the psalms' genre possibilities.

The Canonical Shape of the Psalter in the Work of Brevard S. Childs

As might be expected, the recent interest in the canonical shape of the book of Psalms may be traced back to the work of Brevard S. Childs. The previous chapter discussed Childs's argument that the psalm titles function as guidelines for the continued appropriation of the psalms. This is, of course, a canonical argument in that these titles are now part of the final form of the text.

These titles are not, however, the only aspects of the text's final form that are significant, as Childs has clearly seen. Also of considerable importance is the way certain psalms have made use of earlier material so as to produce 'a new form with its own individual integrity'.[1] In such a way, 'the psalms have been loosened from a given cultic context and the words assigned a significance in themselves as sacred scripture. These words of promise could be used in a variety of new contexts.'[2]

Childs specifically mentions two ways in which individual psalms have been shaped in a decisive new direction. First of all, a number of psalms now have an orientation towards the future that Childs calls eschatological.[3] Secondly, several psalms of the individual were either reshaped in a communal direction or used in a communal way.[4] As a result, the 'final form of the Psalter' has both an eschatological and communal orientation.

What we have seen of Childs's analysis so far concerns his perception of how individual psalms were given a different shape consistent with their new canonical role in the continuing community of believers. It is, however, important for understanding his successors to note that

---

1. Childs, *Introduction to the Old Testament*, p. 514.
2. Childs, *Introduction to the Old Testament*, p. 515.
3. Childs leaves open the question of whether this eschatological orientation stems from the presence of a prophetic oracle in its original setting (so Begrich) or from a conscious editorial reworking in the postexilic period (so Becker). 'However one explains it, the final form of the Psalter is highly eschatological in nature' (*Introduction to the Old Testament*, p. 518).
4. Childs, *Introduction to the Old Testament*, pp. 519-20. As Childs notes, 'there is evidence to suggest that the individual psalms were often understood collectively by the later generation of worshippers... It is significant in again showing a new function which ancient psalms had already acquired within ancient Israel.'

Childs to a certain extent also discusses the way these individual psalms have been arranged in the Psalter to make a specific point.

Along these lines, Childs points out the fact that the royal psalms have not been transmitted within a collection but have instead been 'thoroughly scattered throughout the Psalter'.[5] In contrast to their original function in the setting of the Israelite monarchy, these psalms now serve in their present canonical context as 'a witness to the messianic hope which looked for the consummation of God's kingship through his Anointed One'.[6]

Psalm 2 is particularly significant in this respect because of its prominent position at the beginning of the Psalter. In fact, there are signs that 'the redactor sought to link' this psalm together with Psalm 1 as an introduction to the Psalter as a whole. It is significant that Childs sees the latter psalm as having 'assumed a highly significant function as a preface to the psalms which are to be read, studied, and meditated upon'.[7]

Given the importance of Psalm 1 in some of the works to be discussed below, it might be useful to look at Childs's treatment of it in a bit more detail. For Childs, this psalm is especially significant since it testifies to a fundamental hermeneutical shift in the way the psalms are to be understood. 'The prayers of Israel directed to God have themselves become identified with God's word to the people.'[8] The Torah alluded to in the psalm itself includes 'the faithful meditation on the sacred writings which follow', that is, the rest of the Psalter itself, which now serves as 'a guidebook along the path of blessing'.[9] In such a way, the introduction to the Psalter 'testifies to a new theocentric understanding of the psalms in the continuing life of the people of God'.[10]

This understanding of the psalms as God's word and an object of faithful meditation may well be seen as foundational for those authors who emphasize the canonical shape of the Psalter. It should, however, be noted that for Childs the hermeneutical shift indicated by Psalm 1 is but one hermeneutical move among others. In fact, Childs specifically notes that 'the most characteristic feature of the canonical shaping of

5. Childs, *Introduction to the Old Testament*, pp. 515-17.
6. Childs, *Introduction to the Old Testament*, p. 517.
7. Childs, *Introduction to the Old Testament*, p. 513.
8. Childs, *Introduction to the Old Testament*, p. 513.
9. Childs, *Introduction to the Old Testament*, p. 513.
10. Childs, *Introduction to the Old Testament*, p. 514.

the Psalter is the variety of the different hermeneutical moves which were incorporated within the final form of the collection'. Childs continues:

> Although the psalms were often greatly refashioned for use by later generations, no one doctrinaire position received a normative role. The material was far too rich and its established use far too diverse ever to allow a single function to subordinate all others. The psalms were collected to be used for liturgy and study, both by a corporate body and by individuals, to remind of the great redemptive acts of the past as well as to anticipate the hopes of the future.[11]

It is possible to understand this quote in two somewhat different ways. On the one hand, Childs could simply be pointing to the diversity of hermeneutical moves now to be found within the Psalter. In this view, some psalms would have a liturgical function, while others might have been shaped so as to be an object of study. The final form of the Psalter may be seen as including both 'types' of psalms. As such, the role of the interpreter is first of all to determine the function of a particular psalm and then to come to terms with how these different psalms have been incorporated into the present book of Psalms.

A second way of understanding Childs's comments is to see these different functions not as specific to individual psalms but as hermeneutical possibilities for all the psalms. In this view, all the psalms are at least potentially capable of being used for either liturgy or study, for communal or individual appropriation, depending on the circumstances. The 'richness of the material' is to be seen in its ability to support a number of functions, as attested to by the diversity of this material's 'established use'.

This discussion of how to understand Childs's comments will undoubtedly remind the reader of some of the discussions about genre found in previous chapters. It is, of course, highly suggestive that Childs is so concerned with the 'function' and 'established use' of the psalms and that he very possibly sees the psalms as 'rich enough' to be able to function in a number of different ways. Given the previous discussion of this book, such a multiplicity of function would mean a certain flexibility in genre terms, one which would be specified only in the usage of particular individuals or communities.

Even, however, a narrow reading of Childs's statement would have significant implications for how one understands the genre of the

---

11. Childs, *Introduction to the Old Testament*, p. 522.

psalms. In this case, one could distinguish the genre of the psalms on the basis of their function, with some having liturgical purposes and others didactic purposes. Further specificity is, of course, possible, but once again the basic definition of each psalm would be either liturgical or didactic. Each of these would, in turn, entail a different setting in the life of the interpreter, and this setting would often be very different from a setting in the life of ancient Israel.

Given Childs's obvious familiarity with the varied interpretive history of the psalms, it seems more likely to this reader that his words should be taken in the wider sense. Along these lines, the final shape of the book of Psalms is such as to provide a number of functional possibilities for its individual texts. In other words, a certain genre ambiguity may be seen as having been built into the psalms. This is the case because even at the time of their final redaction their usage was such as to disallow any attempt to restrict them to one particular function. That later generations have found this ambiguity to be a rich resource is clear from the history of their interpretation and use.

The Editing of the Hebrew Psalter: The Work of Gerald Henry Wilson

Childs's approach obviously constitutes a major departure from the psalms interpretation that has dominated much of this century. Recently, a number of scholars have begun to pick up on the suggestions outlined in his *Introduction*. Among the most notable of these has been one of Childs's students, Gerald Henry Wilson.

Wilson's Yale dissertation, 'The Editing of the Hebrew Psalter', is a detailed analysis of the way in which and the purpose for which the Psalter has been shaped.[12] Wilson has subsequently developed his thesis in an impressive series of articles. These studies first of all attempt to isolate the editorial techniques that lie behind the organization of the present book of Psalms. As an aid in this pursuit, Wilson has paid careful attention to the way hymnic collections from both the ancient Near East and Qumran have been organized.

After distinguishing the editorial 'indicators' that determine the present shape of the Psalms, Wilson has been able to evaluate the hermeneutical and theological significance of that shape. Beginning with his initial work, he has argued that three features of the Psalter are of particular importance in this respect: the 'introductory' Psalm 1, the

12. This dissertation was later published as *The Editing of the Hebrew Psalter*.

five-book division and the final Hallel (Pss. 146–50).[13] It will be useful to look at these basic elements in more detail.

Psalm 1 as a Hermeneutical Guide to the Psalter

Wilson's discussion of the way Psalm 1 functions as an introduction to the Psalter follows the lines of Childs's insights on this matter.[14] Particularly important here is the *hermeneutical* function of this psalm.[15] For Wilson, Psalm 1 subtly alters 'how the reader views and appropriates' the rest of the psalms. 'The emphasis is now on meditation rather than cultic performance; private individual use over public, communal participation'.[16] Citing Childs, Wilson sees this psalm as instrumental in transforming Israel's words of response to her God into the Word of God to Israel.[17]

Because of this transformation, Wilson strongly objects to seeing the book of Psalms as a 'hymn book'.[18] The latter phrase has the adverse effect of focusing a 'disproportionate amount of attention on the individual compositions contained within'.[19] It is best to quote Wilson at length on this:

13. Wilson, *Editing of the Hebrew Psalter*, p. 204.

14. See Wilson, *Editing of the Hebrew Psalter*, p. 206, where he quotes Childs at length citing the passage discussed above. See also his 'The Shape of the Book of Psalms', p. 137, and 'Shaping the Psalter: A Consideration of Editorial Linkage in the Book of Psalms', in J.C. McCann, Jr (ed.), *The Shape and Shaping of the Psalter* (JSOTSup, 159; Sheffield: Sheffield Academic Press, 1993), pp. 72-82 (74).

15. At the end of his discussion of Psalm 1 in *Editing of the Hebrew Psalter*, Wilson argues that 'while it provides hermeneutical principles for the correct approach to the pss, it does not provide a key to the nature of the *message* contained within. We know only that we are to find the "Word of God" there. The *content* of that word is not specified' (p. 207). As will be seen below, other scholars will emphasize the content aspect of this psalm more than Wilson.

16. Wilson, *Editing of the Hebrew Psalter*, p. 206. One may also note his comment in 'Shaping the Psalter' (p. 74) that Psalm 1 'shifts the function' of the psalms which follow in such a way.

17. Wilson, *Editing of the Hebrew Psalter*, p. 206.

18. Wilson, *Editing of the Hebrew Psalter*, pp. 206-207, and 'Shaping the Psalter', pp. 72, 81-82.

19. Wilson, *Editing of the Hebrew Psalter*, p. 206. For this reason, Wilson prefers to see the Psalter as a 'musical score', a 'symphony' or an 'oratorio', each of which is a 'whole'. As such, it has an 'integrity that cannot and must not be ignored', despite the ability of each individual composition to stand on its own in a way similar to an aria from an oratorio. So 'Shaping the Psalter', p. 82.

A 'hymn book' collects hymns so that they may be readily available for individual use in worship. Emphasis is placed on the secondary use of the individual members of the collection rather than the collection itself. While some hymn books evidence a limited attempt to group their contents by theme, interest or liturgical function, there is seldom any sustained, organizational purpose at work in consecutive arrangement.[20]

For Wilson, the Psalter is not a 'source book from which to extract individual pss which are then read in another context which is provided for our own purposes'. Rather, in its 'final form', it is 'a book to be *read* rather than to be *performed*; to be *meditated over* rather than to be *recited from*'.[21] The placement of Psalm 1 means that 'the psalms are no longer to be sung as a human response to God but are to be meditated upon day and night as the source of the divine word of life to us'.[22]

The Books of the Psalter
After using Psalm 1 to establish the proper way of approaching the Psalter, Wilson then examines the rest of the book in an attempt to uncover its underlying theological perspective. Once again, it is the editorial indicators that have shaped the book which provide the key to this perspective. Particularly important in this respect is the way the fivefold division of the Psalter works.

For Wilson, there is an important break that occurs between the first three books of the Psalter and the last two books. First of all, the two groups have different principles for organizing their individual psalms. Thus, the two groups use the *hllwyh* and *hwdw* psalms and the doxologies differently to introduce and conclude their sections and books. They also differ in the way their author/genre groupings function and in the number of 'titled' or 'untitled' psalms that they contain.[23] According to Wilson, 'this difference in organizational technique between the earlier and later books points to the possibility of a separate redactional history for these two segments and the editorial process which lies behind them'.[24]

20. Wilson, *Editing of the Hebrew Psalter*, p. 206.
21. Wilson, *Editing of the Hebrew Psalter*, pp. 206-207. Emphasis original.
22. Wilson, 'Book of Psalms', p. 127. The same argument is to be found in 'Shaping the Psalms', p. 72, though later in that work Wilson does seem to leave the door open to seeing the psalms as eloquently 'mirroring' human cries to God (p. 74).
23. Wilson, *Editing of the Hebrew Psalter*, p. 207.
24. G.H. Wilson, 'The Use of Royal Psalms at the "Seams" of the Hebrew Psalter', *JSOT* 35 (1986), pp. 85-94 (87).

Most importantly, however, the first three books differ from the last two in their purposeful placement of 'royal' psalms at the 'seams' of these books.[25] According to Wilson, the strategic placement of these psalms allows one to view Psalms 2–72 'as a celebration of YHWH's faithfulness to the [Davidic] covenant', especially as this found its fullest expression during the time of David and Solomon.[26] Psalm 2 introduces this overwhelmingly Davidic collection by presenting a 'positive evaluation of the Davidic covenant which is divinely instituted and continues to experience divine support'.[27] The Solomonic Psalm 72, on the other hand, 'functions as David's attempt to transfer the blessings of his covenant with YHWH to his descendants'.[28]

Psalm 89 ends the third book by explicitly repeating the covenant promises made to David. However, in contrast to the earlier 'seams' of Psalms 2 and 72, this psalm also laments the apparent breaking of these promises and pleads for their restoration.[29] For Wilson, this seems 'perfectly suited to express the exilic hope for the restoration of the Davidic kingship and the nation'.[30] Nevertheless, it is God's failure to keep the Davidic covenant that concludes the first major segment of the Psalter.

In such a way, the first three books of the Psalter end with a 'problem'. It is, moreover, this problem to which the fourth book provides the 'answer'. For Wilson, the fourth book is the 'editorial "center" of the final form of the Hebrew Psalter'. Indeed, this book 'is especially the product of purposeful editorial arrangement'. The fact that it consists of a large number of 'untitled' psalms is a key indication of its editorial purposefulness, as is the 'close interweaving of theme and verbal correspondences' in its 17 psalms.[31]

Wilson sees the fourth book's answer to the crisis of the Davidic

25. See Wilson, *Editing of the Hebrew Psalter*, pp. 207-214, and 'Use of Royal Psalms'. Also 'Shaping the Psalter', pp. 133-34.

26. Wilson, *Editing of the Hebrew Psalter*, p. 208. In his later work, Wilson explains the lack of a royal psalm at the end of the first book by arguing for a redactional movement to combine the first two books into a single Davidic collection, a movement reflected in the Davidic postscript of 72.20 ('Use of Royal Psalms', p. 87).

27. Wilson, 'Use of Royal Psalms', p. 88.

28. Wilson, 'Use of Royal Psalms', p. 89.

29. Wilson, *Editing of the Hebrew Psalter*, pp. 212-14.

30. Wilson, 'Use of Royal Psalms', p. 91.

31. Wilson, *Editing of the Hebrew Psalter*, pp. 214-15.

covenant as one that focuses on the rule and continued faithfulness of God. Indeed, this book helps to shift 'the emphasis away from hope in human, Davidic kingship back to the premonarchic period with its (supposed) direct reliance on God's protection'.[32] The presence of both the Mosaic Psalm 90 at the beginning of the collection and the enthronement psalms at its center help to establish these themes. The book concludes with psalms that emphasize the need to trust in God and to remember both God's previous gracious acts and Israel's past rebellions.

The fifth book picks up on some of these themes and develops them further. It is, according to Wilson, 'intended to stand as an answer to the plea of the exiles to be gathered from the diaspora'.[33] The answer is one of dependence on and trust in God alone, an attitude that David is seen to model in this book's two Davidic collections (Pss. 108–110 and 138–45).

There are two other aspects of this book's answer to the problem found in Psalm 89. First of all, the monumental Psalm 119 highlights the role of the Law as a means of guaranteed individual access to God.[34] Secondly, the book ends in an extended declaration of praise (Pss. 146–50), one which comes in response to David's vow of praise in Ps. 145.21.[35] Both of these shift the focus in the book to the Mosaic covenant and the kingship of God.

Larger Structures and Genre Distribution

According to Wilson's most recent writings on the subject, the final compilation of the Psalter has two 'competing editorial frames'.[36] The 'royal covenant frame' is primarily associated with the first three books, as may be seen in the presence of the royal psalms at the 'seams' of these books. In contrast, the last two books may be seen to have a wisdom frame, as indicated by the strategic placement of 'wisdom' psalms at their 'seams' (Ps. 90 + 91; 106; 145).

There is some overlap between these two frames, as may be seen by

---

32. Wilson, 'Use of Royal Psalms', p. 92.

33. Wilson, *Editing of the Hebrew Psalter*, p. 227.

34. Wilson, *Editing of the Hebrew Psalter*, pp. 222-24; 'Use of Royal Psalms', p. 92. This psalm picks up on both the themes of Ps. 1 and the Mosaic direction of Ps. 90.

35. According to Wilson, Pss. 146–50 take the place of the expected doxology at the end of the fifth book. *Editing of the Hebrew Psalter*, pp. 225-26.

36. Wilson, 'Book of Psalms', pp. 133-34; 'Shaping the Psalter', pp. 74-81.

the presence of the royal Psalm 144 near the end of the fifth book and the wisdom Psalm 73 at the beginning of the third book. However, the fact that the wisdom frame is now dominant is clear from the 'wisdom shaping of the important royal Psalms 2 and 144, and the primary placement of wisdom compositions at the beginning and conclusion of the unified Psalter (Pss. 1 and 145)'.[37]

It is, of course, especially significant for the present book that Wilson sees the strategic placement of these psalm 'types' as a key aspect of the final shape of the Psalter. This is not, however, the only place where Wilson sees genre as playing a significant role in this shape.[38] Again, in his latest works, Wilson specifically discusses two other cases of genre distribution that, in his words, profoundly influence the theology of the Psalter.[39]

The first of these is what Wilson sees as the shift from the 'significant collection of lament psalms' that one finds in the first half of the Psalter to the increasingly dominant praise of the second half. For Wilson, this movement from lament to praise means that although the Psalter acknowledges the dark side of human existence, it 'still points to an alternative view of reality in which there is room in the human heart only for praise'. This praise 'constitutes another reality in which the presence of God has become so real that anger has no point, pain has no hold, and death lacks all power to sting'.[40]

The other example of genre distribution that Wilson sees as significant in the Psalter's final shape is one that involves individual and communal psalms. Just as the Psalter moves from lament to praise, it also moves from psalms of the individual to those that have a more communal voice. For Wilson, this movement indicates a shift from moments of individual 'weakness, failure, and doubt' to 'identity, affirmation, renewal, restoration, and a hope for the future' in the community of

37. Wilson, 'Book of Psalms', p. 34. Cf. also 'Shaping the Psalter', pp. 80-81, where Wilson sees such elements as resolving the 'tense dialogue (or a dialogue in tension) between the royal covenantal hopes associated with the first two-thirds of the Psalter and the wisdom counsel to trust YHWH alone associated with the final third' in favor of the latter.

38. That is to say, genre in the modern sense of the term. Wilson, of course, talks at considerable length about the significance of the genre terms in the psalm titles for the way the psalms are put together.

39. Wilson, 'Book of Psalms', p. 139; 'Shaping the Psalter', p. 81.

40. Wilson, 'Book of Psalms', pp. 138-39.

faith.[41] It is in the community that one can re-experience the steadfast mercy of God and be given reason to praise.

Wilson's Analysis: A Summary

Wilson's basic insight is that the shape of the Psalter is not accidental but rather 'purposeful' and 'intentional'.[42] Both the way that different types of psalms have been grouped together and the way individual psalms have been situated at strategic points throughout the larger whole are to be seen as the result of conscious editorial decisions. Moreover, the resulting shape of the Psalter is one that has a specific hermeneutical and theological purpose.

It is significant that Wilson sees the present shape of the Psalter as one that was called into being by the particular historical circumstances of Israel's national life. Thus, the question posed by the crucial Psalm 89 is specifically a question that arises from the disruption of the exile, and the answer of the fourth and fifth books which follows is specifically a postexilic answer.[43] Furthermore, the psalms' basic move from a setting in the temple cult to one in the 'heart and experience of the faithful reader' seems to have taken place as a result of the specific historical circumstances of the temple's destruction in the first century CE.[44] In such a way, the assessment of the purpose of the final shape of the Psalter is, at least in part, a historical enterprise.[45]

41. Wilson, 'Book of Psalms', p. 139. Despite the fact that Wilson sees the Psalter as ending in 'public, communal proclamation of praise', he still argues for a 'shift of function away from public performance to private meditation and appropriation'. So 'Shaping the Psalter', p. 81.

42. These terms recur throughout Wilson's writings on the shape of the Psalter. Note, for example, the title of 'Understanding the Purposeful Arrangement of Psalms in the Psalter: Pitfalls and Promise', in J.C. McCann, Jr (ed.), *The Shape and Shaping of the Psalter* (JSOTSup, 159; Sheffield: Sheffield Academic Press, 1993), pp. 42-51. See also his comments on p. 48 of that work, 'In my opinion, the only valid and cautious hypothesis with which to begin is that the present arrangement is the result of purposeful editorial activity, and that its purpose can be discerned by careful and exhaustive analysis of the linguistic and thematic relationships between individual psalms and groups of psalms'.

43. Wilson, *Editing of the Hebrew Psalter*, pp. 209-228; 'Use of Royal Psalms;' 'Book of Psalms', p. 140.

44. Wilson, 'Book of Psalms', pp. 137-38. Cf. also his 'A First Century CE Date for the Closing of the Psalter?', in *Haim M.I. Gevaryahu Memorial Volume* (Jerusalem: World Jewish Bible Center, 1990), pp. 136-43.

45. On this, see the comments of R.E. Murphy, O. Carm., 'Reflections on the

This historical situating of the Psalter is related to one of Wilson's more important methodological perspectives, namely, that the Psalter is to be approached sequentially. As noted above, Wilson argues that the last two books were crafted as a response to the theological questions raised by the first three books in the postexilic period. This is, on the one hand, a historical judgment about priority of composition and standardization, one with much supporting evidence in its favor. It also, however, leads directly to Wilson's sequential reading of the Psalms in order from the first to the last.

To understand the Psalter correctly, one needs to begin at the beginning and work through to the end. Thus, one needs to feel the force of the royal claims of the first three books (as well as the problem raised by these claims in the postexilic period) before one can move on to the answer provided by the last two books. One also needs to feel the problems raised by the lament in the first half of the Psalter before one can appreciate the 'alternate vision' of the praise of the second half. Finally, one needs to experience the problems associated with the individual psalms before one can understand the strength found in Israel's communal life.

Given this sequential perspective, it is not surprising that Wilson locates the 'editorial center' of the psalms in book four, since that book constitutes the point of transition in many of these cases. It is in this book that one hears what Wilson considers to be the dominant theological note of the Psalter, as it is presently shaped. The implications of this sequential and historical reading will be considered further below.

Other Approaches to the Final Shape of the Psalms

In the last few years, a number of other scholars have begun to devote serious attention to the final shape of the Psalms along the lines proposed by Childs and Wilson. Among these authors there is much agreement about some aspects of the Psalter's shape, such as the importance of Psalm 1. There are also, however, some differences that are significant, especially when these are considered in terms of the main interests of this book. With this in mind, it will be useful to look at some of these other authors before moving to a more general analysis of

Contextual Interpretation of the Psalms', in J.C. McCann, Jr (ed.), *The Shape and Shaping of the Psalter* (JSOTSup, 159; Sheffield: Sheffield Academic Press, 1993), pp. 21-26 (21-22).

the implications of this approach for the genre definition of the psalms.

The Canonical Argument of Walter Brueggemann

One of the more interesting of these recent attempts to come to terms with the canonical shape of the Psalter is that of Walter Brueggemann.[46] Brueggemann, of course, has already been much discussed in the present book. His arguments for a comprehensive theological order and existential setting for the psalms have been analyzed in some detail, as has his attempt to retrieve an awareness of these texts' world-making potential. Given this background, Brueggemann's insights about the canonical shape of the Psalter take on considerable significance.

One may begin by noting those aspects which Brueggemann's argument shares with that of Childs and Wilson. The basic agreement is, of course, that Brueggemann joins these authors in seeing the presence of a certain 'theological intentionality' in the canonical shape of the present book of Psalms. Beyond this, he also accepts their view that the beginning and end of the Psalter manifest this intentionality in a special way. As a result, it is necessary to read the Psalms sequentially if one is to understand the role of these psalms correctly.

For Brueggemann, the Psalms begin in obedience and end in praise.[47] As the entry point into the Psalter, Psalm 1 'asserts that the Psalter is intended for and intends to evoke and authorize a community of trusting, joyous obedience'.[48] Psalm 150, on the other hand, ends the collection 'in glad, unconditional praise, completely, and without embarrassment or distraction, focused on God'.[49] The sequence of these psalms is purposeful and cannot be reversed. Their place in the canonical shape of the Psalms is, in fact, 'an assertion about the shape of life lived in Israel's covenant'.[50]

---

46. Brueggemann, 'Obedience and Praise', and W. Brueggeman and P. Miller, 'Psalm 73 as a Canonical Marker', *JSOT* 72 (1996), pp. 45-56. See also his 'Response to James L. Mays, "The Question of Context"', originally presented at the 1989 Annual Meeting of the Society of Biblical Literature and now published in J.C. McCann, Jr (ed.), *The Shape and Shaping of the Psalter* (JSOTSup, 159; Sheffield: Sheffield Academic Press, 1993), pp. 29-41.

47. It is noteworthy that Brueggemann explicitly argued for this progression earlier in *Message of the Psalms*, p. 183 n. 32. At that time, however, he did not develop the canonical argument as fully as he does in 'Obedience and Praise'.

48. Brueggemann, 'Obedience and Praise', p. 66.

49. Brueggemann, 'Obedience and Praise', p. 68.

50. Brueggemann, 'Obedience and Praise', p. 68.

There is, of course, much that occurs in both the Psalter and life between these parameters of obedience and praise. As one might expect from his previous work, Brueggemann is specifically interested in those psalms and events that challenge what he sees as the overly simple world envisioned in the first psalm. In particular, it is the laments with their underlying 'crisis of God's *hesed*', that are a crucial step on the road from the duty of obedience to the delight of praise. To quote Brueggemann:

> Thus it is my thesis that Israel's struggle with God's *hesed*, in suffering and hope, in lament and in hymn, in candor and in gratitude, and eventual acceptance of God's *hesed* as the premise of life permits Israel to make the move from the obedience of Psalm 1 to the doxology of Psalm 150.[51]

According to Brueggemann, it is Psalm 73 that best enacts the transformation necessary to make the theological move from *hesed* doubted to *hesed* trusted, a move that is crucial to the larger move from obedience to praise.[52] This psalm is, in fact, the 'center' of the Psalter, the 'pivot' of its canonical structure.[53] Significantly, it does not conclude with a judgment of whether 'the world is morally coherent or not', but rather asserts that what finally matters is 'communion *with* God in which all other issues are derivative and subordinate'.[54] It is this position that allows one to move to praise in the midst of all the realities of

51. Brueggemann, 'Obedience and Praise', p. 78.

52. Brueggemann, 'Obedience and Praise', p. 81.

53. For Brueggemann, Ps. 73 'performs a function for Books III–V not unlike that of Psalm 1 for Books I–II. That is, Ps. 73 reiterates the thesis of Ps. 1 and then enters into dispute with that thesis. On the other hand, the stance taken by Ps. 73, of affirmation and then dispute, is a stance taken over and over again in the Psalter. Thus I suggest that Ps. 73 assumes a paradigmatic function, providing a normative example of the frequently reiterated, re-enacted argument made in the Psalter concerning, (a) the reliability of God's *hesed*, (b) the doubting of that *hesed*, and (c) the ultimate embrace of it in trust and confidence' ('Obedience and Praise', pp. 80-81 n. 3). See also the more recent article of Brueggemann and Miller, 'Psalm 73', which elaborates on the canonical placement of this psalm in light of what the authors see as its similarity to the royal and torah features of Pss. 15–24. On the latter, see P. D. Miller, 'Kingship, Torah Obedience, and Prayer: The Theology of Psalms 15–24', in K. Seybold and E. Zenger (eds.), *Neue Wege der Psalmenforschung* (Herders Biblische Studien, 1: Freiburg: Herder, 1994), pp. 127-42.

54. Brueggemann, 'Obedience and Praise', p. 86.

life, and it is here in the heart of the Psalter that Israel mostly lives.[55]

Brueggemann's focus on Psalm 73 as the pivot of the Psalter is, of course, at some variance with Wilson's argument that it is the fourth book (Pss. 90–106) which is the Psalter's 'editorial center'. In one of his most recent articles, Wilson admits that Brueggemann's insights have a certain appeal, though he still opts for seeing the psalms that follow Psalm 89 as 'the clearest articulation of the crisis of identity and faith that precipitates the theological response one finds in the final form of the Psalter'.[56]

Obviously, there is room for scholarly disagreement over the exact way in which the Psalter is structured. Nevertheless, what needs to be seen here is that this disagreement is actually the result of some much more significant differences in these scholars' approaches to the Psalms.

Brueggemann and the Wider Context of Canon
The clue to this difference in approach is to be found in the way that Wilson and Brueggemann see the wider theological issue of the Psalter. As has been noted above, Wilson sees the final shape of the Psalter as an attempt to answer the crisis of the Davidic monarchy that resulted from the events of 587 BCE. In such a way, the shift from books I–III to books IV–V is such as to lead the believer away from reliance on human kingship to a celebration of the eternal kingship of God.

Brueggemann, on the other hand, does not talk about this theological crisis of the postexilic period, at least in his first 'canonical' article.[57]

---

55. Brueggemann, 'Obedience and Praise', pp. 90-91.

56. Wilson, 'Book of Psalms', p. 140; see also pp. 134-35. Wilson is attracted to Brueggemann's suggestions about the role of Ps. 73 especially because of its place after the editorial divide of Ps. 72.20. Nevertheless, he does admit that Brueggemann's lack of attention to a number of the Psalter's other structural features leaves him with 'a vague sense of incompleteness in understanding the final form of the Psalter' ('Book of Psalms', p. 136 n. 26). As a result, 'what the full implications of Brueggemann's insight for our understanding of the final shaping of the Psalter might be remains to be seen'.

In this connection, Wilson also notes the work of J. Clinton McCann who has shown that the argument of the last two books concerning human and divine kingship can already be found in the third book. See McCann's 'Books I–III and the Editorial Purpose of the Hebrew Psalter', in *idem*, *Shape and Shaping*, pp. 93-107.

57. In the later article, 'Psalm 73', Brueggemann sees the language of that psalm as indicating a concern with royal behavior. In such a way, Ps. 73 sets forth an 'alternative script' for the monarchy which Ps. 89 shows is not taken.

Instead, he paints on a much wider existential canvas.[58] As in his other writings, his concern is with the believer of every age, whose movement from obedience to praise must proceed through the crisis of God's hiddenness in everyday life. As Brueggemann freely admits, his argument about the centrality of Psalm 73 is first of all 'theological', though he does see it as being confirmed by critical features such as the editorial comment in 72.20.[59]

One should not miss the significance of Brueggemann's statement that his initial decision about the centrality of Psalm 73 was made on 'substantive theological grounds' and was not at first 'informed by any critical category of form-, literary, or canonical criticism'.[60] There is in this a firm link between Brueggemann's earlier work on the psalms and his most recent canonical analysis. Indeed, it seems quite clear that Brueggemann sees Psalm 73 as theologically central because it contains within itself the basic dynamic of his earlier schema of orientation–disorientation–new orientation.

One sees the influence of Brueggemann's earlier schema in other areas as well. One may, for example, compare the role of Psalm 1 in the work of Wilson and Brueggemann. For Wilson, Psalm 1 has a hermeneutical function with respect to the rest of the Psalter, in that it helps to establish the latter as a book to be read rather than performed. Brueggemann also sees Psalm 1 as having something of a hermeneutical function, though it is one a bit different from that put forward by Wilson. For Brueggemann, Psalm 1 intends that 'all the Psalms should be read through the prism of torah obedience'.[61] The rest of the Psalter

58. In this respect, one may note Brueggemann's comments about the relationship between book as context and history as context, a relationship which he sees as having a certain ambiguity and which he notes may result in two very different construals of the book of Psalms. 'Response', p. 33.

59. Brueggemann, 'Obedience and Praise', pp. 81-83. Brueggemann's arguments about how Ps. 72 leads into Ps. 73 through the reader's awareness of Solomon's failures to fulfill the former's hopes are not entirely convincing in this work. For a somewhat more detailed argument along similar lines, see Brueggemann and Miller, 'Psalm 73'.

60. Brueggemann, 'Obedience and Praise', p. 81.

61. Brueggemann, 'Obedience and Praise', p. 64. It is significant that Wilson specifically argues with Brueggemann's reading of this psalm as an exhortation to obedience. He instead sees it as an encouragement to constant 'meditation' upon the Torah, including the Torah which follows in the rest of the Psalter ('Book of Psalms', pp. 136-37).

can be sung only by those who gladly participate in a community of trusting obedience.[62]

In other words, Psalm 1 does not so much specify 'how' the psalms are to be approached as it specifies 'who' will be able to use them (those with the requisite praxis).[63] Given the present shape of the Psalter, 'only the obedient can praise God'.[64] There is, however, another aspect of Psalm 1, one which ties in closely with Brueggemann's previous analyses. Along these lines, Psalm 1 evokes a world that 'operates according to a reliable pattern of deeds leading to consequences'.[65] It is a world of 'trustworthy outcomes of a life of obedient faith'.

One should note that according to this view Psalm 1 not only has a 'hermeneutical function'. It also has a very definite 'content'. Furthermore, the claims of this psalm are, for Brueggemann, at 'considerable tension' with the markedly less sanguine view of life that characterizes the rest of the Psalter. This tension 'makes clear that Psalm 1 intends to insist on a certain reading of the Psalter which seems against the grain of the poems themselves'. Indeed, the canonical purpose of Psalm 1 is to preclude an awareness of those aspects of life which are not so neatly ordered.[66]

Psalm 1 is, in other words, a classic psalm of orientation.[67] As such, its position at the beginning of the Psalter mirrors its position in Brueggemann's schema of orientation–disorientation–new orientation. One will, of course, remember that for Brueggemann the psalms of orientation are the psalms most in need of 'further development'. Their

---

62. Brueggemann, 'Obedience and Praise', p. 66.

63. There is an interesting ambiguity in Brueggemann's comments about this psalm. On the one hand, he sees that 'as an entry point into the Psalter, this poet asserts that the Psalter is intended for and intends to evoke and authorize a community of trusting, joyous obedience'. On the other hand, he asserts that 'the songs that follow in the Psalter, according to the categories of Ps. 1, can be sung only by those who gladly participate in this community of obedience' (both quotes are from 'Obedience and Praise', p. 66.) Once again, the issue is one of whether the psalms have the *power* to shape an individual or a community or whether they can only be used by those already oriented in a certain direction. The first quote at least allows for the former possibility, whereas the second quote would seem to imply the latter. This issue is discussed at length in the fourth chapter of the present work.

64. Brueggemann, 'Obedience and Praise', p. 69.

65. Brueggemann, 'Obedience and Praise', p. 65.

66. Brueggemann, 'Obedience and Praise', p. 66.

67. So Brueggemann, *Message of the Psalms*, pp. 38-39.

easy harmonies are not sufficiently in touch with the less ordered realities of life. It is only when they have been challenged by what underlies the psalms of disorientation that they can develop into a more mature faith, as reflected in the psalms of new orientation.

When seen in this light, Psalm 1 is less a guide to the rest of the Psalter than the starting point of a journey through the whole. It has, in this respect, only a transient value, since it reflects at best an incomplete picture of the relationship between God and humanity. Some psalms, such as Psalm 73, are much more theologically comprehensive, while others, such as the laments, are at least closer to the reality of the relationship.

Brueggemann shows that he senses the ambiguity of Psalm 1 when he offers two different 'interpretive comments' on the Psalter's movement from obedience to praise. His first argument has already been seen in the idea that it is only the obedient who can praise God. Real praise can take place only when one comes to terms with the reality of a God who keeps the world as safe and reliable as Psalm 1 anticipates.[68]

Brueggemann's second interpretation of this movement is, as he notes, more dialectical in nature. In this perspective, the obedience demanded in Psalm 1 is still necessary but incomplete. It is 'a beginning point beyond which the faithful characteristically move', something that is transcended in favor of 'joyous communion'.[69] This movement from willing duty to utter delight takes place in the rest of the Psalter, through which the believer comes to trust in God beyond the dictates of the simple moral coherence seen in Psalm 1.

What one should note here is that Brueggemann's two interpretive comments reflect two different aspects of Psalm 1. That aspect of Psalm 1 that has enduring value throughout the entire Psalter is the human duty of obedience. That which is transcended as one moves through the rest of the book is the moral symmetry implied by the world the psalm evokes. Once again, this fits well with Brueggemann's previous description and evaluation of the psalms of orientation.

In such a way, Brueggemann's latest canonical arguments dovetail nicely with his previous schema of relationship between the psalms. One should, however, remember that this previous schema was not, on the whole, dependent on any particular order within the psalter.[70] As

---

68. Brueggemann, 'Obedience and Praise', p. 69.
69. Brueggemann, 'Obedience and Praise', p. 70.
70. Though note Brueggemann's comments about the place of Ps. 1 and Ps. 150

such, the psalms he placed in his different orientation–disorientation–new orientation categories do not reflect the consistent movement through the Psalter suggested by his canonical article. There are psalms of orientation that are to be found towards the end of the Psalter, and psalms of new orientation to be found near the beginning. Similarly, psalms of disorientation are not restricted to any one place, even though they are to be found especially in the beginning of the collection.

Significantly, Wilson has challenged Brueggemann's description of the Psalter by noting the presence of the torah Psalm 119 towards the end of the book.[71] The massive quality of this psalm makes it hard to explain away as an unimportant feature of the later Psalter. For Wilson, this psalm is a significant support for the 'Mosaic' character of the final two books. If, as Brueggemann, has argued, the Psalter moves from obedience to praise, what is the function of this torah psalm in its present position?[72] On the other hand, one might ask how Wilson would see the function of either Psalm 19 so early in the collection[73] or Psalm 110 so late?[74]

These questions concerning individual psalms point toward a larger issue. To what extent do canonical analyses of the psalms need to go beyond looking at strategically placed psalms towards an inclusive interpretation of the placement of all the psalms? Certainly, scholars such as Wilson do not think that the final redactors of the Psalter had complete freedom in their arrangement of the psalms. At least to a certain extent, the presence of earlier collections limited their editorial liberty. Given these constraints, should one expect the final shape of the

---

in *Message of the Psalms*, pp. 166-67. While these comments do not play an important part in his earlier argument, they do anticipate his later canonical work.

71. Wilson, 'Book of Psalms', p. 137 n. 28.

72. One should note that Brueggemann has argued that this psalm 'probes beyond the simplistic formulation of Psalm 1' (*Message of the Psalms*, p. 41). As such, he might well be able to make a case for its presence late in his movement from obedience to praise.

73. One may also note here Patrick Miller's contention that the of all the books of the Psalter it is the first which has a primary emphasis on Torah. See his 'The Beginning of the Psalter', in J.C. McCann, Jr (ed.), *Shape and Shaping of the Hebrew Psalter* (JSOTSup, 159; Sheffield: Sheffield Academic Press, 1993), pp. 83-92 (86).

74. So N. Whybray, *Reading the Psalms as a Book* (JSOTSup, 222; Sheffield: Sheffield Academic Press, 1996), p. 94.

Psalter to present a completely coherent picture?[75]

On the other hand, if one cannot go beyond broad strokes, what is the nature of the context that the canon affords to those psalms that do not have such strategic importance? To be sure, the strategic presence of individual psalms does serve to guide the reader along certain lines in his or her interpretation of the remaining psalms. On the other hand, Wilson himself has warned against what he sees as the tendency (such as he finds in Brueggemann) to generalize and to focus on certain points of structure while passing over others without comment.[76] There is obviously much work still to be done in determining the extent and significance of the editorial signposts in the Psalter.[77]

Brueggemann and the Wider Question of Use

There is another issue that Brueggemann's analysis raises for the canonical interpretation of the Psalter. One will remember that one of the areas of disagreement between Wilson and Brueggemann is the extent to which Psalm 1 has a determining hermeneutical function with respect to the rest of the Psalter. Far from being a simple disagreement about the nature of this one particular psalm, this difference between Wilson and Brueggemann goes right to the heart of the nature of the entire Psalter, as well as to the concern of this book, the nature of genre itself.

Again, for Wilson, the introductory position of this psalm means that the Psalter has become 'a book to be *read* rather than to be *performed*; to be *meditated over* rather than to be *recited from*'.[78] For Brueggemann, on the other hand, this psalm determines who it is that may use the rest of the psalms. It does not, however, determine how those psalms are to be used. Indeed, in terms of content, this psalm is, to some extent, superseded by what follows.

As noted above, Brueggemann agrees with Wilson that the sequence of the psalms is important for their interpretation. This is, of course, especially the case since he sees the general outline of that sequence as similar to his earlier schema. It is, however, precisely this similarity

---

75. On the question of whether 'meticulous attempts to account for every detail in the structuring of the Psalter' are possible, see the detailed argument of Whybray, *Reading the Psalms*.

76. Wilson, 'Book of Psalms', p. 136 n. 27. See also his comments in his 'Understanding Arrangement'.

77. Again see the extended analysis of Whybray, *Reading the Psalms*.

78. Emphasis Wilson's, *Editing the Hebrew Psalter*, p. 207.

between Brueggemann's view of the sequence of the Psalter and his earlier schema that indicates the difference between the ways in which Wilson and Brueggemann approach the psalms.

Both in Brueggemann's earlier work and in his later canonical analysis, the psalms do not function solely as a text to be 'read' and 'meditated over'. Whatever their value as theological texts to be 'meditated over', their continued use in the prayer life of individuals and communities is of obvious importance for Brueggemann. It is inconceivable that Brueggemann would concur in Wilson's statement that the psalms are 'no longer to be sung'. Only through the psalms' use in the context of life do they have the significance that Brueggemann attributes to them.[79]

For Brueggemann the psalms do not have their setting only in the literary context of the Psalter. They also continue to have a setting in the life of believers. For Brueggemann, these two contexts overlap insofar as the sequence of a person's life and relationship with God is mirrored in the sequence of the psalms within the Psalter. Indeed, as he himself admits in the case of Psalm 73, Brueggemann's understanding of the book's literary shape is at least chronologically secondary to his understanding of the individual psalms' life settings.

As may be seen from Wilson's objection, Psalm 119 might be less amenable to Brueggemann's overlapping contexts of life and literature. Again, as a psalm of orientation, this psalm seems somewhat out of place so late in the Psalter's movement from obedience to praise. To the extent that Brueggemann still regards this psalm as a psalm of orientation, he needs to nuance his views of the movement of the Psalter. On the other hand, it is possible that this psalm's position in the Psalter might prompt Brueggemann to reconsider its status in his schema of orientation–disorientation–new orientation.

There are, however, problems for Brueggemann in both of these possibilities. The movement from obedience to praise, or from orientation to new orientation, is one that is grounded in the readily observable reality of the believer's life. As such, it is not really something that is

---

79. Brueggemann's explicit insistence on a continued cultic setting may be seen in his response to the canonical proposals of James Luther Mays at the 1989 meeting of the Society of Biblical Literature. In that response, he sees cult as an ongoing process of symbolization and resymbolization and argues that the term 'post-cultic' is a misnomer. 'Response to James L. Mays', pp. 31-32. One might also mention Brueggemann's *Praying the Psalms* (Winona, MN: St. Mary's Press, 1982) as further evidence for his view of the continued use of the psalms.

open to a great deal of flexibility. Similarly, the status of a particular psalm is for Brueggemann also determined primarily by its use in the life setting of believers. It is important to note that this too is an empirical reality, not something dictated solely by the literary context.

To point out this difficulty is not necessarily to criticize Brueggemann's attempt to do justice to the psalms' setting in the life of believers. Rather, it is to acknowledge that psalms are complex texts, whose setting in life may well exist in some tension with their setting in literature. Actually, there is flexibility in both of these settings. Just as different believers use individual psalms in different ways, so different interpreters understand the literary context in different ways.

It may be that Brueggemann's great contribution to the canonical analysis of the psalms is his recognition that the Psalter's present shape does not negate the psalms' continuing function as prayer. The relationship between an individual psalm's settings in life and literature may not be quite as smooth as he has envisioned. He has, nevertheless, seen the different dimensions of the question. It remains to consider the genre implications of this double setting in more detail after looking at some other scholars who have studied the canonical shape of the Psalter.

Torah-Piety and the Kingdom of God: The Work of Gerald Sheppard, James Luther Mays and J. Clinton McCann

A number of the issues discussed by Brueggemann have also been raised by some of the other scholars who have recently turned their attention to the canonical shape of the Psalter. While this book cannot discuss the work of every scholar who has taken this approach to the Psalms, it will be helpful to look at three such scholars whose work has helped to define the field at the present time: Gerald Sheppard, James Luther Mays and J. Clinton McCann. It is significant that these scholars share a concern for such issues as the role of Psalm 1 as the introduction to the Psalter and the relationship between the psalms' literary context and their context in the life of believers.[80] A brief overview of their work will be helpful here.

One may begin with the views of Gerald Sheppard, another of Childs's students who has written on the psalms. As was the case with Wilson, Sheppard sees Psalm 1 as playing a crucial role in determining

---

80. For a dissenting view as to the significance of Psalm 1, see Whybray, *Reading the Psalms*, pp. 38-42.

how one approaches the rest of the psalms. For Sheppard, however, the royal Psalm 2 shares this broader introductory function, rather than simply being an introduction to the first section of the Psalter, as argued by Wilson.[81]

Whereas Psalm 1 invites the reader to view the Torah as the means of attaining sacred wisdom, Psalm 2 identifies David as 'both the author of the Psalms and as one who qualifies under the injunction of Psalm 1 to interpret the Torah as a guide to righteousness'.[82] The result is that the

> entire Psalter is made to stand theologically in association with David as a source book of guidance for the way of the righteous. In this fashion, the Psalter has gained, among its other functions, the use as a source for Wisdom reflection and a model of prayers based on such a pious interpretation of the Torah.[83]

One will, of course, recognize in Sheppard's argument many standard elements of the canonical interpretation of the Psalms. The disagreement between Sheppard and Wilson as to the role of Psalm 2 is a canonical disagreement similar to that between Wilson and Brueggemann over the role of Psalm 73. No difference in method is necessarily implied here, only a difference in the application of a shared canonical approach. Such diversity of interpretation is to be expected and in itself does not reflect badly on the method.

More important, however, is Sheppard's recognition that the Psalter's function as a source for Wisdom reflection is a function that exists 'among its other functions'. One of these other functions is obviously prayer. As the introductory summary of his recent article notes: 'While the Psalter imparts instruction to the faithful on the ways of God, it also teaches them to pray'.[84]

81. See his *Wisdom as a Hermeneutical Construct: A Study in the Sapientializing of the Old Testament* (BZAW, 151; Berlin: W. de Gruyter, 1980), pp. 136-44; also 'Theology', p. 149. For Wilson's views, see *Editing the Hebrew Psalter*, pp. 173, 204-208; 'The Use of "Untitled" Psalms in the Hebrew Psalter', *ZAW* 97 (1985), pp. 403-13 (405); 'Use of Royal Psalms'. It should be noted that the question of the precise nature of the introductory role of Ps. 1 is not solved by settling the question of whether Pss. 1 and 2 should be seen as a single psalm. For the present MT it is also not solved by noting other traditions in which Ps. 1 was an untitled introductory psalm.

82. Sheppard, *Wisdom as a Hermeneutical Construct*, p. 142.

83. Sheppard, *Wisdom as a Hermeneutical Construct*, p. 142.

84. Sheppard, 'Theology', p. 143. Along these lines, Sheppard also quotes Bonhoeffer's statement that 'we must learn to pray' (p. 144).

As one might expect from his view of Psalm 2, Sheppard sees the psalms as working through the figure of David. Through the psalms we are given an insight into the humanity of this one person from God's point of view.[85] As the narrative superscriptions make clear, David is not a 'unhistorical ideal, or typological figure, an "everyman"'. Rather 'we are invited by the biblical portrayal more to identify with some of David's ordinary actions and feelings than to compare our experiences with his'. David's life is less 'typical' and 'universal' than it is 'thoroughly human' and 'psychologically deep'.[86]

As Sheppard notes, 'the Bible provides no guarantee that our daily lives will be any less traumatic than that of David or that we will need to resort to prayers of lamentation less than he'.[87] In such life settings, it is through the 'model prayers' of this thoroughly human figure that we 'learn to pray'. This is clearly something more than a wisdom meditation on the theological content of the psalms.

The next scholar under consideration, James Luther Mays, is someone whose name has for a long time been synonymous with the sensitive and perceptive study of the Psalms. In his 1986 presidential address to the Society of Biblical Literature, Mays picked up on Childs's challenge of reading the Psalms as a book by looking at 'the place of the torah-psalms in the Psalter'.[88] This address was followed by a series of other important works along these lines.[89]

A number of canonical emphases show up repeatedly in Mays' work. Previous chapters of the present book have already noted Mays' arguments that both the kingship of God and the figure of David undergird the entire Psalter.[90] On a more structural level, Mays has emphasized

85. Sheppard, 'Theology', p. 148. Sheppard sees the psalms' depiction of David's humanity as 'reminiscent of the wisdom literature, for they provide a 'God's eye view of the interplay of trouble and tranquility in a particular human life' (p. 149).

86. Sheppard, 'Theology', p. 148.

87. Sheppard, 'Theology', p. 148.

88. This address was published as 'The Place of the Torah-Psalms in the Psalter', *JBL* 106 (1987), pp. 3-12.

89. See, among other works, his 1989 address to the SBL Psalms group, 'The Question of Context in Psalms Interpretation', in J.C. McCann, Jr (ed.), *Shape and Shaping of the Hebrew Psalter* (JSOTSup, 159; Sheffield: Sheffield Academic Press, 1993), pp. 15-20; his masterful commentary, *Psalms*; the various essays in *The Lord Reigns*; and his recent 'Psalm Study'.

90. See also the presence of these themes in the specifically canonical essay,

the important introductory role of Psalm 1 in underlining the connection between 'torah-piety' and the book of Psalms. Together with the other torah psalms, Psalm 1 works to shift 'the context for the construal of language in the Psalms'.[91]

Two aspects of Mays' analysis are especially worthy of note. The first is his assertion that in the present shape of the Psalter 'form-critical and cult-functional questions are subordinated and questions of content and theology become more important'.[92] For Mays, 'semantic horizons are more those of intratextual relations and less groups of types and reconstructed cultic occasions'. In such a way, Mays explicitly raises the question of the connection between genre and final shape. This obviously needs to be discussed further below.

The second feature that needs to be noted here is Mays' acceptance of Sheppard's argument that Psalm 2 now functions as the second half of the introduction to the book of Psalms.[93] For Mays, the complete introduction brings together 'the topics of torah and the kingship of the Lord', as well as questions of the individual and of history. Significantly, Mays sees the combination of these psalms as providing 'an eschatological context for a piety based in torah'.[94]

For Mays, 'the torah psalms point to a type of piety as setting-in-life for the Psalms, a piety that used the entire book as prayer and praise'. 'The Psalms were reread in the light of this piety and it in turn was constantly shaped by the use of the Psalms'.[95] These last comments are perhaps particularly significant in view of Mays' previous 'intratextual' statements. In his later works, Mays is even more explicit about the dual function of the psalms as both instruction and prayer.[96] More will be said below about the dialectic implied in these last statements.

J. Clinton McCann draws on the work of Mays in his concern for the way the torah psalms 'orient the reader to hear the entire collection as

'Going by the Book: The Psalter as a Guide to Reading the Psalms', in *idem*, *The Lord Reigns*, pp. 119-27.

91. Mays, 'Torah-Psalms', p. 12. Mays also claims that 'it identifies the function of the book'. 'Going by the Book', p. 121.

92. Mays, 'Torah-Psalms', p. 12. See also 'Going by the Book', p. 127.

93. Mays, 'Torah-Psalms', p. 10; *Psalms*, pp. 17-18; 'Going by the Book', pp. 120-23.

94. Mays, 'Torah-Psalms', p. 11.

95. Mays, 'Torah-Psalms', p. 12.

96. See, for example, his comments in *Psalms*, pp. 14, 36, and *passim*.

instruction'.[97] Quoting Mays, McCann recognizes that 'to approach the Psalms as instruction is to reorient the customary form-critical and cult-functional search for the setting-in-life of the Psalms'.[98] For McCann, the Psalms were 'appropriated as scripture, and their setting-in-life is in the faith of God's people'. Further, 'the interpretive task is not complete until we ask about the content and theology of the Psalms for our generation, our setting-in-life: What do the Psalms *teach us now* about God, ourselves, the world, the life of faith?'[99]

It is clear that McCann sees the Psalms in a predominantly 'instructional' way, a view that is clear in his characterization of the Psalter more as a 'catechism' than a 'hymnbook'.[100] Nevertheless, like Sheppard and Mays, McCann also sees that the Psalms 'should be prayed and sung'. Even though he argues that these texts have been preserved and passed on as God's word to humanity rather than in their original function as human words to God, they 'have been and should continue to be used as human words to God'.[101]

As with many of the above scholars who look at the Psalter from a canonical point of view, McCann sees Psalm 1 as playing a crucial role in support of understanding that book as instruction.[102] Like Mays, McCann also sees Psalm 2 as playing an important introductory role, especially in terms of its emphasis on the reign of God.[103] It may be that this understanding of Psalm 2 is in some tension with his desire to agree with Wilson about the historical setting and editorial intention of the

97. J. Clinton McCann, Jr, 'The Psalms as Instruction', *Int* 46 (1992), pp. 117-28 (119).

98. McCann, 'Psalms as Instruction', p. 121.

99. Emphasis McCann's. One should note that this concern for the present relevance of the Psalms goes hand in hand with a concern for the intent of the book's final redactors ('Psalms as Instruction', p. 121).

100. J. Clinton McCann, Jr, *A Theological Introduction to the Book of Psalms: The Psalms as Torah* (Nashville: Abingdon Press, 1993), p. 15. Such a concern for the instructional nature of the Psalter is also obvious from the titles of both his article ('The Psalms as Instruction') and his book.

101. McCann, *A Theological Introduction*, p. 15; 'Psalms as Instruction', p. 128. McCann sees liturgy as instructional in the sense that it moves and transforms, as well as creating a new vision of reality.

102. So 'Psalms as Instruction', pp. 118-20; *A Theological Introduction*, pp. 25-40.

103. McCann, 'Psalms as Instruction', pp. 122-23; *A Theological Introduction*, pp. 41-50; 'The Book of Psalms', in *NIB*, IV, pp. 664-65.

Psalter's canonical shapers.[104] The issues raised by this tension will be discussed further below.

Canonical Shape and Genre Definition

Obviously, psalms scholarship has traveled a great distance from the form-critical consensus that prevailed 20 years ago. Close attention to the final shape of the Psalter has yielded a number of important insights that cannot be ignored. Such research will undoubtedly continue to bear much fruit for some time. There is, however, at least one issue that needs to be looked at a bit more closely, one that bears directly on the subject matter of the present work. This is the issue of how attention to the canonical shape affects the way in which one approaches the genre analysis of the psalms.

One may begin by distinguishing between two different levels on which canonical analysis makes a difference for how the psalms are seen in terms of genre. First of all, one needs to take note of how the way in which one sees the final shape of the Psalter affects the way in which one perceives the genre of the individual psalms. Secondly, one needs to understand how the way in which one perceives the genre of the individual psalms affects the way in which one understands the final shape of the Psalter.

There is, in other words, a hermeneutical circle here with respect to the way genre works in the Psalter. The way that one sees the whole affects the way one sees the parts, and the way that one sees the parts affects the way one sees the whole. It is instructive to look at this hermeneutical circle in light of the work of the above authors.

104. McCann, 'Editorial Purpose'; 'Psalms as Instruction', pp. 122-23; and *A Theological Introduction*, pp. 41-45; *NIB*, IV, pp. 659-66. One may note that for McCann the exile is not simply a historical event of the sixth century but a continuing theological problem after that time as well. While McCann agrees with Wilson that this problem is addressed in books four and five, he also sees it as addressed already in book three and prepared for in books one and two.

McCann shares Wilson's historical-critical concern for the intentionality of the Psalter's shapers. In part, this seems to be a defense of his canonical method. Note, for example, his defense of canonical interpreters against the charge of being 'pre-critical': 'After all, what could be more *historically* honest and *critically* appropriate than to approach the book of Psalms the way its shapers intended...?' (*A Theological Introduction*, p. 20). It is not clear that all of the interpreters he wishes to defend would wish to tie their method to a historical quest for the intentionality of the canonical shapers.

The Effect of the Whole on the Parts

One may begin this twofold analysis by looking at the big question. What kind of book is the Psalter? To what genre does it belong? This is perhaps the ultimate question that is raised by those who take a canonical approach to this text. It is, significantly, a question that has been addressed directly by a number of the above authors.[105]

In such a vein, both Wilson and McCann have argued against seeing the Psalter as a 'hymnbook'. Rather than being a collection of hymns from which one can excerpt individual texts as needed, these authors see the Psalter as a coherent whole with a specific theological message. Wilson especially sees it as a book of instruction, meant for meditation and reading rather than personal or communal actualization. Along similar lines, one will recall McCann's characterization of it as a 'catechism'.

Such descriptions are based on what has been called the hermeneutical function of Psalm 1. Scholars such as Wilson see this psalm's injunction to meditate on the Torah as changing the way the other psalms are to be appropriated. No longer are they to be taken in a way appropriate to their original cultic setting in the life of ancient Israel. Instead, they are now to be seen as 'instruction' similar to that which is found in the wisdom literature.[106]

This may, of course, be seen as a genre shift of the first magnitude, especially if, like Gunkel, one sees setting as important to genre definition. What this genre classification of the Psalter has done is to substitute the reconstructed setting of the Psalter's final redactors for

---

105. On this, see also E.S. Gerstenberger, 'Der Psalter als Buch und als Sammlung', in K. Seybold and E. Zenger (eds.), *Neue Wege der Psalmenforschung* (Herders Biblische Studien, 1: Freiburg: Herder, 1994), pp. 3-13. Gerstenberger objects to seeing the Psalter as a 'book' with a unified outlook on both redaction-historical and theological grounds. Gerstenberger also sees all of the 'canonical' authors as taking essentially the same position on this question. The discussion that follows in the text shows that this is not necessarily the case.

106. To such scholars one may also add K. Seybold (*Introducing the Psalms* [Edinburgh: T. & T. Clark, 1990], p. 27). For Seybold, Pss. 1 and 119 help the existing Psalter to take on 'the character of a documentation of divine revelation, to be used in a way analogous to the *Torah*, the first part of the canon, and becomes an instruction manual for the theological study of the divine order of salvation, and for meditation'. Seybold does, however, note that in Pss. 120–50, 'the centre of gravity of the Psalter archive shifts once again in favour of the hymnic component'.

the settings of the individual psalms' original users—and, one might add, for the settings of its subsequent users, many of whom have obviously used the psalms for more than meditation and reflection.

One may easily accept this characterization of the Psalter as *a* plausible definition of its genre.[107] What is more problematic is the implication that this is the only possible genre definition of the Psalter, an implication that is especially to be found in the writings of Wilson. It is significant that none of the other authors considered above have attempted to deny the continued use of the psalms in prayer. This is even the case with McCann, particularly in his more recent works.

On this issue, it would be good to recall Childs's insistence on seeing a 'variety of different hermeneutical moves which were incorporated into the final form of the Psalter'. Even though a feature like the introductory psalm allows one to approach the book in a certain way, other features that point in different directions are also to be seen in the text. In such a way, the Psalter does not insist upon, or even allow for, one exclusive way in which its texts function.

Childs gives two reasons for this hermeneutical complexity. The first is the 'richness' of the material itself. This implies that the psalms have a surplus of theological meaning that cannot be exhausted by any one hermeneutical move.

Childs's second reason is even more interesting from the perspective of the present work. One cannot reduce the psalms to a single 'function' because its 'established use' was 'far too diverse' to allow such a reduction. That is to say, even at the time of their canonical shaping the psalms were being used in different ways. As such, they were incapable of being shaped in favor of one exclusive function at the expense of all others.

Given Childs's appreciation of the richness of the Psalms and the diversity of their use, it comes as no surprise that he specifically argues

---

107. Gerstenberger argues that this view of the Psalter as a book for continuous meditative reading is 'monastic' in origin ('Der Psalter', p. 10). While this may well be the case, one still needs to ask whether this is a productive interpretive strategy for the present time. Similarly, Gerstenberger certainly may be correct when he asserts that such a way of reading the Psalms is one that meets our contemporary interests. It is, of course, the position of the present work that reading a text in line with such interests is to some extent inevitable and even necessary. As such, it need not be subject to a negative evaluation on those grounds alone.

that these texts were collected to be 'used for liturgy and for study'.[108] In terms of genre categories, this would seem to argue for what Wilson tries so hard to rule out. The book of Psalms can indeed be seen as a collection of hymns for liturgical use, just as it can be seen as a theological text to be meditated upon. The book as a whole is capable of more than one genre definition because the texts within it cannot be restricted to one 'function'.

Significantly, Childs takes the question of the psalms' use beyond the time of the final redactors of the material. One of the reasons for looking at the history of the psalms' exegesis is 'to be made aware of many different models of interpretation which have all too frequently been disparaged through ignorance'.[109] Because these earlier commentators 'stand firmly within the canonical context, one can learn from them how to speak anew the language of faith'. For Childs, it is precisely the diversity of the history of interpretation which does justice to the canonical nature of the material. Through this history, one becomes aware of the many hermeneutical possibilities that this text allows.

One might well contrast this position with the views of Wilson and Brueggemann. For different reasons, both of these scholars see the psalms in a more one-dimensional way. In Wilson's case, it is his concern for the intentions of the final redactors that leads him to see the final shape in a certain way. For Brueggemann, on the other hand, it is his conviction that the shape of the Psalter mirrors the experience of life as presented in his earlier orientation–disorientation–new orientation schema.[110]

Childs's view of the psalms is more complex in large part because it is open to the empirical diversity of the psalms' past use and interpretation. Because he sees this history as at least potentially illuminative of

---

108. As noted above, other authors, such as Sheppard and Mays, are similar to Childs in their affirmations of the different uses of the psalms. In addition to Mays's previously cited comments, see his statement that the psalms' 'functions are opened up to a variety of uses for prayer, praise and study that reflect their role as both liturgy and Scripture' ('Context in Psalm Interpretation', p. 20).

109. Childs, *Introduction to the Old Testament*, p. 523.

110. Brueggemann is somewhat more historical in 'Psalm 73'. In that article, he and Miller suggest that Ps. 73 is part of a postexilic reflection on the end of the monarchy, a suggestion that is clearly part of a larger conversation with such scholars as Wilson and McCann. It is, nevertheless, significant that at the end of that article the authors see the choice posed by the psalm as one that will eventually need to be made by Israel as a whole.

the canonical shape of the psalms, he also sees the final redaction as one in which 'no doctrinaire position received a normative role'. Which hermeneutical possibilities of the text's final shape are actualized at any given time would seem to depend on the function that it is being called on to perform in a particular setting.

Given the present work's appreciation for the role of the history of interpretation as a hermeneutical guide to the biblical text, it should come as no surprise that this author is more inclined toward Childs's view. One does, however, need to look a bit further at the implications of this more flexible view for how one sees the genre of the individual psalms.

As noted above, Childs allows for at least two different genre definitions of the Psalter as a whole. What remains to be seen is that the way one defines the genre of the Psalter has a definite effect on how one sees the genre of the individual psalms. If one sees the Psalter as a collection for liturgical use or individual prayer, one will tend to emphasize those aspects of the psalms that fit the interpersonal dynamics of the divine–human relationship. If, on the other hand, one sees the Psalter as a text to be studied and meditated upon, one will tend to emphasize those aspects that lend themselves to such didactic purposes.

The significance of this difference in emphasis is perhaps seen most clearly in the case of the so-called 'mixed psalms'. These psalms have long been a problem for form-critical scholars because their final form contains elements from different genres. Particularly problematic are psalms that combine didactic and liturgical elements, since such texts do not readily admit of any plausible setting in life.[111] Recent authors have tended to see such psalms as resulting from a wisdom redaction of earlier liturgical texts for a 'post-cultic' setting.[112]

If one sees the Psalter as a book of instruction in keeping with the intentions of Wilson's final didactic redactors, one will undoubtedly privilege the didactic elements of such psalms. On the other hand, if one views the Psalter more in keeping with liturgical use or individual

---

111. It might be noted here that pre-critical authors had far less of a problem in accounting for these psalms. As Kuczynski notes about the medieval view: 'The fact that David is doing two things at once in his poetry, expressing himself subjectively and using himself as an objective moral example for others, accounts for some of the remarkable shifts in tone one encounters in the psalms' (*Prophetic Song*, pp. 10-11).

112. See, for example, Stolz, *Psalmen*.

prayer, it is the earlier liturgical material that becomes central in allow-ing the didactic material to be appropriated in relational terms.[113]

The real issue is that of whether the final form of the Psalter is sufficiently clear as to mandate only the genre definition of the Psalter as a book of instruction, along with the resulting effects on the genre definition of its individual parts. Clearly, the fact that the psalms have never ceased to be appropriated as prayer or liturgy would seem to make it hard to argue for an exclusive genre definition of the Psalter as a book of instruction. The fact that most of the canonical scholars cited above are concerned to allow the psalms to continue to function as prayer seems to indicate the need for flexibility in this regard.

Tehillim: *The Psalter's Own Genre Definition*

One may conclude this consideration of the genre definition of the Psalter as a whole by looking at the genre designation that one finds in the book itself. At least in its Masoretic form, the book of Psalms is known as *Tehillim* or 'praises'.[114] According to Childs, 'this is not a literary classification and does not accurately describe the various genres of prayer, songs and liturgies which the Psalter contains, but it does accurately reflect the theology of Israel. The psalms have to do with the praise of God'.[115]

What Childs seems to be saying here is that the Hebrew title of the Psalter does not fit the standard form-critical categories to which the individual psalms belong. However, despite the fact that the psalms do not fit any such 'literary' genre of praise, they are still described as praise for theological reasons. Mays is even more explicit along these

---

113. It is, of course, important to see that the canonical issue of how a particular psalm is to be understood in the light of the entire Psalter is not necessarily the same as the redaction-historical question of how the final redactors of a particular psalm intended that psalm to be understood. This is the case even if one identifies the redactors of a particular psalm with the final redactors of the Psalter as a whole. At least as seen by such scholars as Childs, canonical interpretation is not entirely the same as redaction criticism, even redaction criticism of the final form of the text.

114. For an account of how the Psalter received this title, see K. Koch, 'Der Psalter und seine Redaktionsgeschichte', in K. Seybold and E. Zenger (eds.), *Neue Wege der Psalmenforschung* (Herders Biblische Studien, 1; Freiburg: Herder, 1994), pp. 243-77.

115. Childs, *Introduction to the Old Testament*, p. 514.

lines, seeing the title as one of the ways in which the book 'defines all
its contents, the prayers and instruction, as the praise of the LORD.
Their literary genre remains, but their function is transposed to another
canonical genre'.[116] That this subsequent 'genre definition' is related to
a transposition of 'function' is very much in keeping with the larger
argument of the present work.

Along these lines, the overarching categorization of the psalms as
Tehillim may be seen as a prescriptive genre definition. The presence of
the title *Tehillim* serves to define these texts first and foremost as those
which have to do with the praise of God. As such, this title functions in
much the same way as the genre definition of Psalms 6, 32, 38, 51, 102,
130 and 143 as the 'seven penitential psalms' was seen to function in
the second chapter of this work.

It will be recalled that the latter definition worked in two ways. First
of all, it emphasized the penitential aspects of these seven psalms, with
the result that their other aspects were seen in a 'penitential' light.
Secondly, it enabled the less 'penitential' of these psalms to be read in a
way consistent with their more penitential fellows.

In a similar way, the title *Tehillim* emphasizes the feature of praise
that is to be found in almost all the psalms, even the psalms of
lament.[117] Even more importantly, this title mandates the way in which
all the psalms are to be understood, even those that are manifestly not
songs of praise in any modern form-critical sense. Just as the genre
definition of Psalm 102 as a penitential psalm led to its functioning as
such for generations of believers, so the definition of all the psalms as
Tehillim has become the means of their functioning as praise of God.

Such a genre definition does not, as both Childs and Mays note, fit
the modern literary or form-critical definitions of many of the psalms. It
does, however, fit the function such psalms were felt to have in their
later history of reception. In such a vein, even the psalms of lament
were felt to be a means of praising God.

It is helpful to compare this understanding of the title *Tehillim* with
the understandings of it found in Wilson and Brueggemann. According
to Wilson, the designation of the Psalter as *Tehillim* might seem at first
'somewhat odd and inadequate' as a description for a book that knows

116. Mays, *The Lord Reigns*, p. 62, also 41.
117. For a modern affirmation of the same theological judgment, see Westermann, *Praise and Lament*.

'the whole gamut of human experience from praise to lament and thanksgiving'.[118] Nevertheless, the title reflects the final shape of the Psalter, especially the fact that the last half of the book 'is increasingly dominated by forms of praise'. For Wilson, the final shape of the Psalter, 'though it acknowledges the reality and pain of human suffering...nevertheless still points to an alternative view of reality in which there is room in the human heart only for praise'.[119]

For Brueggemann, the Psalms move from obedience to praise through the crisis of God's *ḥesed*. In such a way, Brueggemann shares with Wilson the view that the final half of the Psalter represents the place where praise is to be found in a special way. It is this part of the Psalter that represents the ultimate goal of the faithful life, despite the fact that Brueggemann sees a somewhat more dialectical relationship between the different parts of the Psalter.

The present analysis would see the title *Tehillim* as a safeguard against such arguments for seeing a fundamental dichotomy in the Psalter. According to the title, all the psalms are 'praises', including those that extol the rewards of the obedient life and those that complain of God's absence. The psalms that conclude the Psalter may be 'praises' according to modern form-critical analysis,[120] but according to the Psalter's own genre definition all the psalms are to be seen in this way. That is to say, all the psalms function as praise for those who accept the canonical designation of the Psalter itself.

The Effect of the Parts on the Whole

This section turns to the other part of the hermeneutical circle and asks about the way the genre definition of individual psalms affects the way that one sees the nature of the larger Psalter. One may begin by recalling that such genre definition is of some importance to the scholars considered in this chapter. For authors such as Wilson and Brueggemann, the question of where particular genres occur in the larger book is a major aspect of their analysis of the Psalter's final shape.

It is important to recognize that there are two steps in the process of

118. Wilson, 'Book of Psalms', p. 138.

119. Wilson, 'Book of Psalms', pp. 138-39.

120. It should in any case be noted that praise in itself is not really a form-critical category like the hymn or thanksgiving. It is really more of a content category or a theological stance.

understanding how the genres of the individual psalms work in the larger whole. The first step is, of course, the basic act of defining the genres of those texts. Only after this act of genre definition can one move to the further question of what the placement of these genres implies for the meaning of the larger work. It is useful to look at how those interested in the Psalter's final shape have approached each of these steps.

Genre Definition and Canonical Analysis

As is clear from the earlier chapters of the present work, the task of defining the genres of the individual psalms is not simply one of deciding where they fit in Gunkel's system. The history of these psalms' interpretation shows that there have been other genre possibilities in both the pre- and post-Gunkel periods. Significantly, the fact of these other genre possibilities was explicitly recognized by Wilson in his analysis of the Psalter.

Throughout his work, Wilson operates with an awareness of two different types of genre categories in the Psalms. There is, in the first place, the type of genre categories that Wilson sees as present in the superscriptions of the psalms themselves.[121] That these terms are genre categories may be seen from the fact that they never occur together in the same psalm superscription. As Wilson notes, however, there is almost no attempt to group together all of the psalms of a particular genre category. This is the case even though there are a number of places where their distribution in successive psalms seems to serve an organizational purpose in the Psalter as a whole.

The other type of genre terminology that Wilson uses is that of modern form-critical analysis.[122] Once again, Wilson does not see this type of genre category as furnishing a 'primary' editorial principle for the organization of the Psalter, at least to the extent that all the psalms of a particular form-critical category might be grouped together. He does, however, view the predominance of such genres as lament and praise in different parts of the Psalter as significant for understanding the final shape of that book and the intentions of the final redactors.

In such a way, Wilson's analysis talks of two types of genre that were

121. Wilson explicitly calls these genre categories in *Editing the Hebrew Psalter*, pp. 143, 158-62.

122. Wilson, *Editing the Hebrew Psalter*, pp. 143, 161; 'Book of Psalms', pp. 138-39.

of significance for those who were responsible for the canonical shape of the Psalter. Wilson's argument concerning ancient genre terms is, on the whole, rather persuasive, since he has been able to show a fairly regular pattern in the way these terms now appear in the Psalter. The final redactors may not have been aware of the exact meaning of the genre terms attached to the psalms, but, as Wilson has demonstrated, they were able to use both these terms and the designations of authorship to organize the book in a certain way.

His argument concerning the placement of the psalms as seen from the perspective of modern form-criticism is, on the other hand, somewhat less compelling. According to Wilson, the present arrangement of these form-critically identified genres offers a clue to the final redactors' intentions as to the meaning of the larger book. This argument would thus seem to imply that the redactors had at least some intimation of the psalms' status in terms of modern form-critical genres. One wonders, however, whether one can really assume such an awareness, especially if the psalms no longer retained their original cultic setting in life.

A division into lament and praise might seem obvious to modern critics reared on Gunkel's form-critical consensus. It is, however, by no means certain that such a division was either obvious or important to the ancient editors.[123] Indeed, the fact that such editors could call all the psalms *Tehillim* may well be an indication of a type of genre consciousness different from that of modern form-critics. The diversity of the psalms' genre definitions throughout the history of their interpretation should also make one cautious about assuming that an earlier era shared one's genre categories.

If, however, one is unable to assume that the editors of the Psalter shared the genre categories of modern biblical scholars, one cannot really use the distribution of the latter categories as a clue to the former's redactional intent. This does not mean, of course, that one cannot use our modern definition of these genres to inform our understanding of the Psalter's final shape. It does, however, mean that our interpretation of the Psalter's final shape is proper to our own time, since it depends on genre definitions that are proper to our own time.[124]

---

123. On this one may quote Mays: 'The use of contemporary form-critical categories for descriptive purposes also introduces considerations that do not appear to have played much of any role in arranging the psalms' (*The Lord Reigns*, p. 127).

124. One should also remember the argument of the earlier chapters which

Because other times defined the genres of the psalms differently, they also may have had a different view of the overall shape of the Psalter.

Genre Evaluation and the Interpretation of the Psalter

Once one has defined the genres of the individual psalms, one can then move to an analysis of how these genres work together to inform the whole of the Psalter. One should, however, not expect that scholars who agree on the genre definition of the psalms will necessarily agree on the implications of the placement of such psalms for the larger meaning of the Psalter. A comparison of the canonical work of Wilson and Brueggemann is a good example of such differing interpretations of similarly defined genres.

In keeping with their form-critical definitions of psalm genres, both Wilson and Brueggemann see a 'movement' in the Psalter from the laments that are concentrated in the first part of that book to the praise with which it concludes. Both of these scholars see the lament as a necessary stage in the move to what Wilson calls an alternate view of reality, one dominated by the praise of God.[125] For Wilson, however, the laments are more a way of setting up the problem for which God's kingship is the answer. Wilson sees the individual laments of the first half of the Psalter as connected to 'human weakness', 'the failure of nerve and power', 'the lack of will to obey', and 'the successful forays of enemies'. In contrast, the communal praise of the second half provides the isolated individual with 'identity, affirmation, renewal, restoration, and a hope for the future'.[126] Lament might be necessary at some point, but praise is the desired human response for the reader who takes the present shape of the Psalter seriously.[127]

Brueggemann, on the other hand, tends to focus on those psalms that reflect the recurring crises of human existence that are also crises of God's *ḥesed*.[128] It is the psalms in the midst of the Psalter, especially

cautioned about the unquestioned identification of ancient psalm categories with modern theological interests.

125. Wilson, 'Book of Psalms', p. 139.

126. Wilson, 'Book of Psalms', p. 139.

127. Note Wilson's statement that the concluding *hallel* in Pss. 146–50 'do not *end* the psalter but rather catapult the reader onward into an open and unending paean of praise for Yahweh' ('Book of Psalms', p. 138).

128. So 'Obedience and Praise', p. 91: 'The literature of the Psalms articulates the shape, not only of a biblical book, but of Israel's faith and of Israel's life.'

those that incorporate the lament, that provide the means by which one moves from the simple obedience of that book's beginning to the ecstatic praise at its end. Because these psalms more closely address the place where 'Israel mostly lives', they remain central for Brueggemann even while he argues that the praise is the ultimate goal of human existence.[129]

On one level, the difference in emphasis between Wilson and Brueggemann may be attributed to the different ways in which they see the setting of the Psalter. Wilson is more consistently concerned with the historical setting of the redactors (in both the postexilic period and the first century CE). For him, the final shape of the Psalter is an attempt to answer the questions raised by the political upheavals of Judaism. As a result, he sees as central those psalms that affirm and praise God as the only trustworthy king.

Brueggemann, on the other hand, is more inclined to emphasize the broader setting of the psalms in human life. For him, 'the shape of the Psalter correlates with the shape of Israel's life with God'.[130] Just as suffering is at the center of that life, so those psalms that are rooted in suffering are at the center of the Psalter.

There is, however, a more fundamental reason why different scholars might disagree as to their interpretations of the genre distribution in the Psalter, even if those scholars were to agree as to how they see both the genre definition of individual psalms and the setting of the larger work. That reason is the fact that while such scholars may define the individual psalm genres in a similar way they may still differ as to how they *evaluate* those genres. The interpretive importance of privileged genres was, of course, a major concern of the third chapter of the present work. Clearly, one of the reasons why Wilson and Brueggemann interpret the final shape of the Psalter in different ways is because they place a different value on the lament psalms. Because a genre that has central importance for Brueggemann is of only passing interest for Wilson,

Brueggemann's more recent work, 'Psalm 73' (co-authored with Patrick Miller) is to a certain extent more in keeping with Wilson's concern for the contrast between human and divine kingship.

129. One might well recall here Brueggemann's earlier caution that one should not move too quickly to the kind of praise that ends the Psalter. So *Israel's Praise*, p. 155.

130. Brueggemann, 'Obedience and Praise', p. 88.

these scholars will invariably disagree as to their interpretations of the Psalter as a whole.

One should remember that different ages have evaluated psalm genres differently, often preferring one genre over another for theological or other reasons. Such genre preferences have almost certainly had an effect on the way the message of the larger Psalter has been understood. In such a way, the historical context of the reader is an important factor in the way that reader interprets the shape of the Psalter.

The Hermeneutical Circle of Genre: The Royal Psalms

This chapter will conclude with a consideration of a specific example of the way genre definition may have a decisive effect on the way one sees the canonical shape of the Psalter. The example is that of the royal psalms, a category of some importance for most of the authors considered above. An examination of the different ways these psalms have been viewed in terms of genre will help to sharpen the issues treated in this chapter.

One may begin by recalling the prominent place the royal psalms play in Wilson's analysis of the final shape of the Psalter. These psalms are now to be found at the 'seams' of the Psalter, especially in its first three books.[131] Of some importance for Wilson's analysis is the shift in emphasis between the individual examples of this genre that one finds at the beginning and end of these three books. Thus, Psalm 2, the first of these psalms, is full of confidence in the royal promises which are being delivered in the psalm itself. On the other hand, Psalm 89, at the end of the third book, contains a lament about their apparent failure at some later date.

It is this movement from confidence to lament that sets up what Wilson sees as the central 'problem' of the Psalter, namely, the apparent failure of the Davidic covenant in the postexilic period. One finds the answer to this problem in the fourth and fifth books of the Psalter, with their emphasis on the need for confidence in the true King of Israel who alone is worthy of praise.[132]

For Wilson, then, the royal psalm genre plays a crucial role in helping us to understand the intentions of those responsible for the final

---

131. And near the end of the final book in Ps. 144. See 'Shaping the Psalter'.

132. This problem is also addressed through the dominance of the wisdom frame in the book. So 'Shaping the Psalter'.

shape of the Psalter. By taking note of the strategically placed royal psalms at the beginning and end of the first three books of the Psalter, one is also able to understand why the Psalter moves from lament to praise in terms of its genre distribution. Read sequentially from beginning to end, the Psalter sets up and answers a crucial theological problem of the postexilic period.

What is striking about Wilson's analysis is the way it depends on the modern form-critical understanding of the royal psalms. For the first three books to set up the problem of the Psalter as Wilson has argued, these psalms must be understood with reference to the actual Davidic kings of ancient Israel. The promises of Psalm 2 must be understood as dynastic promises in accord with that psalm's setting in the life of Judean monarchy. Similarly, the lament of Psalm 89 must be seen as a lament concerning the apparent failure of that royal line in the post-exilic period, thus setting up the problem to be addressed by the last two books of the Psalter.[133]

It is, however, far from clear that those responsible for the final shape of the Psalter understood the royal psalms along such modern form-critical lines.[134] At the time of the Psalter's final redaction, the royal psalms were in all probability understood instead along eschatological and messianic lines, as a number of the scholars considered above have pointed out.[135] To quote Childs on Psalm 2: 'Indeed, at the time of the final redaction, when the institution of kingship had long since been destroyed, what earthly king would have come to mind other than God's Messiah?'[136]

Although the royal psalms once had a specific function in the historical setting of ancient Israel, 'they were treasured in the Psalter for a different reason, namely as a witness to the messianic hope which looked for the consummation of God's kingship through his Anointed

---

133. In addition to the argument which follows in the text, one might also note the reservations of Whybray who questions Wilson's interpretation of Ps. 89 as an expression of despair. Like the rest of the laments, this psalm is actually an expression of hope which looks forward to God's future actions on behalf of Israel. See *Reading the Psalms*, pp. 94-96.

134. On this, see Mays, *The Lord Reigns*, p. 127.

135. So Childs, *Introduction to the Old Testament*, pp. 515-17. See also Westermann, *Praise and Lament*, p. 258; and Mays, 'Torah-Psalms', pp. 10-11.

136. Childs, *Introduction to the Old Testament*, p. 516. Whybray sees Pss. 2, 72 and 89 as having been placed 'in prominent positions which support the notion of an orientation along messianic lines' (*Reading the Psalms*, p. 99).

One'.[137] If this is true of the time of the Psalter's canonical shaping, it is even more true of the Psalter's subsequent history of interpretation in both Judaism and Christianity.

If, however, Psalm 2 functions eschatologically as a messianic promise, it no longer helps to set up the problem that Wilson has seen as central to the Psalter. Indeed, in such a case, the Psalter has already addressed the question of the continuing validity of the divine promises in a definitive way at its very beginning. Moreover, it has done so not by shifting the theological focus from the Davidic promises to the kingship of God as much as by affirming that God's kingship will ultimately result in the fulfillment of those very promises.

One should be clear as to what exactly is at stake here. How one defines the genre of the royal psalms seriously affects the way in which one understands the final shape of the Psalter. If one sees these psalms in accord with their original setting in ancient Israel as determined by form-critical analysis, Wilson's understanding of the final shape has some plausibility.[138] If, on the other hand, one adopts a more eschatological understanding of these psalms in accord with the way they functioned at a later time, Wilson's reading becomes much more problematic.

The genre definition of the royal psalms also affects another issue related to the canonical shape of the Psalter. The question is whether Psalm 2 shares with Psalm 1 the distinction of being part of the general introduction to the Psalter as a whole. Given the great importance attributed to the beginning and end of the Psalter by those interested in that work's canonical shape, this is clearly an important question. Here too, the way one defines the genre of these psalms makes a crucial difference.

For Wilson, Psalm 2 is not part of the introduction to the entire Psalter, but rather the introduction to the first book of the Psalter. As such, it helps to set up the problem that has been discussed at length above. The importance of this way of seeing Psalm 2 for Wilson's overall interpretation of the Psalter may be seen in his early discussion

---

137. Childs, *Introduction to the Old Testament*, p. 517.

138. Though whether it could still be maintained as the intention of the final redactors would remain problematic. One would have to argue that the final redactors' understanding of these psalms' genre was the same as that of modern form-critics.

of the relationship between this psalm and Psalm 1.[139]

Many of the other scholars considered above see Psalm 2 in the other way, as part of the introduction to the Psalter as a whole. It is no coincidence that they also tend to see this psalm in an eschatological light.[140] Thus, Childs sees the prominent position of Psalm 2 as a way of emphasizing 'the kingship of God as a major theme of the whole Psalter'.[141] Mays is even stronger in seeing Psalms 1 and 2 as a larger literary unit which introduces the entire Psalter. The point of the combination is to 'put the torah piety of Psalm 1 in an eschatological context'.[142]

In addition to having an effect on one's view of the message of the Psalter (especially with regard to its eschatological contours), how one sees Psalm 2 affects the way one views the genre of the Psalter. This is especially the case with regard to the much disputed question of whether the Psalter is able to be seen as a 'hymnbook'. Thus, if one follows Wilson in taking Psalm 2 (and the other royal psalms) with reference to the historical Davidic monarchy, it is very hard to see such psalms as 'hymns' to be appropriated in the present. As a result, it is also hard to define the Psalter as a hymnbook. On the other hand, if one follows the dominant Jewish and Christian tradition in taking these

139. Wilson, *Editing of the Hebrew Psalter*, pp. 204-206. Important for Wilson is the article of J.T. Willis, 'Psalm 1: An Entity', *ZAW* 91 (1979), pp. 381-401.

140. Even Sheppard, who sees Ps. 2 as pointing to David as the one who fulfils the description of Ps. 1, sees 'the foundations for messianism' being laid in Ps. 2. 'Theology', p. 154. Childs and Mays are more direct in seeing an eschatological reference here.

141. Childs, *Introduction to the Old Testament*, p. 516. Childs notes that while there are 'some signs the redactor sought to link the two psalms together', there is not 'sufficient evidence' to decide 'whether or not Psalm 2 was conceived as a formal part of the introduction'. It is, nevertheless, clear that for Childs this psalm's 'prominent place' has given it a role with respect to the rest of the Psalter.

142. Mays, 'Torah-Psalms', p. 10. Mays sees a number of similar juxtapositions throughout the rest of the psalter.

Of particular interest is the position of McCann on this issue. McCann sees Psalms 1–2 as introducing Book 1, Books 1–3, and the entire Psalter (*NIB*, p. 664). It is possible that the two former introductory functions reflect McCann's sympathies with Wilson's historical interests and analysis. The last introductory function seems to reflect his sympathies with Mays' more purely canonical reading of the text, as does his desire to see an eschatological perspective from the beginning of the Psalter. While all of these approaches are clearly valid, it is not always apparent how they can coexist with each other in a single reading of the text.

psalms in a more eschatological light, one can more easily appropriate them as 'hymns' and understand the Psalter as a hymnbook.

As one would expect in the case of a hermeneutical circle, the converse is, of course, also true. Thus, if one understands the larger Psalter as a hymnbook for communal or individual worship, one needs to understand the genre of such psalms as Psalm 2 in a way that allows them to be used for that worship. In the absence of an actual Davidic king, this would clearly favor an eschatological reading of such psalms. Seeing the genre of the Psalter as a wisdom book would allow other non-eschatological understandings of the royal psalms (although it does not necessarily exclude an eschatological approach to those psalms).

The point of this look at the royal psalms is not to assert that they provide a decisive clue as to how the genre of the Psalter is to be understood. It is rather to argue once again that genre is a term that is inevitably related to function and setting. This is no less true of the entire Psalter than of the individual psalms.

Conclusions

With this consideration of the royal psalms, the present chapter concludes its discussion of the canonical analysis of the Psalter on a note consistent with what has gone before in this book. Despite the very different approach of recent canonical scholars, their work in many respects turns on the same issues discussed in earlier chapters. Because genre remains an important question for such scholars on a number of levels, questions of function and setting turn out to be the decisive questions. Any attempt to understand either the final shape of the Psalter or the role of the individual psalms within that shape must come to terms with both the fundamental issue of what constitutes a genre and the diverse genre definitions found in the history of the Psalter's interpretation.

It is important to note that the diversity of genre possibilities for the Psalter does not arise from a lack of textual evidence. Rather, there are a number of indicators in the book that can be picked up on, some of which point in different directions. Thus, as has been seen, Psalm 1 may well point to a didactic function for these texts. On the other hand, a very different function is apparently indicated by the call to worship which is a part of many individual psalms and which constitutes the ending to the Psalter as a whole. As Childs has argued, the final shape of the Psalter makes no attempt to eliminate either of these functions, both of which have been prominent throughout the history of the Psalter's interpretation.

One is faced with the same overabundance of evidence when one attempts to come to terms with what the placement of psalm genres means for the overall message of the Psalter. One can obviously take note of the unequal distribution of praise and lament psalms throughout the Psalter. One can also argue for the strategic placement of such genres as torah and royal psalms. To do so, however, means that one must in some way come to terms with those psalms that run counter to one's interpretive schemas.

As Whybray has recently noted, one of the problems for understanding the redaction of the Psalter lies in 'the evident complexity of its composition'.[143] The result of such complexity is that there are simply too many rough edges in the placement of psalm genres to allow for a completely consistent reading of the Psalter as a whole. One might well quote Whybray further on the larger problem: 'However hard one may try to account for the arrangement of the Psalter, it is difficult to dismiss the impression of randomness in the positioning of many of [the psalms]'.[144]

Whether this 'impression of randomness' stems from a complex redactional history or from an intentional editorial attempt to preserve a number of interpretive possibilities, the effect is the same. The interpreter of the Psalter is faced with the necessity of making a number of genre and thematic choices. As always, such choices will be guided by both the interpreter's present context and the tradition in which that interpreter stands, as well as by the clues found in the canonical text itself.[145]

One choice facing the interpreter is that of which psalms form the

---

143. Whybray, *Reading the Psalms*, p. 35.

144. Whybray, *Reading the Psalms*, p. 86. Whybray also argues throughout against any systematic redaction of the Psalms in either a wisdom/Torah or an eschatological direction or in a way which attempts to reinterpret ritual sacrifice.

145. One might well note here Whybray's explicit recognition of a 'consistent, silent, reinterpretation' of the Psalms which takes place as individual readers and 'church and synagogue tradition' 'struggled to make the Psalter relevant to later generations', *Reading the Psalms*, pp. 119, 124. It is, of course, the thesis of this book that this reinterpretation has important implications for the present genre definition and interpretation of the psalms.

context in which to read the others. As was noted above, such a choice is clearly rooted in the interpreter's larger theological stance and historical circumstances. It is, for example, instructive that the privileging of the lament which was found in Brueggemann's earlier work on the psalms continues in his more recent canonical interpretation. Indeed, the central place of the lament in Brueggemann's canonical analysis is remarkably similar to its central position in his earlier orientation–disorientation–new orientation schema, a position that was seen to owe much to Brueggemann's contemporary theological concerns.[146]

One could, of course, argue that other ages saw other psalm genres as the structural underpinning for the Psalter's final shape and overall message. One will, for example, recall that many medieval authors saw the seven penitential psalms as involving the reader in a 'journey' with distinct stages. Like modern canonical scholars, such authors clearly assume an approach to the Psalter that begins at the beginning and moves consecutively through the whole of the Psalter. Given the centrality of these psalms for the medieval period, one might well expect that these psalms provide the key for understanding that period's approach to the Psalter as a whole.[147]

It may well be that earlier ages were less concerned with the final shape of the Psalter than our own, perhaps as a result of a more thoroughgoing liturgical appropriation of that book. This would, of course, not rule out the current interest in that shape, which has already shown itself theologically fruitful and for which there is ample support in the text. At the same time, however, the modern canonical analysis of the Psalter cannot ignore what an analysis of the Psalter's interpretive history has shown us about the nature and role of genre in that history.

It is no accident that some of the most fruitful canonical analyses of the Psalter have been provided by those scholars who have also taken account of that book's interpretive history. Perhaps because of their awareness of the diversity of that history, such scholars seem to be more open to the multiple possibilities built into the Psalter's present

146. One will recall Brueggemann's admission that certain aspects of his canonical analysis stem in the first instance from his own theological considerations. So 'Obedience and Praise', pp. 81-83.

147. Implicit in this is, of course, the question of whether other ages put any emphasis on the canonical shape of the Psalter in a manner similar to that of modern canonical scholars. More research is clearly needed here.

shape. They also seem to be more aware that coming to terms with those possibilities involves the reader in a many layered hermeneutical process.

The present chapter has attempted to show that defining the canonical shape of the Psalter involves genre questions throughout. Like every act involving genre definition, this is a task that needs to be situated in both tradition and community. As such, it is both a descriptive and a constructive task.

Chapter 7

CONCLUSIONS

The preceding chapters have taken the reader on a somewhat kaleido-scopic tour of many of the latest trends of contemporary research on the psalms. The first impression made by such a tour is undoubtedly that psalms scholarship has entered a new post-Gunkel era in which genre questions are no longer the pre-eminent concern that they have been for most of this century. Certainly, this conclusion is accurate if terms such as form and setting are understood in their classical form-critical sense.

If, on the other hand, one takes a more expansive view of such terms, it becomes quite clear that questions of genre remain just as crucial as ever to any understanding of the psalms. Indeed, it can easily be argued that scholars will never come close to achieving anything like this century's methodological consensus until they address genre questions in as direct and persuasive a manner as that of Gunkel.

It may, of course, be that such a consensus is an unrealistic goal for a time as methodologically fragmented as the present. At the very least, however, an awareness of the way that different methods approach questions of genre will help to illustrate the distinctiveness of such methods with reference to an important common issue. It will also allow for an understanding of how such approaches relate to their methodological predecessors.

The conclusions that follow attempt first of all to account for why genre has continued, and will continue, to be an important category in psalms scholarship. They then draw on the preceding chapters to argue for an expansive definition of the task of genre analysis, one that is both descriptive and constructive. Finally, they offer some suggestions for the future of psalms research, suggestions which, I hope, are open to the many strands of contemporary endeavors in the field.

The Indispensability of Genre

A popular refrain of the present post-Gunkel era is that traditional form-criticism has tended to pay too much attention to biblical texts' common elements at the expense of a proper appreciation of such texts' distinctive individual aspects. This charge of concentrating on the general category to the neglect of the individual text is, of course, one which has sometimes been an important one in the wider humanities as well.[1] In biblical scholarship, one may conveniently take note of James Muilenburg's influential Society of Biblical Literature presidential address as a major impetus to a more comprehensive analysis of individual texts.[2]

The move to devote more attention to the singularities of individual texts is certainly one which is very much alive in contemporary psalms scholarship. Some of the most recent works on the psalms have argued for a shift in priorities along these lines and have undertaken extensive analyses of individual psalms.[3] There is no doubt that such studies are part of an inevitable swing in the pendulum of psalms research.

It is, however, important to note that few of those who have argued for paying more attention to individual psalms have completely turned away from classifying those psalms according to form. Thus, even as one of these authors, LarsOlov Eriksson, argues passionately for appreciating the peculiar artistry of Psalm 34, he still devotes considerable space to questions about that psalm's form.[4] This may, of course, simply be a nod to his immediate methodological predecessors. It may also, however, say something important about the role of genre in biblical scholarship.

What continued attention to genre provides even to scholars like Eriksson is a vital background against which to appreciate the individual texts that are their special concern. For Eriksson, much of what is distinctive about Psalm 34 is apparent only after one has seen it in the company of other psalms with similar thanksgiving and wisdom elements. In other words, paying attention to genre questions helps

1. The most extreme form may be seen in the arguments of Croce.
2. Printed as 'Form Criticism and Beyond', *JBL* 88 (1969), pp. 1-18.
3. See among others, Fuchs, *Die Klage als Gebet*, and LarsOlov Eriksson, *Come, Children, Listen to me! Psalm 34 in the Hebrew Bible and in Early Christian Writings* (ConBot, 32; Stockholm: Almqvist & Wiksell, 1991).
4. Eriksson, *Psalm 34*, pp. 56-81.

Eriksson to establish an interpretive framework within which he can better pursue the analysis of his psalm's individual features. His is indeed an attempt to go, in Muilenberg's words, 'beyond' form-criticism, rather than an attempt to replace it completely.

The persistence of form-critical analysis even in works such as that of Eriksson is not just a holdover from a previous scholarly era. Rather, it is an indication that one cannot really do a detailed study of individual texts unless one is able to understand those texts in relationship to other texts. It is only in the interplay of similarities and differences with other texts that what is truly distinctive about a particular text becomes apparent. Again, genre categories furnish such scholars with an important literary context within which to situate their texts.

The continued attention to form among the psalms scholars discussed in this work would seem to indicate an abiding, even essential, role for genre definition. One should not, however, overlook the reluctance of such scholars to pursue genre definition in the traditional Gunkel mode. As was seen throughout much of the present work, what appears to be most problematic for these scholars is Gunkel's concern for social setting.

One can certainly understand the impatience of recent scholars with the increasingly speculative arguments about life setting that have tended to plague form criticism in its later stages. The fact that the psalms are texts of ancient literature whose historical context remains largely unknown despite the best efforts of critical scholarship certainly makes the more purely 'literary' approaches of recent scholars quite attractive. To think, however, that even such literary approaches can afford to ignore questions of social context would be very much mistaken.

What the preceding chapters have shown is that genre is neither expendable nor able to be confined to questions of literary taxonomy. Texts relate to other texts not only in terms of their vocabulary and structure but also in terms of the functions that they perform in a particular community. Gunkel's genius lay in his recognition that genre is both a literary and social category. As a historian, he was primarily interested in the way that genre groupings functioned in ancient Israel. The fact that those who do not share his historical concerns continue to use his categories is understandable to the extent that Gunkel's categories often have a clear basis in the vocabulary and structure of the psalms.

To focus on these elements often means seeing the psalms in a primarily literary mode, something that is usually accomplished by bracketing or minimizing their social situation. It is, however, important to recognize that such an emphasis on the literary features of the psalms actually assigns these texts a social role as an 'aesthetic object' in the present time. These texts are undoubtedly capable of playing such a role for modern readers who are interested in reading them in the context of other such aesthetic objects. Nevertheless, one should not ignore the fact that one is making a reader-based genre definition here. Moreover, this genre definition is one that the psalms have almost never had for most of the communities that have valued them, including those communities active at the present time.

Towards a More Comprehensive Understanding of Genre Analysis

The challenge of the present moment is to preserve Gunkel's insight that genre has both a literary and a social dimension while moving beyond his primary concern with the historical context of ancient Israel. In the view of the present author, such a challenge should not be met by ignoring the efforts of the generations of critical scholars who have attempted to define the genres of ancient Israel. While such efforts were often overly speculative, they also resulted in many insightful readings of the texts in question. In addition, such scholars' investigations of these texts' social role in ancient Israel might well serve as an important reminder that they continue to play such a social role in the present. Finally, one should not be too dismissive of an interest in historical origins, even if one is properly suspicious of exaggerated claims made on the basis of limited evidence.

On the other hand, the challenge of a genre analysis that is both literary and social should also not be met by fixing the genres of the ancient period as definitive for all successive generations of biblical readers. As the history of interpretation clearly shows, the same texts have often been assigned to different genre categories at various stages of that history. An awareness of this interpretive history helps one to see the genre potential of a given text. It also helps to pose the question of that text's present genre definition in the sharpest possible way.

What the present work has argued for throughout is an approach to genre that is both descriptive and constructive. The task of defining a text's genre is descriptive in so far as it attempts to determine how that text has been seen in genre terms throughout its history. This task would include attention to the genre status of a text at the time of its origins in ancient Israel, to the extent that such information can be ascertained. It would also include a recognition of that text's genre history during the biblical period, including, if possible, an understanding of its genre definition at the time of its being recognized as canonical. Finally, it would include at least an overview of the text's post-canonical genre history, down to and including the present time.[5]

The constructive aspect of genre definition entails an interpretive decision as to which texts should be read together at the present time. Such a decision would obviously need to take into account a number of factors. First of all, one would certainly expect that such literary features as lexical and structural similarities would play a role in most decisions to group texts together. Also of importance, however, for any constructive genre definition is an awareness of the social purpose for which this definition is being made. In other words, one should be conscious of what function the text is being asked to perform. This necessarily involves an awareness of the community for which the text is being interpreted.

What needs to be seen clearly here is that the constructive aspect of genre definition is in reality a twofold act of interpretation. It is, on the one hand, an interpretation of the text in that it involves a judgment about which elements of that text are to be brought into conversation with similar elements of other texts. It is also, however, an interpretation of one's life setting in that it involves a judgment about which historical concerns are important at any given time. Other interpreters may obviously interpret both the textual features and the historical situation differently, and this will naturally result in different genre definitions.

It is obvious that one should not draw a hard and fast line between the descriptive and constructive tasks of genre definition.[6] In such a vein, it is helpful to remember that scholars' attempts at descriptive historical conclusions have almost inevitably manifested at least some

---

5.   The description of these stages in a text's genre history should, of course, include attention to the social settings of these genre definitions, at least to the extent that these can be determined.

6.   Along these lines, one might recall Roland Murphy's wise call for a 'continuity' between the contexts in which the biblical text is read. Murphy sees such a continuity as providing an interpretive guideline which both points in a certain direction and eliminates arbitrary proposals. So 'Reflections', p. 27.

constructive tendencies rooted in such authors' own present sensibilities. On the other hand, one might well expect the genre definitions of the past to have some influence on present interpreters and their choice of textual groupings. This is especially the case if these interpreters have both a historical connection and a continued allegiance to the past communities responsible for such interpretations. This connection and allegiance are in fact part of such interpreters' present life setting.

The fact that a modern interpreter lies on this side of the historical-critical divide means that that interpreter has the obligation to be aware of the genre classifications of a text's origins and subsequent interpretive history. This obligation does not, however, mean that such an interpreter is exempt from situating that text among other texts according to the needs of his or her own social setting, unless he or she wishes to restrict his or her task to that of a historian. If one wishes to go beyond the historical task, one is at least somewhat similar to previous interpreters who felt themselves to be informed by the genre choices of tradition but who also saw themselves as able to address the needs of their own times.

Keeping in mind the fact that texts continue to have a social dimension helps one to understand the connection between the descriptive and the constructive aspects of genre definition. Because the genre definition of a particular text changes according to its social setting, the present interpreter may be seen as simply the latest in a series of interpreters who have read that text in the company of texts which he or she feels are 'significant others'.

All of this means that one should not expect any genre definition to have a once and for all status. As was seen in the third chapter, the tendency of modern interpreters to accept what they see as a biblical text's ancient genre as binding for present practice is actually a prescriptive or constructive move in its own right. Furthermore, it is a move that is usually possible only because the interpreter also interprets the social setting of the modern period as being in some way similar to that of the text's origins. That other interpretations of the social setting are quite possible is, of course, one of the insights gained from an awareness of the text's interpretive history.

Diversity and Validity in Genre Definition
It might be objected that taking account of settings beyond that of the author is simply siding with those modern theorists who grant the

reader authority over the interpretation of texts. Such an objection might run as follows: If the reader can group texts together on the basis of community need, the reader becomes a tyrant over the text and all readings become relative. Such a situation is exactly what Hirsch feared and what he tried to prevent by tying genre questions to the time of the author.

One must acknowledge the importance of such a concern, especially in the case of the Bible. Since most of its readers see the Bible as a text that has some kind of authority over their lives, such readers are naturally reluctant to see themselves as having authority over the text. These readers expect the biblical text to have at least a certain amount of independence over against its interpreters.

At the same time, however, these readers also expect the Bible to be in some way relevant to their own life situations. This expectation persists despite the fact that these situations vary even within a single lifetime. For such readers, biblical texts are, therefore, authoritative but not static. They must be flexible enough to address different circumstances in a manner that is both authoritative and relevant.

Genre plays a key role in mediating these somewhat contradictory expectations, precisely because it is both a literary and a social category. It is, on the one hand, flexible enough to allow continued relevance because a particular text may be read in conjunction with different groups of other texts depending on the needs of different social situations. On the other hand, genre provides for a number of interpretive safeguards on both the literary and social levels, which help to maintain the text's independence and authority. This is especially so in the case of the Bible. These safeguards have been discussed throughout this book, but they may be conveniently mentioned again here.

The first kind of safeguard for the definition of biblical genres is a literary one, arising from the fact of the canon itself. While biblical texts may be read alongside similar extra-canonical texts (especially for historical purposes), their primary genre grouping is usually constructed from other canonical texts. In such a way, the canon provides an authoritative literary guide to the genre definition of biblical texts. In the case of the psalms, this canonical guideline means that the most appropriate genre grouping for a psalm will be composed of other psalms and similar prayers found elsewhere in the Bible.

As may be seen from Chapters 5 and 6 of the present work, the canon also provides two other literary guides to the genre definition of the psalms. The first of these is the narrative context of the canonical story of David, which helps to provide both a general model for those who pray the psalms and a number of more specific genre guidelines. (For Christians, the Gospel accounts of Jesus constitute an additional narrative context of this kind.) The second canonical guide is the literary context provided by the Psalter as a whole, which helps to place the individual psalms in a variety of genre relationships with each other.

The second set of safeguards for genre definition are those connected with the psalms' social context and the way these texts function in real life. Primary among these safeguards is the fact that the individuals who use these texts are usually rooted in a community that has both an established pattern of using these specific texts and a distinctive mode of life. As noted throughout the present work, the way a text functions is a major factor in that text's genre definition. In addition, the connection of a genre with a particular community's mode of life is a major way that genre has the power to shape individual lives.

An additional safeguard provided by the social context is the fact that the community in which texts function is usually a community with a history of using these texts. While this history often sanctions the present usage of these texts, it also often provides equally sanctioned alternative models of usage rooted in the different circumstances of the past. These alternative models remain available as acceptable resources for the present or, at the very least, as valid conversation partners for current thought.

A similar argument can be made for taking into account the genre definitions of communities other than one's own. These communities include both other religious communities and those communities from within one's own religious affiliation but from different social, economic and/or national backgrounds. One might further include both the genre definitions that inform the present use of such communities and those that may be found in these communities' previous interpretive traditions.

Such an awareness of the text's full genre history has the benefit of preventing an overly easy dominance of situation over text. It would be a mistake to see the text as infinitely malleable according to the needs of the present community. On the contrary, texts have an unexpected way of 'pushing back' against their interpreters, causing them to rethink their preconceptions and even to re-evaluate their needs and those of their community. An awareness of previous and alternate interpretations simply adds to the independence of such texts, since any attempts to define them according to the present must be done in the presence of numerous other conversation partners.

This does not mean that the interpreter is restricted to either present genre definitions or those of the past. It does, however, mean that any new genre definition will need either to fit into an already existing mode of life or to support the emergence of a new one. At the very least, an awareness of one's social context helps to ensure that the genre definition of a biblical text will not be restricted to a narrowly historical treatment alone.

The history of psalms interpretation makes it clear that acknowledging the social dimension of genre necessarily means accepting a certain diversity in the genre possibilities of biblical texts. However, despite the fears of some modern interpreters and the hopes of others, such a diversity is neither infinite nor lacking in criteria for adjudicating validity. Indeed, what the literary and social safeguards detailed above show is that the very factors that allow for a diversity of genre definitions in the first place are also those that guarantee a certain continuity. They also are responsible for the relevance and power of genre definitions in real life.

It is, of course, not accidental that the safeguards outlined above have had an honored place throughout much of the Jewish and Christian interpretive traditions. At least in their pre-critical manifestations, both Judaism and Christianity have placed great emphasis on the need to read an individual text in the context of both the larger canon and the accepted interpretive traditions of the past. Both Judaism and Christianity are also explicit in according an active interpretive role to the ongoing use of texts within their communities.

One may conclude this section by recalling that even someone as concerned for validity in interpretation as Hirsch has seen the Bible as belonging to a genre that seems to 'require that meaning go beyond anything which a human and historical author could possibly have willed'.[7] It is, of course, a bit ironic to realize that this is, in fact, a prescriptive genre definition on Hirsch's part, since it is quite possible to read the Bible as simply a collection of ancient literature whose meaning is restricted to the past.[8] Such a prescriptive definition is, however,

7. Hirsch, *Validity*, pp. 122-23.
8. In this respect, one cannot accept Hirsch's claim that in the type of genre to which the Bible belongs 'the author submits to the convention that his willed impli-

one that has considerable empirical support throughout the history of its interpretation.

Hirsch has, however, seen that crucial to this type of text is the presence of an extra-textual authority that is capable of distinguishing between valid and invalid interpretations. In such a vein, one can see Hirsch's reference to such concepts as the 'consensus ecclesiae' as supportive of the idea that the social context provides a valid interpretive safeguard for biblical texts.[9] It simply needs to be emphasized that this 'consensus ecclesiae' has often worked through the genre definition of its sacred texts.

Future Directions in Psalms Research

The type of genre analysis proposed in this book moves beyond Gunkel's form criticism in ways that are very different from those proposed by such scholars as Muilenburg. By attempting to maintain Gunkel's literary and social settings in a larger historical context and by including a constructive as well as a descriptive element, the present argument significantly expands the role of genre definition. What are the implications of this more expansive version of genre analysis for the psalms, those texts that have generally been seen as the most successful objects of Gunkel's research?

First of all, it must be said that just as few biblical texts were more suitable for Gunkel's genre analysis, few are more congenial for the new type of genre analysis outlined in this work. The present work has barely touched upon the raw material available for a comprehensive genre history of these texts. Almost all of the most perceptive biblical commentators from every period have written major commentaries on the psalms, and these often address genre questions in a direct way. One can certainly expect that increased attention to such sources will produce new insights into these texts, as well as opening up avenues for constructive dialogue with scholars outside the immediate biblical area.

Furthermore, the fact that the psalms continue to play a central role in both individual and communal religious practice makes them obvious

---

cations must go far beyond what he explicitly knows' (*Validity*, p. 123). Few parts of the Bible were written as explicitly 'biblical literature' of the sort that Hirsch has in mind. It is only much later in their interpretive history that these texts came to be seen in such a way. As such, Hirsch's attempt to maintain even a minimal tie to authorial intention cannot be sustained.

9.   Hirsch, *Validity*, p. 123 n. 35.

candidates for a form of analysis that recognizes the social as well as the literary nature of genre. While other biblical texts also play important roles in contemporary religious practice, the psalms present perhaps the clearest example of how social function affects genre definition and overall interpretation. Once again, such an analysis opens up significant avenues for dialogue with scholars outside the biblical field.

Finally, one should at least mention the potential for ecumenical dialogue that arises from an approach to the genre definition of the psalms that includes a full appreciation of their interpretive history. Because such an appreciation should ideally include an awareness of the genre possibilities found in other traditions, the interpreter is inevitably engaged in a conversation with others. Moreover, this conversation must needs be ongoing, since genre definition never is settled once and for all.

One would certainly expect that some of the more recent emphases in psalms research—such as the greater focus on the literary aspects of individual psalms and the new interest in the canonical shape of the Psalter itself—will continue to produce much fruit. On this front, what the present book has argued is that the results of such research depend on both continued attention to genre analysis and a clearer understanding of what that analysis entails. Even such questions as psalm authorship and the relationship of the psalms to the larger canon of Scripture have been seen to be inevitably intertwined with genre questions.

Conclusions

In looking back over the long process by which this book has come into being, I have come to realize that its central purpose has been to reclaim as a topic for modern psalms research something that was once an important feature of these texts' interpretive history—namely, the peculiar ability of these texts to affect the lives of those who use them. The modern authors who have had the most influence on the development of this work have been those who were willing to look beyond the standard literary and historical analyses of these texts to ask larger questions about their continued religious use and contemporary theological significance. At the same time, the book was driven by what was felt to be the need to reflect further on the crucial role that genre has played in the appropriation of these texts.

The first step towards appreciating the power of the psalms is to look at the concrete ways they have been appropriated. Only once one has begun to appreciate the variety and richness of the psalms' interpretive history and practical usage can one begin to reflect upon questions such as how the psalms do what they do. It is this book's contention that genre concerns are crucial for an understanding of this history and a continued appropriation of these texts.

No one is more aware than the present author how much important material has been overlooked in this work. The study of the psalms is clearly the work of a lifetime. Indeed, it is a work that cries out for collaboration between scholars of many disciplines. One longs to see a commentary that would provide access to the full history of the psalms.

It is, however, hoped that this book has been able to use at least some parts of the psalms' interpretive tradition to shed light on one aspect of their peculiar nature. If this work helps other scholars to recognize the potential of this tradition for engaging these texts in the present, its author will be happy indeed.

BIBLIOGRAPHY

Ackroyd, P.R., *Doors of Perception: A Guide to Reading the Psalms* (London: SCM Press, 1983).

Anderson, B.W., *Out of the Depths: The Psalms Speak for Us Today* (Philadelphia: Westminster Press, 1983).

Austin, J.L., *How To Do Things With Words* (Oxford: Clarendon Press, 1962).

Barth, K., *Church Dogmatics*, 4/1 (Grand Rapids: Eerdmanns, 1981).

Berger, P., and T. Luckmann, *The Social Construction of Reality* (Garden City, NY: Doubleday, 1966).

Bernini Giuseppe, S.I., *Le preghiere penitenziale del salterio: Contributo alla teologia dell' A.T.* (Analecta gregoriana, 62; Romae: Universitas Gregorianae, 1953).

Berry, D.K., *The Psalms and their Readers: Interpretive Strategies for Psalm 18* (JSOTSup, 153; Sheffield: JSOT Press, 1993).

Bonhoeffer, D., *Psalms: The Prayer Book of the Bible* (Minneapolis: Augsburg, 1970).

Braude, W.G., *The Midrash on Psalms* (New Haven: Yale University Press, 1959).

Brown, R.E., *The Sensus Plenior of Sacred Scripture* (Baltimore: St Mary's, 1955).

—'Hermeneutics', *New Jerome Biblical Commentary* (Englewood Cliffs, NJ: Prentice–Hall, 1990), pp. 1146-65.

Broyles, C.L., *The Conflict of Faith and Experience in the Psalms: A Form-Critical and Theological Study* (JSOTSup, 52; Sheffield: JSOT Press, 1989).

Brueggemann, W., *Abiding Astonishment: Psalms, Modernity, and the Making of History* (Louisville, KY: Westminster/John Knox Press, 1991).

—'Bounded by Obedience and Praise: The Psalms as Canon', *JSOT* 50 (1991), pp. 63-92.

—'The Costly Loss of Lament', *JSOT* 36 (1986), pp. 57-71.

—'The Formfulness of Grief', *Int* 31 (1977) , pp. 263-75.

—'From Hurt to Joy, from Death to Life', *Int* 28 (1974), pp. 3-19.

—*Israel's Praise: Doxology against Idolatry and Ideology* (Philadelphia: Fortress Press, 1988).

—*The Message of the Psalms: A Theological Commentary* (Minneapolis: Augsburg, 1984).

—*Praying the Psalms* (Winona, MN: St. Mary's Press, 1982).

—'Psalms and the Life of Faith: A Suggested Typology of Function', *JSOT* 17 (1980), pp. 3-32.

—'Response to James L. Mays, "The Question of Context", in McCann (ed.), *Shape and Shaping*, pp. 29-41.

—'Response to John Goldingay's "The Dynamic Cycle of Praise and Prayer"', *JSOT* 22 (1982), pp. 141-42.

Brueggemann, W., and P. Miller, 'Psalm 73 as a Canonical Marker', *JSOT* 72 (1996), pp. 45-56.

Buss, M.J., 'The Idea of Sitz im Leben: History and Critique', *ZAW* (1978), pp. 157-70.

—'The Study of Forms', in Hayes (ed.), *Old Testament Form Criticism*, pp. 1-56.

Buttenwieser, M., *The Psalms, Chronologically Treated with a New Translation* (2nd edn; New York: Ktav, 1969).

Childs, B.S., *The Book of Exodus: A Critical Theological Commentary* (Philadelphia: Westminster Press, 1974).

—*Introduction to the Old Testament as Scripture* (Philadelphia: Fortress Press, 1979)

—'Psalm Titles and Midrashic Exegesis', *JSS* 16 (1971), pp 137-50.

—'Reflections on the Modern Study of the Psalms', in F.M. Cross, W.E. Lemke, P.D. Miller, Jr (eds.), *Magnalia Dei: The Mighty Acts of God. Essays on the Bible and Archaeology in Memory of G. Ernest Wright* (Garden City, NY: Doubleday, 1976), pp. 377-88.

Cohen, R., 'History and Genre', *New Literary History* 17 (1986), pp. 203-217.

Cooper, A., 'The Life and Times of King David According to the Book of Psalms', in R.E. Friedman (ed.), *The Poet and the Historian: Essays in Literary and Historical Biblical Criticism* (HSS, 26; Chico, CA: Scholars Press, 1983), pp. 117-132.

Culler, J., *Structuralist Poetics: Structuralism, Linguistics, and the Study of Literature* (Ithaca, NY: Cornell University Press, 1975).

Davis, E.F., 'Exploding the Limits: Form and Function in Psalm 22', *JSOT* 53 (1992), pp. 93-105.

Engnell, I., *Studies in Divine Kingship in the Ancient Near East* (Uppsala: Almqvist & Wiksell, 1943).

Eriksson, L., *Come, Children, Listen to Me! Psalm 34 in the Hebrew Bible and in Early Christian Writings* (ConBOT, 32; Stockholm: Almqvist & Wiksell, 1991).

Fichtener, Johannes, 'The Wrath of God', *TDNT*, V, pp. 395-409.

Fisch, H., *Poetry with a Purpose: Biblical Poetics and Interpretation* (Bloomington: Indiana University Press, 1988).

Fishbane, M., *Biblical Interpretation in Ancient Israel* (Oxford: Clarendon Press, 1985).

Fowler, A., *Kinds of Literature: An Introduction to the Theory of Genres and Modes* (Cambridge, MA: Harvard University Press, 1982).

Fuchs, O., *Die Klage als Gebet: Eine theologische Besinnung am Beispiel des Psalms 22* (Munich: Kösel, 1982).

Gadamer, H.G., *Truth and Method* (New York: Crossroad, 1975).

Gerhart, M., 'Generic Studies: Their Renewed Importance in Religious and Literary Criticism', *JAAR* (1977), pp. 309-27.

—'Genre as Praxis: An Inquiry', *PreText* 4 (1983), pp. 273-94.

—*Genre Choices, Gender Questions* (Norman: University of Oklahoma Press, 1992).

Gerstenberger, E.S., 'Psalms', in Hayes (ed.), *Old Testament Form Criticism*, pp. 179-224.

—'Canon Criticism and the Meaning of *Sitz im Leben*', in D. Petersen, G. Tucker, and R. Wilson (eds.) *Canon, Theology, and Old Testament Interpretation* (Philadelphia: Fortress Press, 1988), pp. 20-31.

—'Der Psalter als Buch und als Sammlung', in Seybold and Zenger (eds.), *Psalmenforschung*, pp. 3-13.

Goldingay, J., 'The Dynamic Cycle of Praise and Prayer', *JSOT* 20 (1981), pp. 85-90.

Goulder, M., *The Prayers of David: Psalms 51–72. Studies in the Psalter II* (JSOTSup, 102; Sheffield: Sheffield Academic Press, 1990).

Gunkel, H., *Die Psalmen* (Göttingen: Vandenhoek & Ruprecht, 1929).

—*Einleitung in die Psalmen: Die Gattungen der religiösen Lyrik Israels, zu Ende geführt von Joachim Begrich* (Göttingen: Vandenhoek & Ruprecht, 1933).

—*What Remains of the Old Testament* (New York: Macmillan, 1928).

Hayes, J.H. (ed.), *Old Testament Form Criticism* (San Antonio, TX: Trinity University Press, 1974).

Hirsch, E.D., *Validity in Interpretation* (New Haven: Yale University Press, 1967).

Holladay, W.L., *The Psalms through Three Thousand Years: Prayerbook of a Cloud of Witnesses* (Minneapolis: Fortress Press, 1993).

Jauss, H.R., *Toward an Aesthetic of Reception* (Minneapolis: University of Minnesota Press, 1982).

—'Literary History as a Challenge to Literary Theory', in *idem*, *Toward an Aesthetic of Reception*, pp. 3-45.

Kim, Ee Kon, ' "Outcry": Its Context in Biblical Theology', *Int* 42 (1988), pp. 229-39.

Knierem, R., 'Criticism of Literary Features, Form, Tradition, and Redaction', in D. Knight and G. Tucker (eds.), *The Hebrew Bible and its Modern Interpreters* (Chico, CA: Scholars Press, 1985), pp. 136-46.

—'Old Testament Form Criticism Reconsidered', *Int* 27 (1973), pp. 435-68.

Koch, K., 'Der Psalter und seine Redaktionsgeschichte', in Seybold and Zenger (eds.), *Psalmenforschung*, pp. 243-77.

Kraus, H.J., *Die Königsherrschaft Gottes im Alten Testament: Untersuchungen zu den Liedern von Jahwes Thronbesteigung* (Tübingen: J.C.B. Mohr, 1951).

—*Psalms 1–59: A Commentary* (Minneapolis: Augsburg, 1988).

—*Theology of the Psalms* (Minneapolis: Augsburg, 1986).

—*Worship in Israel* (Richmond, VA: John Knox Press, 1966).

Kuczynski, M.P., *Prophetic Song: The Psalms as Moral Discourse in Late Medieval England* (Philadelphia: University of Pennsylvania Press, 1995).

Kugel, J.L., 'David the Prophet', in *idem*, (ed.), *Poetry and Prophecy*, pp. 45-55.

—*In Potiphar's House: The Interpretive Life of Biblical Texts* (San Francisco: Harper & Row, 1990).

—*The Bible As It Was* (Cambridge, MA: Harvard University Press, 1997).

—*The Idea of Biblical Poetry: Parallelism and its History* (New Haven: Yale University Press, 1981).

—'Topics in the History of the Spirituality of the Psalms', in A. Green (ed.), *Jewish Spirituality from the Bible through the Middle Ages* (New York: Crossroad, 1986), pp. 113-44.

Kugel, J.L. (ed.), *Poetry and Prophecy: The Beginnings of a Literary Tradition* (Ithaca, NY: Cornell University Press, 1990).

Levenson, J.D., *Sinai and Zion: An Entry into the Jewish Bible* (New York: Harper & Row, 1985).

—'A Technical Meaning for *N'M* in the Hebrew Bible', *VT* 25 (1985), pp. 61-67.

Levine, H.J., *Sing unto God a New Song: A Contemporary Reading of the Psalms* (Bloomington: Indiana University Press, 1995).

Linton, O., 'Interpretation of the Psalms in the Early Church', *Studia Patristica* IV, TU 79 (1961), pp. 143-56.

Mailloux, S., *Interpretive Conventions: The Reader in the Study of American Fiction* (Ithaca, NY: Cornell University Press, 1982).

Mays, J.L., 'The David of the Psalms', *Int* 40 (1986), pp. 143-55.

—'The Center of the Psalms: "The LORD Reigns" as Root Metaphor', in *idem*, *The Lord Reigns*, pp. 12-22.

— 'Going by the Book: The Psalter as a Guide to Reading the Psalms', in *idem, The Lord Reigns*, pp. 119-27.

—*The Lord Reigns: A Theological Handbook to the Psalms* (Louisville, KY: Westminster/John Knox Press, 1994).

—'Means of Grace: The Benefits of Psalmic Prayer', in *idem, The Lord Reigns*, pp. 40-45.

—'Past, Present, and Prospect in Psalm Study', in Mays, Petersen, and Richards (eds.), *Old Testament Interpretation*, pp. 147-56.

—'The Place of the Torah-Psalms in the Psalter', *JBL* 106 (1987), pp. 3-12.

—*Psalms* (Louisville, KY: John Knox, 1994).

—'The Question of Context in Psalms Interpretation', in McCann (ed.), *Shape and Shaping*, pp. 15-20.

Mays, J.L., Petersen, D.L., and K.H. Richards (eds.), *Old Testament Interpretation: Past, Present, and Future* (Nashville: Abingdon Press, 1995).

McCann, J.C., Jr, 'The Book of Psalms', in *The New Interpreter's Bible*, IV, pp. 639-1280.

—'Books I–III and the Editorial Purpose of the Hebrew Psalter', in *idem* (ed.), *Shape and Shaping*, pp. 93-107.

—'The Psalms as Instruction', *Int* 46 (1992), pp. 117-28.

—*A Theological Introduction to the Book of Psalms: The Psalms as Torah* (Nashville: Abingdon Press, 1993).

McCann, J.C., Jr (ed.), *The Shape and Shaping of the Psalter* (JSOTSup, 159; Sheffield: Sheffield Academic Press, 1993).

Miller, P.D., 'The Beginning of the Psalter', in McCann (ed.), *Shape and Shaping*, pp. 83-92.

—'Kingship, Torah Obedience, and Prayer: The Theology of Psalms 15–24', in Seybold and Zenger (eds.), pp. 127-42.

—*They Cried to the Lord: The Form and Theology of Biblical Prayer* (Minneapolis: Fortress Press, 1994).

Mowinckel, S., *Psalmenstudien*. II. *Das Thronbesteigungsfest Jahwäs und der Ursprung der Eschatologie* (Amsterdam: Schippers, 1961 [1922]).

—*The Psalms in Israel's Worship* (Nashville: Abingdon Press, 1962).

Muilenburg, J., 'Form Criticism and Beyond', *JBL* 88 (1964), pp. 1-18.

Murphy, R.E., 'Patristic and Medieval Exegesis: Help or Hindrance?', *CBQ* 43 (1981), pp. 505-16.

—*The Psalms Are Yours* (New York: Paulist Press, 1993).

—'Reflections on the Contextual Interpretations of the Psalms', in McCann (ed.), *Shape and Shaping*, pp. 21-26.

—*The Song of Songs* (Hermeneia; Minneapolis: Augsburg–Fortress, 1990).

Nasuti, H.P., 'Identity, Identification, and Imitation: The Narrative Hermeneutics of Biblical Law', *The Journal of Law and Religion* 4 (1986), pp. 9-23.

Neubauer, A., 'The Authorship and the Titles of the Psalms According to Early Jewish Authorities', in *Studia Biblica et Ecclesiastica*, II (5 vols.; Oxford: Clarendon Press, 1890).

Omont, H., *Catalogue des manuscrits français de la Bibliothèque Nationale* (Anciens Saint-Germain francais, 2; Paris: Leroux, 1898).

Pietersma, A., 'David in the Greek Psalms', *VT* 30 (1980), pp. 213-26.

Pleins, J.D., *The Psalms: Songs of Tragedy, Hope, and Justice* (Maryknoll, NY: Orbis Books, 1993).

Preus, J.S., *From Shadow to Promise: Old Testament Interpretation from Augustine to the Young Luther* (Cambridge, MA: Harvard University Press, 1969).

Rains, Ruth Ringland, *Les sept psalmes allégorisés of Christine de Pisan: A Critical Edition from the Brussels and Paris Manuscripts* (Washington, DC; Catholic University Press).

Recanati, F., *Meaning and Force: The Pragmatics of Performative Utterances* (Cambridge: Cambridge University Press, 1987).

Richter, W., *Exegese als Literaturwissenschaft* (Göttingen: Vandenhoek & Ruprecht, 1971).

Ricoeur, P., *Essays on Biblical Interpretation* (Philadelphia: Fortress Press, 1980).

—'Toward a Hermeneutic of the Idea of Revelation', in *idem, Essays on Biblical Interpretation*, pp. 73-118.

Rosmarin, A., *The Power of Genre* (Minneapolis: University of Minnesota Press, 1985).

Schauber, E., and E. Spolsky, *The Bounds of Interpretation: Linguistic Theory and Literary Text* (Stanford: Stanford University Press, 1986).

Searle, J.R., *Expression and Meaning: Studies in the Theory of Speech Acts* (Cambridge: Cambridge University Press, 1979).

—*Speech Acts: An Essay in the Philosophy of Language* (Cambridge, MA: Cambridge University Press, 1969).

Seybold, K., *Introducing the Psalms* (Edinburgh: T. & T. Clark, 1990).

Seybold, K., and E. Zenger (eds.), *Neue Wege der Psalmenforschung* (Herders Biblische Studien, 1; Freiburg: Herder, 1994).

Sheppard, G., 'Theology and the Book of Psalms', *Int* 46 (1992), pp. 143-55.

—*Wisdom as a Hermeneutical Construct: A Study in the Sapientializing of the Old Testament* (BZAW, 151; Berlin: W. de Gruyter, 1980).

Simon, U., *Four Approaches to the Book of Psalms: From Saadiah Gaon to Ibn Ezra* (Albany: State University of New York Press, 1991).

Slomovic, E., 'Toward an Understanding of the Formation of Historical Titles in the Book of Psalms', *ZAW* 91 (1979), pp. 350-80.

Snaith, N., *The Seven Psalms* (London: Epworth Press, 1964).

Stendahl, K., 'The Apostle Paul and the Introspective Conscience of the West', *HTR* 56 (1963), pp. 199-215.

Stolz, F., *Psalmen im nachkultischen Raum* (Zürich: Theologischer Verlag, 1983).

Thistleton, A.C., *New Horizons in Hermeneutics: The Theory and Practice of Transforming Biblical Reading* (Glasgow: HarperCollins, 1992).

Tracy, D., *The Analogical Imagination: Christian Theology and the Culture of Pluralism* (New York: Crossroad, 1981).

Walsh, P.G. (trans.), *Cassiodorus: Explanation of the Psalms* (3 vols.; Ancient Christian Writings, 51; New York: Paulist Press, 1990–91).

Weiser, A., *The Psalms: A Commentary* (Philadelphia: Westminster Press, 1962).

Westermann, C., *The Living Psalms* (trans. J.R. Porter; Edinburgh: T. & T. Clark, 1989).

—*Praise and Lament in the Psalms* (Atlanta, VA: John Knox Press, 1981).

—'The Role of the Lament in the Theology of the Old Testament', in *idem, Praise and Lament in the Psalms*, pp. 259-80

Whybray, N., *Reading the Psalms as a Book* (JSOTSup, 222; Sheffield: Sheffield Academic Press, 1996).

Willis, J.T., 'Psalm 1: An Entity', *ZAW* 91 (1979), pp. 381-401.

Wilson, G.H., *The Editing of the Hebrew Psalter* (SBLDS, 76: Chico, CA: Scholars Press, 1985).

—'Evidence of Editorial Divisions in the Hebrew Psalter', *VT* 34 (1984), pp. 337-52.

—'A First Century CE Date for the Closing of the Psalter?' in *Haim M. I. Gevaryahu Memorial Volume* (Jerusalem: World Jewish Bible Center, 1990), pp. 136-43.

—'The Shape of the Book of Psalms', *Int* 46 (1992), pp. 129-42.

—'Shaping the Psalter: A Consideration of Editorial Linkage in the Book of Psalms', in McCann (ed.), *Shape and Shaping*, pp. 72-82.

—'Understanding the Purposeful Arrangement of Psalms in the Psalter: Pitfalls and Promise', in McCann (ed.), *Shape and Shaping*, pp. 42-51.

—'The Use of Royal Psalms at the "Seams" of the Hebrew Psalter', *JSOT* 35 (1986), pp. 85-94.

—'The Use of "Untitled" Psalms in the Hebrew Psalter', *ZAW* 97 (1985), pp. 404-13.

Wittgenstein, L., *Philosophical Investigations* (Oxford: Basil Blackwell, 1967).

Zim, R., *English Metrical Psalms: Poetry as Praise and Prayer 1535–1601* (Cambridge: Cambridge University Press, 1987).

Defining the Sacred Songs